Lecture Notes in Economics and Mathematical Systems 467

Springer
Berlin
Heidelberg
New York
Barcelona
Hong Kong
London
Milan
Paris
Singapore
Tokyo

Heike Hennig-Schmidt

Bargaining in a Video Experiment

Determinants of Boundedly Rational Behavior

Springer

Author

Dr. Heike Hennig-Schmidt
University of Bonn
Wirtschaftstheorie II
Adenauerallee 24–26
D-53113 Bonn

Cataloging-in-Publication Data applied for

Die Deutsche Bibliothek - CIP-Einheitsaufnahme

Hennig-Schmidt, Heike:
Bargaining in a video experiment : determinants of boundedly rational behavior / Heike Hennig-Schmidt. - Berlin ; Heidelberg ; New York ; Barcelona ; Hong Kong ; London ; Milan ; Paris ; Santa Clara ; Tokyo : Springer, 1999
(Lecture notes in economics and mathematical systems ; 467)
ISBN-13: 978-3-540-65415-5 e-ISBN-13: 978-3-642-45775-3
DOI:10.1007/978-3-642-45775-3

ISSN 0075-8442
ISBN-13: 978-3-540-65415-5 Springer-Verlag Berlin Heidelberg New York

Softcover reprint of the hardcover 1st edition 1999

Typesetting: Camera ready by author
Gedruckt mit Unterstützung der Deutschen Forschungsgemeinschaft D5
SPIN: 10649678 42/3142-543210 - Printed on acid-free paper

To my family:
Heiko, Heidi, Holger
and my parents

Acknowledgements

There are many persons who inspired and helped me during the long process of preparing this study. First of all I want to thank Reinhard Selten who suggested to me the project of videotaping groups of players and evaluating the discussions on their joint decisions. I readily accepted this advice not knowing how much hard work this decision would imply and how many interesting results I would be going to obtain. I am deeply indebted to my supervisor for trusting me to be able to achieve this task, for his support, advice and critique.

Working in the field of boundedly rational behavior as opposed to or at least amplifying traditional neoclassical economics was also inspired by Werner Hildenbrand with whom I work together now for more than 15 years. His methodological critique on microeconomic theory that hypotheses should be falsifiable, at least in principle, and should be based on observable entities which then could be evaluated by data analysis had a great influence on my thinking and encouraged me to have a close look on data.

I am obliged to Jürgen Arns who plotted all the graphics in Appendices B, C, D, E, and F on negotiation processes, allocations, aspiration levels and break offs. In addition to the transcripts these diagrams proved to be extremely helpful in getting the comprehensive insight into aspiration level based behavior of subjects and into determinants of potential and actual break offs which is reported in this study.

I thank my colleagues in the Bonn Laboratory of Experimental Economics, Karim Sadrieh and Bettina Kuon, as well as Klaus Abbink and Bernd Irlenbusch who always had time to exchange views on open questions of my research. Thanks to Inge Baßmann for proof reading the manuscript of this study as well as to Sophie Hentschel and Karl Schlag who translated parts of the transcripts into English in order to subtitle a video showing break off discussions.

Wulf Albers devoted many hours to make me familiar with the research area of prominence, and Axel Ostmann handled over to me a lot of his experience in videotaping experiments. Alastair Fischer read an earlier version of my work and heavily improved my English. Wolff-Dietrich Amerling was indefatigable in tracing particular economic and psychological literature. Discussions with participants of several congresses, workshops and seminars where I presented parts of this study induced me to have a critical look on my findings. Thanks to all those persons whom I do not mention by name but who in some way or the other enabled me to do this research.

Special thanks to Dagmar Müller who patiently prepared the numerous versions of this study. She managed to overcome most of the difficulties TEX has in store for users with unusual demands.

Last but not least I thank my family not only for their understanding with respect to my time-consuming research. They all provided me with active help: Due to my father's connections to the Trade Corporation (Handwerkskammer) I received several answers for the questionnaire study. My three children who during the years became quite familiar with my work proved to be valuable partners when discussing my work. Three of us have been working on experimental projects: two have been writing their diploma theses, one (me) the PhD thesis. Since the academic subjects of all four of us are different there have been many fruitful discussions, also on methodological questions. Not to mention Heiko's invaluable help when solving apparently unsolvable TEX-problems.

Finally, I gratefully acknowledge the financial support by the Deutsche Forschungsgemeinschaft, Sonderforschungsbereich 303. Without this funding I could not have done the kind of research reported in this study.

Contents

Chapter 1

Introduction

In this study we will analyze an experiment which is designed to observe experimental subjects in decision situations. The design of our experiment was motivated by the fact that experiments clearly show that subjects do not behave according to the assumptions of neoclassical microeconomics. As Tversky and Kahneman (1986) put it "...the deviations [...] are too widespread to be ignored, too systematic to be dismissed as random error and too fundamental to be accommodated by relaxing the normative system" (p. 68).

Subjects do not behave according to full rationality, i.e. making decisions according to Baysianism and the game theoretic notion of Nash equilibrium. They behave according to bounded rationality, the goal-oriented systematic behavior human beings show when taking actual decisions. It is an empirical question to discover the determinants of boundedly rational behavior.

Human beings are bounded concerning the access and processing of information as well as their computational capacities. The complexity of optimization goes beyond their cognitive capabilities. This fact was pointed out by Herbert Simon already in the 1950s. He introduced the concept of bounded rationality in human subjects, and stressed the necessity to take into account the empirical behavior of individuals instead of deriving it from abstract principles. He demanded that the global rationality of economic men should be replaced by boundedly rational behavior (Simon, 1955).

In addition to cognitive limitations, also motivational and emotional bounds of rationality may be a feature of bounded rationality: It is not the lack of cognitive capability but the failure of behavioral trust into abstract induction arguments that is likely to guide human behavior (Selten, 1978a, 1993).

Research has provided clear evidence that subjects do behave according to rules that are not guided by full rationality. Yet many experiments show that the typical behavior of experimental subjects is not irrational even if it is nonoptimizing. It is rational in the sense that it is grounded on reasonable systematic principles which are quite different from those normative decision and game theory assumes (Selten, 1990, 1997).

Since we still have only limited knowledge of boundedly rational economic behavior, the aim of this exploratory study is to look for behavioral regularities in the context of our bargaining experiment, and to learn about subjects' reasoning and motivations. As will be shown later, we found such regularities that facilitate handling the subjects' difficult task of problem solving during a decision process. How do we get the data in order to achieve our aim?

When conducting experiments in a computer laboratory we do get a great number of data in a quick and very efficient way. However, the disadvantage of this method is that only formal decisions can be observed. We get the results of the individuals' decision processes, but we obtain no or only few verbalizations of the players' decisions that allow an interpretation of their motives. Since we are interested in the way how subjects actually behave and in the motives for their behavior, people have to be observed in decision situations and, moreover, they have to be induced to verbalize their thought processes. There are several methods to address the problem:

1. At the beginning, at the end or during the experiment subjects are asked to report on the motives for their decisions by *questionnaires* or other means[1].

2. Interviewing people in field studies could reveal the intentions of decision makers without using questionnaires in order not to impose structure on an interview which might not capture the important aspects of the problem (Bewley, 1997).

3. Strategies can be made observable by the *strategy method* (Selten, 1967). Subjects have to write computer programs for a given problem. For every possible situation they have to program a corresponding solution (see for example Selten, Mitzkewitz, and Uhlich 1997, Keser 1992).

4. The method of *thinking-aloud* asks subjects to vocalize their thoughts, thought processes, motives and reasons when solving a problem. Yet there is evidence that deliberately verbalizing motives or reasons for one's thinking leads to different outcomes than spontaneous remarks (c.f. Ericsson and Simon 1984, pp. 78).

[1]Nagel (1998) reports on two experiments the participants of which have been readers of newspapers. They have been asked to comment on their choices. The evaluation of these extensive statements will certainly further the understanding of subjects' reasoning.

5. Subjects are observed during experiments by recording their spontaneous remarks during their decision process either on audio (Klemisch-Ahlert, 1996) or on videotapes (Ostmann, 1990). Two or three subjects act together in a group and have to perform a common task. The discussions between the group members are transcribed into text protocols, and these protocols are investigated.

In our experiment we decided to follow the latter approach. The methodology of videotaping does provide a unique opportunity to observe the spontaneous behavior of subjects during their decision processes, and therefore extremely well meets the methodological requirement that hypotheses and conclusions in economics should be based on entities that are observable and thereby are falsifiable.[2]

Controversies about how to explain deviations from normative predictions on behavior in equilibrium provoked a lot of papers hypothesizing on the motivations that might have led people to the observed behavior[3]. Most of the authors quoted by Roth (1995a) address the deviations from game theoretic predictions by including noneconomic concerns into utility functions. Other authors strictly reject this approach since their results from ultimatum bargaining indicate that subjects are not maximizing (Güth, 1994, 1995, Güth and Tietz, 1990). This statement complies with the findings from our experiment; the videotapes clearly show that subjects do not maximize. Since we have a means of observing directly what people are doing and how they are arguing in a certain experimental setup we should use it to learn which motives might lead subjects to certain actions. If we find behavioral regularities being valid in different setups we possibly can make better predictions and design better descriptive theories.

We will see that the regularities we found are not at all new findings. What is new is that in our experiment they are directly observable in contrast to the most common practice in designing experiments where one can at best hypothesize on the existence of behavioral regularities underlying the obtained results. In this context it is worthwhile to quote Herbert Simon (1962, p. 12) who wrote that if the words could be recorded that accompany the thoughts being induced by problem solving a great deal could be learned about the process. He notes that decision making in groups is "... a means of externalizing the phenomena and making them accessible to observation."[4]

[2]C.f. Hildenbrand (1994a,b, 1998)

[3]See for instance Roth (1995a) for an overview on experiments in ultimatum bargaining.

[4]See also Camerer and Thaler (1995) and Camerer (1997b) who writes that ignoring almost all data but choices in experimental economics "...wastes a valuable opportunity to learn something more from a group of subjects who are often eager to

Looking closely at actual behavior shows that there is a lot more to be discovered than an even intensely contemplating theorist may imagine. People are different, and the behavior of others could be guided by motives that may not be worthwhile thinking about or may even not be conceivable for another person. We found for instance that non of the noneconomist students and less than 50% of the economists knew the concept of "Split the Difference" which, however, is a commonly used solution concept in game theory .

From a game-theoretic point of view the game played in our experiment is classified as a game with complete information. However, there are uncertainties in many respects. The guaranteed payoff is the only information on opponents that groups receive. The number of possible decision alternatives, i.e. the possible divisions of the coalition value, is very large. Moreover, groups don't have any knowledge of their opponents. They have no information on most of the variables game theory assumes as common knowledge, and they don't know all the determinants which may affect decisions and which are possibly different from those game theory takes for granted, e.g. whether opponent's decisions are purely payoff-oriented.

There is a whole range of factors that may affect bargaining behavior , and, as we saw from the experiment, in fact do have influence. Therefore, players have to find guidelines for their behavior that makes the decision problem manageable and criteria that allow them to select the alternative that is to be taken as final decision.

---

explain their thinking processes and inferences. Whether their thoughts are useful or not is difficult to answer, but it is surely <u>less</u> difficult if we collect such data!" (p. 325).

Chapter 2

Description of the Experiment

2.1 Experimental Design

In our experiment a two-person characteristic function game was played. Each of the 'players' comprises a group of three, in some cases two, persons. The groups receive a guaranteed payoff, if they do not form a coalition, but break off the negotiation. These values, being $v(1), v(2)$, where $v(1) > v(2)$, are also called alternative, outside option, threat point or status quo. The coalition value, $v(12)$, can be distributed between the two groups, where $v(12) > v(1) + v(2)$ and $v(1) + v(2) = v(12)/2$.

The experimental setup was arranged as follows: The two groups negotiate on the allocation of the coalition value by alternately making offers to the opponent group. The negotiation ends if one of the groups accepts the proposal of the other group or if one of the groups breaks off negotiation. The subjects in each group are instructed to argue which of the decisions allowed by the rules of the game is to be taken and why this should be done. At the end of this discussion they have to take a joint decision.

The following decisions can be taken if a group is in decision mode:

1. *Making a proposal* on the allocation of the coalition value,
2. *Shift*, i.e. passing the initiative to the other group without making a proposal,
3. *Accepting* the last proposal of the other group,
4. *Breaking off* negotiation.

We gave no rules how the decision was to be taken within the groups. There was no time constraint. The groups did not bargain directly with each other. Only their decisions were transmitted by the experimenter. Each participant received a money payoff proportional to the final payoff of his or her group. Thus we excluded within-group bargaining on the distribution of the amount finally paid. The point-to-cash rate was 1 to 0.10 Deutsche Mark in each session.

Payoffs were calculated such that individuals could gain about 12 Deutsche Mark per hour, an amount students used to earn if they had a job in or outside the university. All but one group either received an offer $\geq$ 12 DM within the first hour of negotiation or could have achieved a fictitious payoff per hour $\gg$ 12 DM had they accepted an early offer.[5]

Both groups received identical information on the alternatives of both groups and all other characteristics of the game. They knew that the other group got the same information[6].

The design of our experiment follows as closely as possible a computer experiment by Uhlich (1988, 1990), and Kuon and Uhlich (1993) which was conducted in the Bonn Laboratory of Experimental Economics. Our experiment, however, was restricted to those two of the games with a positive threat point carried out by Kuon and Uhlich where the two alternatives added up to half of the coalition value. The design concerning the decision alternatives was exactly like in the Kuon/Uhlich-experiment, the essential difference being that subjects did not have to decide on their own, but were grouped with other subjects and had to make a joint decision. Moreover, they were videotaped during the entire experiment.

We had three treatments[7]: two different values for $v(1)$ and $v(2)$, and two levels of experience (cf. Table 2.1).

Groups with a larger alternative $v(1)$ we call S-groups, and those with a smaller alternative $v(2)$ we call W-groups (group 1 or group 2 respectively). The numbers we refer to are the amounts that are attributed to S-groups. Proposed amounts are to be interpreted either as demands of S-groups for themselves or as offers of W-groups to S-groups. To get the figures for W-groups the corresponding amounts have to be deducted from 320, the coalition

[5]Subjects participating in our experiment saw the money they were going to earn as part of their monthly budget. They calculated which goods of their daily expenses they could buy or were not able to buy if they gain or loose certain amounts of money, e.g. a meal in the students' cafeteria (4.1.21; 5.1.9, 5.1.26; 6.1.4; 12.1.18), beverages at the Christmas fair or in the students' cafeteria (8.2.3; 9.2.3, 9.2.35; 10.1.94, 19.1.32; 18.2.17; 19.2.11, 19.2.12, 19.2.31), a ticket for a movie or a concert(5.2.12; 10.1.42), buying Christmas presents (6.1.14; 7.1.24), a meal in a restaurant (10.1.73; 12.1.14; 15.1.4, 15.1.23; 18.2.5), cigarettes (4.1.42).

[6]The introduction to the experimental subjects is to be found in Appendix A.

[7]We use the terminology following Davis and Holt (1992, p. 21): *session*: a sequence of periods involving the same group of subjects on the same day; *treatment*: a unique environment or configuration of treatment variables, i.e., of experience and incentives; *experiment*: the collection of sessions in one or more related cells.

Table 2.1: Coalition values, alternatives, relation between alternatives and number of sessions in different treatments

$v(12)$	$v(1)$	$v(2)$	$v(1)/v(2)$	Number of sessions
Inexperienced (I-)Groups / I-sessions				
320	96	64	3:2	6
320	128	32	4:1	6
Experienced (E-)Groups / E-sessions				
320	128	32	4:1	8

value $v(12)$ that is to be distributed between the two groups in case of agreement. It will be stressed if occasionally we refer to amounts of W-groups.

Inexperienced groups (I-groups) consist of subjects who had not participated in our experiment before or in the computer experiment by Uhlich, and Kuon and Uhlich. Experienced groups (E-groups) are those who had already participated in our experiment. Sessions with inexperienced participants we call I-sessions, those with experienced subjects we call E-sessions.

According to the different treatments we distinguish the following types of groups (see Table 2.2):

Table 2.2: Types of groups according to different treatments

Game Type	Experience of Groups			
	Inexperienced (I)		Experie nced (E)	
	$v(1)$ S-Groups (S)	$v(2)$ W-Groups (W)	$v(1)$ S-Groups (S)	$v(2)$ W-Groups (W)
v(1)/v(2) = 3:2 Low (L)	96 ISL	64 IWL		
v(1)/v(2) = 4:1 High (H)	128 ISH	32 IWH	128 ES(H)	32 EW(H)

If an I-group agreed to play in an E-session, all subjects were asked to participate again to ensure that the composition of the groups did not change. This requirement could not always be met. In addition to two I-groups that consisted of two persons, in another 8 E-groups only two persons participated.[8] E-groups were matched such that the opponent group changed, they did not play against a group which they had met already in I-sessions.

It was our goal to arrange the groups in such a way that in E-sessions all S-groups became W-groups and vice versa. This was not possible in three cases: two strong groups remained strong, one weak group remained weak again.

Sessions are divided into proposal rounds, abbreviatingly called rounds in the following, a ***proposal round*** being the time between two decisions plus the decision of the previous round. We decided to use this definition since mostly extensive discussions started as a reaction to the foregoing proposal of the opponent group. The structure of the discussions becomes more transparent by assigning rounds to the decisions they refer to.

We introduce an abbreviating notation to indicate groups and rounds in particular sessions. 10.1.86, e.g., has the following meaning: the first one or two digits refer to the session number. The sessions are numbered chronologically as they have been conducted. The third digit indicates whether we examine group 1 or group 2, i.e. an S- or a W-group. The next (maximally three) digits indicate the round number. Thus we indicated session no. 10, group no. 1, round no. 86 in the transcripts of this group (Hennig-Schmidt 1996a).

2.2 Organizational Features

When registering for the experiment subjects were informed that they would be videotaped. They signed that they agreed to be videotaped, and that the tapes could be used for scientific purposes. They were told when and where to show up, first mover groups arrived 15 minutes earlier than second mover groups. Groups were assigned randomly to be S- or W-groups. When showing up subjects where gathered in rooms apart from each other. They were seated in front of a videocamera such that all verbal and nonverbal expressions could be recorded. The videocamera was switched on when the session started. Beside each camera there was a student helper in order to ensure that subjects did not stop the recording. Subjects were provided with

[8] In 3 of these 8 groups only one of the original group members was willing to participate. In order to be able to run the session we asked one of the student helpers to join the group having served in one of the I-sessions as a controller and thus could also be seen as experienced.

one copy of the introduction and several copies of the bargaining protocol (see Appendix A). In addition they had to fill in a questionnaire after each decision. The questionnaire asked whether subjects agreed with the group's decision. In case of deviation they were requested to write down their preferred decision and the reasons. Moreover, they were asked to evaluate the atmosphere within the group ranging from 1 (excellent) to 9 (very bad). This questionnaire was meant to give those subjects who might not have been able or willing to articulate themselves before the camera the possibility to write down their thoughts. Yet, this fear proved to be unfounded since all subjects very lively took part in often most controversial discussions. However, in case of deviation they readily used the additional chance to state their different view.

At the beginning of each session the experimenter (the author) gave an introduction to the subjects according to Appendix A. Afterwards subjects were asked to read the introduction carefully and ask questions which were answered. Having finished the introduction the experimenter left the room to instruct the other group in exactly the same way. This was the starting time for proposal round 1. After a decision had been taken, i.e. subjects had agreed on an allocation to be proposed to the opponent group, they had to write it down into the bargaining protocol. Each participant had to sign that he/she assents to this proposal. Then the experimenter was called by the student helper and was informed about the decision. She left the room and transferred the decision to the other group. After acceptance or break off the other group was informed and subjects were paid. Videotaping stopped after the group has left the room.

Chapter 3

Data and Evaluation

Our study was the first videotaped experiment run in the Bonn Laboratory of Experimental at the University of Bonn. Since then a series of follow-up studies based on video experiments have been carried out (e.g. Jacobsen and Sadrieh 1996, Artale 1996 and several diploma theses). Since videotaping subjects' discussions is a new methodology in experimental economics, in this chapter we will thoroughly describe how we obtained the data on which we based our study and how we evaluated them.

73 students of law, economics and other subjects played the game in 20 sessions between December 1991 and February 1992. The number of proposal rounds ranged from 5 to 100 in I-sessions, and from 2 to 37 in E-sessions. The bargaining time in I-sessions took from 10 minutes to 2.5 hours, in E-sessions from 3 to 57 minutes. On average groups bargained for 71 minutes. The videotapes amounted to nearly 45 hours' length, the transcripts to about 900 pages (Hennig-Schmidt, 1996a).

Table 3.1 shows the composition of participants with regard to subject of study, gender and game theoretic background of participants. We see that, according to their statements, only 8 of the 73 experimental subjects took a course in game theory.

3.1 Experimental Setup

Before going into the details of our evaluation we want to discuss some methodological questions concerning the design of our experiment. We particularly will address different aspects that may be or have been criticized. Our main point of justifying the experiment as it was conducted is that the aim of our study was to learn about people's reasoning and motivations and to find regularities in their behavior. Given this goal and the huge amount of information we obtained, we had to bear a tradeoff with respect to videotaping group discussions, the group effect possibly induced by this technique

Table 3.1: Gender and game theoretic background of participants

Students of	H-sessions					L-sessions					Total					
	m	f	course in game theory			m	f	course in game theory			m	f	course in game theory			Σ
			no	yes	–			no	yes	–			no	yes	–	
Economics	16	5	14	4	3	8	3	8	3		24	8	22	7	3	32
Law	9	4	13			20	1	11	1	9	29	5	24	1	9	34
Psychology							1	1				1	1			1
Musical science	1		1								1		1			1
North American studies	1		1				1			1	1	1	1		1	2
Romance language						1		1			1		1			1
Political science	1	1	1		1						1	1	1		1	2
Σ	28	10	30	4	4	29	6	21	4	10	57	16	51	8	14	73

m : male , f : female
– : subjects did not indicate whether they did or did not take a course in game theory

and the relatively small number of sessions in the single treatments as well as in the experiment as a whole.

3.1.1 Spontaneous versus Strategic Behavior

Having subjects discuss in groups and videotaping them may induce behavior that is different from individual choices if subjects decide on their own. In this respect our data may not be comparable to other experiments based on single-person decisions. Yet, if we want to learn anything about other person's thinking and arguments in special situations we have either to ask or to observe them when acting in these situations. Inducing spontaneous discussions in a group setting is more natural than applying the single-person method of thinking-aloud. The information which we hoped to gain, which we did gain and which we are not able to obtain by another method justifies our proceeding.

It has been argued that one never knows whether true motives or strategic reasoning to persuade their companions will induce subjects' behavior. Therefore, what is observable are not the motivations that persuade an individual subject but rather the subject express the motivation that he/she will be most persuasive in getting the other members in his/her group to agree to his/her preferred proposal. Since it cannot be precluded that subjects think and behave strategically and since our method of observing decision making seems to be not the appropriate way of subjecting hypotheses to rigorous examination critics see no scientific role for the technique of videotaping groups of people.

There are several ways to address this critique. The first one is that the aim of this study is *not* hypothesis testing *but* finding regularities of boundedly rational behavior. If the regularities we found give insight into problems that cannot be solved by theoretical modelling based on mere introspection then one can think of designing experiments that test hypotheses based on the information gained by observing individuals.

Videotaping discussions and choices provides a lot of information on individual and group behavior that cannot be gained otherwise. Moreover, this information is in principle in itself interesting and can serve different purposes. Whether it *is* useful or not can, however, only be decided after it has been obtained[9].

Purposely each subject within a group received the same amount, namely the final payoff agreed upon or the alternative in case of conflict. Since no in-group bargaining is involved we assume that subjects' spontaneous remarks reveal their motivations and that they do not or only to a negligible extent reason strategically within groups. Assuming strategic behavior to be the only way "ordinary" boundedly rational people with nearly no game theoretic background (c.f. Table 3.1) behave is the same presupposition as assuming that they show their true motivations. Thus, the same critique should apply that one never knows the "real" motivational background of decisions. Even if choices look like being influenced by strategic reasoning, observing people may reveal that this in fact is not the case. Our method has the major advantage that we can investigate the videotapes displaying subjects' discussions and actions.

Subjects entered our experiment not knowing anything else than that they would be videotaped in a bargaining situation. All other experimental features they did not know beforehand. They plunged into a situation which they could not strategically analyze in advance, and if they had an imagination of what could happen in the experiment they faced the fact that people (in-group and opponents) behaved differently than they had thought. Thinking ahead was most often wasted time[10]. Different subjects but also the same subject during the negotiation showed quite inhomogeneous behavior. All participants very frankly discussed controversial arguments, be they fair or exploitative. They were sitting before the camera up to 2.5 hours and forgot after some minutes that they were videotaped. They freely discussed very private matters with their companions. Keeping strategic behavior under these circumstances seems to be a very difficult task supporting our impression that they behaved spontaneously and not strategically with their in-group partners.

---

[9] C. f. Camerer (1997, p. 325), Camerer (1997a).

[10] C.f. Section 5.5.

The last point we want to make is the following: if the critique applies that we never observe the motivations of human subjects then studies of group decisions - audiotaped, videotaped, questionnaire and interview data - in economics and psychology are worthless since we never can preclude that subjects behave strategically, be it against their in-group companions, the experimenter, the interviewer. On the other hand, if we find evidence that these different methods yield similar or even the same results[11] then the method(s) should be used that serve(s) best to answer the problem in question.

3.1.2 Observation and Group Effect

Subjects in our experiment have been videotaped. Therefore it might be objected that they felt observed and behaved differently before the camera than in "real life". Even though we had no control groups that were videotaped without knowing it (which we think to be impracticable for technical, as well as, and this is much more important, for reasons of destroying our reputation as a sincere experimenter) we, in fact, found no evidence for the validity of such an objection.

There have been only a couple of persons who in the very beginning of the negotiation showed some unfamiliarity with the situation. After some minutes, however, they became so emotionally involved in the discussion and the bargaining process that they hardly even noticed the camera. Moreover, they discussed a lot of very private matters, and were surprisingly frank about their positive and negative opinions on their Bonn professors with whom they, after all, had to pass their exams. If subjects were worried about the camera this was because some of them suspected that the other group might watch them, and not because their discussions were to be looked at and evaluated by the experimenter.

The objection mentioned above may as well be applied to all other experiments since experimental subjects are aware that they are in an artificial laboratory situation.

Acting in groups is likely to induce a "group effect". Thus, it might be expected that outcomes are different from those in single-person decision situations[12]. Yet, our main interest is not the final payoff but the discussions that lead to this final outcome, and in our experiment we are able to observe also single-person arguments even if they have to be aggregated in a group proposal. Moreover, comparing the effects of different experimental setups and techniques on final outcomes, as we will do in Section 6.5, is an interesting issue since in real world situations frequently decisions have to be made in groups.

---

[11] C.f. Chapter 8

[12] See e.g. Bornstein et al. (1996, 1997) as well as our analysis in Section 5.2.3.

3.1.3 Number of Sessions and Statistical Analysis

It might further be objected that the relatively small number of sessions in the single treatments as well as in the experiment as a whole limits the relevance of our results. This objection could be assented if we had confined our evaluation only to statistical analyses. A generalization of conclusions that are based on not more than 6 independent observations can hardly be defended. Yet again, the goal of our analysis and the huge amount of information that we obtained already by this small number of sessions and which had to be handled serves as a justification for our restriction.

Despite the small number of independent observations we conducted statistical analyses whenever it was possible and reasonable. Some hypotheses we could reject regardless of the small number of independent observations. Moreover, being not able to reject hypotheses on the difference of outcomes in different treatments confirmed the impression from the transcripts that these treatment variables were of no decisive influence on final payoffs.

E-sessions are not independent observations since the groups played against each other in I-sessions in different combinations. Therefore statistical tests on data of E-sessions have been carried out if effects of experience could be disentangled, e.g. with respect to final payoffs, proposal rounds, bargaining time, initial demands. Other behavioral features in E-sessions have been explained and interpreted on the basis of the transcripts, using other means of analysis[13].

3.2 Evaluation

We base our evaluation on the data gained by the bargaining protocols[14] and the discussions of the experimental subjects as recorded on the videotapes. These videotapes have been literally transferred into transcripts (Hennig-Schmidt 1996a).[15] Discussions on private matters have been omitted, and this has been stated in the transcripts. The legend to the text protocols presents the terminology used to characterize sessions, group members etc. in the text protocols and also explains comments given in addition to the mere transcription of verbal discussions. It is contained in the introductory part of the transcripts of all sessions. The transcripts are available upon request.

---

[13]C.f. the next section on data evaluation.

[14]C.f. Appendix A.

[15]If subjects started pronouncing the same word several times or if they inserted "äh", "em" etc. this has been left out.

3.2.1 Data

Figure 3.1 gives a schematic representation of the kinds of data we used and the different means of the data analysis.

Our experiment yielded the following types of data:

(i) Purely verbal data:
verbal data from the transcripts that cannot be translated into numerical data

(ii) Quantifiable data:
verbal data which can be translated into numerical data

(iii) Numerical data:
allocation proposals as entered into the bargaining protocols, number of proposal rounds, bargaining time.

Purely verbal data Since our study has an exploratory character we very carefully watched the videotapes and read the transcripts several times looking for behavioral characteristics and regularities to be decisive in the context of our experiment. The most important ones we analyzed in this study: aspiration levels, aspects of equity, fairness and prominence, break off discussions, motivations and emotions. Moreover, references to other important aspects of bargaining have been found which served as an explanation and interpretation of observed behavior, e.g. of the shape of the proposal curves, bargaining patterns, threats, the notion of bargaining etc. which we will refer to in the course of our study.

Quantifiable data In addition to purely verbal statements references have been made by participants that can be characterized as representing verbal data which could be translated into numerical data: the value of payoffs strived for, i.e. of the aspiration levels, all allocations which are discussed during the negotiation and which are not proposed to the other group, prominence aspects, percentages of break off discussions, prevalence of break off characteristics.

All references to the above mentioned items have been marked in the transcripts by two separate persons. Thus, encoding of a special kind has been conducted. We found it important to evaluate our data as closely as possible to the transcripts to understand the dynamics during the negotiation. Even though the prevalence of the features have been marked in the text protocols, for their understanding, interpretation and explanation it was necessary to read the discussions at these marked passages several times.

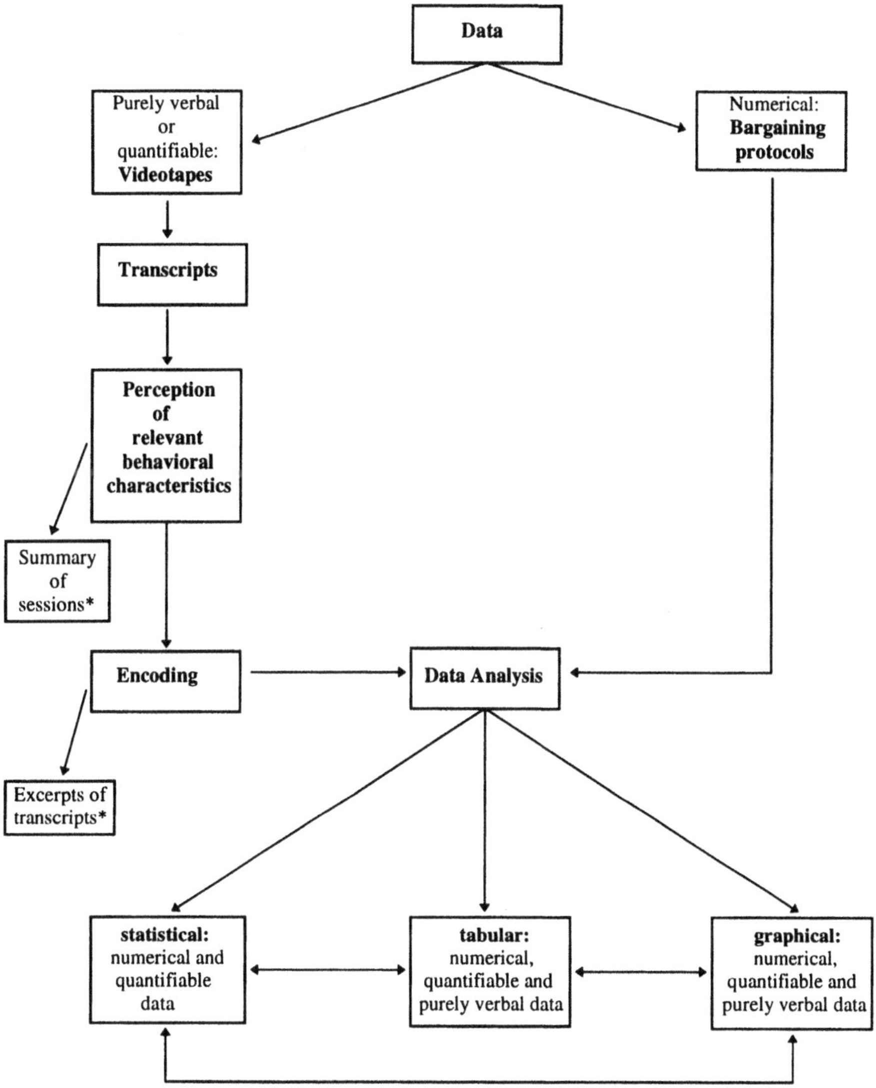

* not included in this study

Figure 3.1: Graphical representation of data and data analysis

3.2.2 Data Analysis

In order to assess the importance of the factors described above we used three different means of data analysis:

(i) Statistical data analysis
(ii) Tabular data analysis
(iii) Graphical data analysis

Statistical data analysis Whenever we had numerical data or data that could be transformed from qualitative into quantitative data and whenever it was reasonable we used statistical tests or statistical measures to be able to make an objective judgement on the importance of the feature under consideration, e.g. payoffs, proposals, bargaining rounds and time, initial demands, prominence level, success of nonmonotone proposals, comparison to the Negotiation Agreement Area, typical bargaining characteristics, break off discussions.

Tabular data analysis In order to structure the discussions according to the behavioral features we perceived to be important and to be able to make a statement on *how* important they are, we used a tabular representation. This was done for all three kinds of data mentioned above. Tables being used for this purpose and having been included in the present study are those on payoffs, threats, formation and adaptation of aspiration levels, first demands and adjustments of proposals, break offs, motivations, answers of business people.

There are also a variety of tables that improved our understanding of the relevant processes but have not been included in this study either because more meaningful tables have been deduced from these original ones or because they have been replaced by diagrams which give a deeper insight than a tabular representation.

Moreover, in order to give readers the possibility to check our statements we quoted the sessions and rounds where the respective arguments can be found in the transcripts. These quotations can be seen as 'quasi-tabular' since as in tables it is shown how frequently a special argument is used.

Graphical data analysis The graphical representation proved to be a very important means for our analysis since the text protocols are condensed under certain aspects. We get an impression which structure of the problems we are focusing on, is predominant.[16] In order to visualize what happened within the groups and to facilitate evaluating the extensive material from the 900-pages transcripts we plotted those features that emerged to be important

[16]For the importance and usefulness of methods of graphical data analysis c.f. Hildenbrand (1994a,b).

for the decision process, e.g. the distribution of payoffs, negotiation processes as displayed by proposal curves, all allocation proposals discussed during the negotiation[17], aspiration levels, proposals, mid-payoffs, Negotiation Agreement Area-hits, break off discussions. The graphical data analysis was of invaluable help when evaluating the determinants of boundedly rational behavior.

[17]Diagrams showing all allocation proposals discussed during the negotiation by members of groups 4.1 and 4.2 are to be found in Appendix D.

Chapter 4

Determinants of Boundedly Rational Behavior

In Chapter 1 we pointed out that the rationality of subjects is bounded in many respects. Yet, experiments show that their typical behavior is not irrational but is based on reasonable systematic principles. Videotaping subjects' decisions in our experiment provides us with the unique opportunity to assess regularities in their behavior by direct observation. The aim of our study is an explorative one: it was not designed to test hypotheses on expected outcomes or behavior. Rather, by looking at the actions of experimental subjects we wanted to find out on which, if any, principles people base their decisions. After having learned about the typical determinants of agents' behavior in our experiment, we found that these principles are well-established in economic, but mainly in psychological literature.

In this chapter we will shortly and in a general manner describe the determinants of boundedly rational behavior we found to be prevalent in our experiment. The subsequent chapters will present a detailed analysis of each of these principles.

4.1 Aspiration Levels

An important phenomenon of human behavior is described by the theory of *aspiration levels* which was developed in experimental psychology by Dembo (1931) and Lewin, Dembo, Festinger, and Snedden Sears (1944) and describes a "goal-striving behavior which occurs within a range of difficulty" (Lewin et al., 1944, p. 333). Simon adopted these ideas into economics and developed theories of boundedly rational behavior which stress the satisficing behavior of human beings in contrast to the maximizing behavior neoclassical microeconomics assume (cf. Simon 1955, 1957). The difficulty in the classical requirement of comparing all alternatives led Simon to pursue the approach of aspiration levels, i.e. criteria that in decision processes perform the function of determining an adequate, or satisfactory, alternative. "The Scottish word 'satisficing' (= satisfying) has been revived to denote problem solving and decision making that sets an aspiration level, searches until an alternative is found that is satisfactory by the aspiration level criterion, and selects that alternative." (Simon, 1972, p. 168)

There is quite a number of other prominent authors who in the Fifties and Sixties developed or proposed to develop economic theories which incorporate aspiration levels (Siegel, 1957, Siegel and Fouraker, 1960, Sauermann and Selten, 1962, Fouraker and Siegel, 1963, Cyert and March, 1963). Roth (1995b) describes the further development as follows: "Interestingly, the aspiration hypothesis has attracted different amounts of attention on different sides of the ocean. American experimenters and theorists have subsequently come to regard aspirations as, at most, an intermediate variable, rather than as a primary explanatory variable. Our German counterparts have been more inclined to regard aspirations as a primary explanatory variable" (p. 88, Fn. 28).

Considering the different views on the explanatory capability of the aspiration hypothesis we found it a striking regularity that the observed behavior of subjects in our experiment does correspond to the concept of *aspiration levels*; an aspiration level being the level of performance a person is striving for when solving a problem (Sauermann and Selten, 1962, p. 577). In all groups very early in the negotiation process goals are formulated concerning the final payoff they are striving for. On average this had happened already in the second round. In all first-moving player groups aspiration levels had been formulated at least by one player already in the first round, i.e. before making their first proposal.

We will analyze aspiration guided behavior in detail in Chapter 6. For the time being we conclude that players' behavior in our experiment corresponds to theories that assume goal striving behavior and an adaptation of aspiration levels.

4.2 Prominence

The idea of *prominence* has been introduced by Schelling (1957); Schelling (1958, 1960). Schelling observed that principles exist which underly tacit coordination and bargaining as well as explicit negotiations when parties involved in a relationship have to coordinate their actions for their mutual benefit. His idea is that people are often able to concert their intentions and expectations with others if each knows that the other is trying to do the same or if by conventions and traditions people inadvertently do the same. Focal points that attract the attention of persons in the sense described above are primarily characterized by some kind of prominence which will depend on cultural and environmental conditions. In bargaining, as Schelling states, there seems to be an "...'intrinsic magnetism' of particular outcomes, especially those that enjoy prominence, uniqueness, simplicity, precedent, or some other rationale that makes them qualitatively differentiable from the continuum of possible alternatives" (1958, p. 247). Schelling points out that this intrinsic magnetism is not a mystical concept but an intellectual phenomenon which is experimentally identifiable. Final outcomes of bargaining may be influenced by focal points characterized by social norms as for instance different appearances of the equity principle (c.f. Section 4.3). If numerical magnitudes are involved, there is a tendency that outcomes are expressed in "round numbers" (1957, p. 28).

This phenomenon of boundedly rational behavior, i.e. certain numbers are preferred when solving a problem since they are perceived as "rounder" than others, is a well established fact in experimental economics. In order to clarify these findings Albers and Albers (1983) developed a theory of prominence in the decimal system the basic idea of which is the determination of a *prominence level of a data set.* An elaboration of their basic ideas is proposed by Selten (1987). His method defines "a prominence level for a whole data set as an estimate of the dividing line separating sufficiently round numbers from other numbers" (Selten, 1997).

The prominence level of a numerical data set is defined as follows:

Let X be the set of all integer multiples of the smallest money unit γ. The prominence level $\Delta \in X$ is of the form

$$\Delta = \mu 10^{\eta} \gamma \text{ where } \mu = 1, 2, 5, 25 \text{ and } \eta = 0, 1, 2, \ldots$$

The prominence level of a number $x \in X$ is the greatest prominence level such that x is an integer multiple of Δ. It has to be adjusted to each data set and is measured in the smallest money unit.

The method of determining the prominence level of a data set will be demonstrated in Section 5.3.3 when proposals are analyzed in our experimental setup. However, we will see that other aspects of prominence influence the behavior of subjects (c.f. Sections 6.3 and 6.4).

4.3 The Equity Principle and Fairness

4.3.1 The Equity Principle

According to the prominence principle described in the previous section, distributions seem to attract the attention of subjects that are focal in other respects than by prominence in the decimal system. They may be influenced by ideas of equity and justice. One of the major results of our study is that equity was found to be most important in that it proves to be another very important guiding principle to determine subjects' behavior in the allocation task to be solved in our experiment. Allocations are chosen which have the particular property that they correspond to social norms. They can be characterized as being selected because the division of the coalition value is to be called equal. However, what is meant by ***equal*** is defined differently by different groups and in different situations. Yet, all these allocations have one common property which is called the equity principle by Selten (1978b, 1987). What is the meaning of this principle?

Consider a number of groups $i = 1, 2, \ldots, n$ and an amount r of money (e.g. rewards or costs) that is to be distributed among these groups. We call x_i the share of group i and w_i the weight of group i. The equity principle proposes a distribution such that the relation between the shares and the weights for each group is equal for all groups

$$\frac{x_1}{w_1} = \frac{x_2}{w_2} = \ldots = \frac{x_n}{w_n}. \tag{4.1}$$

Selten (1987, 1996b) points out that the amount r to be devided between the opponents and the method of finding it may be a point of dispute. As Table 4.1 shows, different equitable distributions imply different r's and thus affect the final payoff.

Allocations which are proposed by participants and are different appearances of the equity principle, e.g. equal shares, "Split the Difference" (Schelling, 1957, p. 28) or shares proportional to some magnitude, are listed below. Table 4.1 shows the formulae for r_i, x_i and w_i in these distributions.

Equal Split (ES) The coalition value is divided into two equal amounts. Both groups receive the same absolute payoff[18] , i.e. $P_S = P_W = \frac{1}{2}v(12)$.

Proportional Split (P) The coalition value is divided proportionally to alternatives. Since $v(1) + v(2) = \frac{1}{2}v(12), P_S = 2v(1)$ and $P_W = 2v(2)$.

Split the Difference (SD) The difference between the sum of alternatives and the coalition value is split equally, and is added to the guaranteed payoff. Thus $P_S = v(1) + \frac{1}{4}v(12)$ and $P_W = v(2) + \frac{1}{4}v(12)$.

Middle between Proportional and Equal Split (MPES) The coalition value is split such that both groups receive a payoff according to the middle between Proportional and Equal Split. Thus in our experiment $P_S = v(1) + \frac{1}{4}v(12)$ and $P_W = v(2) + \frac{1}{4}v(12)$; the values for MPES and Split the Difference are the same.

[18]Payoffs of S-groups will be denoted by P_S, payoffs of W-groups by P_W.

Table 4.1: Allocations according to the equity principle

	r	w_1	w_2	x_1	x_2	x_1 / w_1	x_2 / w_2
P	$v(12)$	$\frac{v(1)}{v(1)+v(2)}$	$\frac{v(2)}{v(1)+v(2)}$	$\frac{v(1)}{v(1)+v(2)}v(12) = 2v(1)$	$2v(2)$	$2(v(1)+v(2))$	$2(v(1)+v(2))$
ES	$v(12)$	$\frac{1}{2}$	$\frac{1}{2}$	$\frac{v(12)}{2}$	$\frac{v(12)}{2}$	$v(12)$	$v(12)$
SD	$v(12)-v(1)-v(2)$	$\frac{1}{2}$	$\frac{1}{2}$	$\frac{v(12)-v(1)-v(2)}{2}$	$\frac{v(12)-v(1)-v(2)}{2}$	$v(12)-v(1)-v(2)$	$v(12)-v(1)-v(2)$
MPES	$2v(1) - \frac{v(12)}{2}$	$\frac{1}{2}$	$\frac{1}{2}$	$v(1) - \frac{1}{4}v(12)$	$v(1) - \frac{1}{4}v(12)$	$2v(1) - \frac{1}{2}v(12)$	$2v(1) - \frac{1}{2}v(12)$
MSDES	(SD - ES) / 2 = $\frac{v(1)-v(2)}{2}$	$\frac{1}{2}$	$\frac{1}{2}$	$\frac{v(1)-v(2)}{4}$	$\frac{v(1)-v(2)}{4}$	$\frac{v(1)-v(2)}{2}$	$\frac{v(1)-v(2)}{2}$

Middle between Split the Difference and Equal Split (MSDES) This allocation gives both groups a payoff according to the middle between Split the Difference and Equal Split. Thus $P_S = \frac{1}{2}v(1) + \frac{3}{8}v(12)$ and $P_W = \frac{1}{2}v(2) + \frac{3}{8}v(12)$.

Only the Equal Split gives the same absolute amount of money to both groups. In all other cases groups receive different payoffs, S-groups get more than W-group.

The above mentioned concepts can be characterized by applying the standard of distribution, e.g. the way to measure the amount to be distributed, and the standard of comparison, the way to assign the weights to each group (Selten, 1987, 1996b). Table 4.2 shows solutions to the equity principle due to different standards of distribution and comparison. Proportional Split of the Difference was not mentioned in our experiment. Middle between Proportional and Equal Split and Middle between Split the Difference and Equal Split are compromises between different standards of distribution and comparison and are found by an "iterated equity principle" (Selten, 1996b).

Table 4.2: Solutions to the equity principle due to different standards of distribution and comparison

Standard of distribution	Standard of comparison	
	egalitarian	proportional to alternatives
Coalition value	Equal Split (ES)	Proportional Split (P)
Surplus	Split the Difference (SD)	Proportional Split of the Difference (SDP) = (P)

4.3.2 Fairness

The issue of fair procedures in exchange and allocation has early attracted the attention of economists and social psychologists. Beginning with Homans's (1961) notion of distributive justice, the problem of "...justice in the distribution of rewards and costs among persons" (p. 74), and the subsequent formulation of the equity model by Adams (1965), equity has been characterized as a rule which allows to define an allocation as fair: in order to be called equitable a distribution of rewards and/or costs should be proportional to inputs or contributions of the persons involved.[19] McClintock, Kramer, and

[19] See e.g. the studies by Leventhal and Anderson (1970) and Greenberg (1978).

Keil (1984) point out that by broadly defining relevant inputs the concept of equity can comprise a diverse set of distributional criteria, e.g. strict proportionallity, equality or the Equal Excess Norm (Komorita and Kravitz, 1979). They stress that these fairness concepts belong to a variety of distributional patterns that may be or have been characterized as fair or just.

Equity and fairness, often used as synonyms, are closely related to each other. In our experiment allocations that are based on the equity principle are intensely discussed and proposed. Most often they are justified by fairness considerations. Groups do not always use the term fairness. They also characterize these allocations as "acceptable, appropriate, comprehensible, ideal, just, justified, legitimate, logical, moral, morally most indisputable, optimal, plausible, rational, realistic, reasonable, satisfactory, an incentive for both parties to agree, a reasonable compromise, the optimum". Yet the transcripts show clearly that these allocations are brought up because they have the equitable division property.

Königstein (1997) conducted an experiment in which two subjects engage in joint advance production. In a second stage the output can be distributed via an ultimatum game. The author reports that in repeated games against the same opponent behavior is "equity anchored" and moves towards equitable allocations: up to 72% of demands are made according to four different equity standards. This result does not only show that different perceptions of equity and fairness exist but also that equity guided behavior plays an important role in other experimental setups, too.

There seems to be no need for a justification that dividing an amount *equally, i.e. being treated equitably, is fair.* As said before, the interpretation of what is equal, i.e. the amount to be distributed and the weights to be chosen, differs considerably, and depends on the status players have in our experiment. Groups explicitly point out the relevance of being an S- or W-group when arguing on what is to be achieved and what is to be seen as fair. Obviously the notion of fairness is situation-dependent. One single fairness concept cannot be assumed to apply for all situations. Thus, fairness does not have an unambiguous meaning.

Similar results have been found by Kelley and Thibaut (1978) and Komorita and Kravitz (1979). If multiple rules of fairness have been available these different concepts do have been used. Kahneman, Knetsch, and Thaler (1986a,b) also state that people's judgements of fairness are ambiguous and are heavily influenced by framing effects as well as by a perceived status quo and other reference points.

4.4 Motivations, Emotions, and Social Norms

Since the behavior of the subjects seems to exhibit some regularities we are interested in knowing whether there are forces and underlying principles behind their actions that allow to identify regularities and to prescribe their behavior. In psychology the notion of *motivation* plays an important role to explain people's behavior. We adopt this notion and define motivation as an *innerpersonal drive or force that makes a subject behave in a particular way for the sake of anticipated consequences* (Heckhausen, 1989, p. 10, Rheinberg, 1995, p. 14).

In neoclassical economics it is assumed that *the* motivational principle underlying people's behavior is maximization[20], i.e. a subject will take that decision which, given the constraints of the situation, will yield the maximal payoff. And the controversy in interpreting the results of ultimatum bargaining centers on whether these outcomes can be explained within the framework of game theory assuming that fully rational players are only motivated by economic or whether also noneconomic factors have to be taken into account.

The videotapes reveal that noneconomic motivations, norms and emotions are of decisive influence on the behavior of subjects. We all know that in everyday life factors influence our behavior that cannot be accounted for by pure economically motivated rationality. Our well-being as well as bad tempers affect our behavior, especially our reactions to the treatment by others.

But only a few attempts have been made to include motivations, emotions and/or other psychological findings into formal economic models (c.f. Akerlof and Dickens, 1982, Geanakoplos, Pearce, and Stacchetti, 1989, Huang and Wu, 1992, and Rabin, 1993). However, also papers that do not directly take into account psychological factors admit that bargainers may be guided by "systematic motivations distinct from simple income maximization" (Ochs and Roth, 1989, p. 380, see also Bolton, 1991). Recently a growing literature started to incorporate phenomena into bargaining models that take into account noneconomic aspects[21].

When analyzing potential and actual break offs by evaluating the videotapes we found that subjects' behavior was guided by economic (i) and

[20] C.f. Simon (1963) for a critical evaluation of neoclassical assumptions on human's motivations. He states (p. 718) "... the assumption of objective rationality [...] permits strong predictions to be made about human behavior without the painful necessity of observing people." "... classical economic theory [...] is deductive theory that requires almost no contact with empirical data [...] to establish its propositions."

[21] C.f. the references in Section 7.4.

noneconomic motivating forces (ii), (iii):

(i) economic efficiency
(ii) power
(iii) reciprocity

As assumed by game theory there is an *economic* motivation that, yet besides others, guides subjects' behavior in our experiment which we call *economic efficiency*. Subjects strive for more than their outside option and thus for an efficient outcome by allocating the total coalition value among the two parties involved. We don't want to use the term income or money maximization (as e.g. Ochs and Roth, 1989, Roth 1995a) since a group's final outcome is contingent on the consent of their opponent group. In this sense a group is not able to maximize their payoff. The behavioral consequence of the economic efficiency motivation is that subjects rather accept an offer if it exceeds their alternative than take the outside option. A break off does not pay in monetary terms; it results in an inefficient outcome in that only half of the coalition value is distributed.

The motivational implications of *power* is an area that has early attracted interest of philosophers[22], sociologists, psychologists[23] and also economists[24] since influence which is constituent to the definition of power affects interactions in social relationships. We define the *motivation of power* as the *intention to influence others in order to make them behave in a way in which they otherwise would not chose to act.*[25] In our context this intention means inducing the opponent to make concessions large enough that the own aspiration level can be enforced.

Another very important *noneconomic* factor motivating people's behavior is *reciprocity*, the existence of which may also displace economic efficiency. Already in the Sixties psychologists addressed the area of reciprocity in social relationships and stressed that reciprocity "may violate certain economic principles" (Goranson and Berkowitz, 1966, p. 228). Gouldner (1960) establishes a "universal, moral norm" of reciprocity which makes the minimal demand that "(1) people should help those who have helped them, and (2) people should not injure those who have helped them" (p. 171). Discussing the problem of equivalence of returns for benefits he rises the question whether also a "norm of retaliation" (p. 172) exists. Berkowitz and Daniels (1964)

[22]Gergen and Gergen (1986, p. 7) quote Thomas Hobbes who believed that people's central motivating force is power. He maintained that people possess "a desire for power after power that ceaseth only in death".

[23]See Heckhausen (1989), and Rheinberg (1995) for an overview.

[24]E.g. Simon (1957, 1961, 1963), Homans (1961).

[25]C.f. Heckhausen (1989, pp. 361), Rheinberg (1995, pp. 93).

as well as Goranson and Berkowitz (1966) contribute to this topic by their findings that reciprocity may work in the direction of retaliation: ".. subjects [...] could have become resentful because they felt they had been treated badly ..." (p. 231) . Similar ideas, without having been termed reciprocity, have been developed by e.g. Simon (1957)[26] and Homans (1961). Recently, reciprocity has been resumed to be investigated as a motivating variable explaining people's behavior.

Emotions, especially anger, are additional factors influencing the behavior of participants in our experiment. Emotions cause subjects to *re-evaluate* the outcome of the game. Monetary issues become totally minor matters.

Decisions that cannot be explained by economically defined rationality we do not want to characterize as irrational since subjects had motives involving a certain logic. We observed that subjects behave as Selten (1997) has described it: the typical behavior of experimental subjects is based on reasonable systematic principles and is quite different from the behavior normative decision and game theory assumes.

[26]Even though Simon (1957, p. 78) states: "... in most situations, all sorts of reciprocal power relations are present ...".

Chapter 5

Analysis of Payoffs and Proposals

In this part of our study we concentrate on the analysis of data that can also be obtained by computer experiments: we investigate the final payoffs, the proposals and the negotiation processes, i.e. the sequence of proposals that were alternately made by the groups. However, since the discussions of the subjects are available via the transcripts we are able to draw conclusions and give interpretations of statistical results that would not have been possible by evaluating just the data.

5.1 Bargaining Models and Related Experiments

Bargaining is a frequent type of social interaction in real world settings. Therefore it is not surprising that not only economists but also social psychologists are interested in phenomena that characterize bargaining situations. Gruder (1970) gives a concise description of the situation bargainers are confronted with in a negotiation process that points out the main features of our experiment: The goal of the participants in a bargaining situation is to reach some agreement as how to devide between themselves the total outcome from their relationship, in our experiment the coalition value of 320 points. They are interdependent since each participant's share of the outcome is determined partly by the other's and partly by his own decision. Each bargainer tries to influence the other in order to make a decision which would yield himself a relatively greater share of the total at the other's expense. Opponents are aware that the other has an alternative to the negotiation, even if this alternative is to opt out and receive much less than by agreement. Each bargainer should be careful not to demand too great a share of the outcome. If his opponent perceives this as a threat he may be forced to opt for his alternative, thus destroying the potentially profitable relationship. However, the relatively attractive outcome attainable by agreement should serve as an incentive for both to continue bargaining in order to achieve a mutually acceptable agreement.

There are two methods to get a theoretical answer to the bargaining problem as described above. The first one is the axiomatic approach defining the outcome of bargaining by a list of desirable properties the solution should satisfy. This approach is used by Nash (1950) the cooperative outcome of which is known as the Nash bargaining solution. Assuming a set of utility pairs representing possible agreement outcomes two persons are bargaining about, and a utility pair representing the utilities in case of disagreement and assuming further that utilities are linear in money, then the Nash bargaining solution assigns each of the two bargainers an amount of money that equals his disagreement payoff plus half of the surplus which is left over after the disagreement payoffs have been deducted.

The second method, called the strategic approach, takes into account the bargaining process. The solution of the bargaining problem is now an equilibrium of a theory which explicitly models the negotiation process.[27] Rapoport, Weg, and Felsenthal (1990) point out that both methods have their advantages and deficiencies: The generality of the axiomatic approach and the difficulty to assess the reasonableness of the axioms are its major drawbacks. The main disadvantage of the strategic method is that the moves in the bargaining game have to be specified completely and in detail.

Since our experiment is designed according to the second approach we in the following will refer to some models, solution concepts and experiments that are based on the social interaction of bargaining accounting for the multistage character of negotiations when alternating offers are made.

Many models incorporating the sequential structure of bargaining are of the following type: Bargainers have the opportunity to alternately make offers how to devide some amount of money. Time is devided into periods and it is assumed that time matters inasmuch as costs arise if an agreement is delayed to the next period. Thus, the amount which can be devided is shrinking from period to period. In odd numbered periods player 1 may propose to player 2 any allocation of the coalition value. If player 2 accepts the proposal the game ends. If player 2 does not accept the proposal he in even numbered periods may make a counterproposal. The game ends if a proposal is accepted by the opponent or in games with a finite horizon if the last period is reached. The amount players receive when accepting the proposal depends on the number of previous proposals and the kind of costs the players face in case of delay, e.g. a fixed amount or a fixed percentage of the amount to be devided. If an offer in the last period is refused both players get nothing. These models are also applicable to infinite horizon cases.

The first to investigate the alternating offer procedure was Ståhl (1972).

[27]For an overview on models using the axiomatic or the strategic approach see Osborne and Rubinstein (1990).

He models bargaining as a multi-stage game assuming a known finite number of bargaining periods and assuming that time is costly. He studies subgame-perfect equilibria by using backwards induction. Krelle (1976) also studies an alternating offer model with a fixed number of periods and bargaining costs arising when agreement is delayed. He applies his model to bargaining between firms as well as between firms and workers' unions, and he shows that a unique subgame perfect equilibrium exists.

Rubinstein (1982) investigates bargaining with infinite time horizon in which time is valuable. He studies a model with fixed bargaining costs for each period as well as a model with a fixed discounting factor for each period. The results he obtains are dependent on the constellation of both bargainers' fixed costs and discounting factors. He shows that a unique subgame perfect equilibrium exists for most of the cases examined. In almost all cases bargaining ends in the first period by immediate agreement.

Shaked and Sutton (1984) introduce a model capturing the asymmetry in bargaining power that might exist between the bargaining parties. In their theory the existence of an outside option which may be used as a threat affects the outcome of the bargaining process.

One of the first bargaining experiments examining some characteristics of the kind of games mentioned in this section are reported by Güth, Schmittberger, and Schwarze (1982). They conducted experiments of one-period games, the so-called ultimatum games, without outside options. They found that experimental subjects did not behave according to game theoretic predictions: on average players 1 did not demand all but the smallest money unit for themselves and if they demanded nearly the whole "cake" for themselves players 2 frequently rejected this proposal. Some participants obviously cared for a "fair" allocation and were willing to punish those who tried to leave them with a split perceived as unjustly uneven.

In a Rubinstein-like setup Binmore, Shaked, and Sutton (1989) experimentally tested the outside option model[28] renamed as "deal-me-out" against Schelling's principle of Split the Difference[29] which is widely used as a solution concept in bargaining theory. Players can opt out of the game in which case the game ends and the player(s) receive(s) a specified amount as outside option. The motivation for their model is that a player can only credibly threat

[28]It should be mentioned that in experimental social psychology a variety of bargaining experiments with outside options have been conducted already in the Sixties and Seventies, c.f. Komorita and Kravitz (1979) who e.g. run an experiment with face-to-face negotiations without the sequence of bargaining being prescribed by the experimenter. However, these experiments were not meant to test formalized theories as the ones reviewed in this section. See Section 6.1 for details on equity based allocations.

[29]C.f. Schelling (1960). This principle is called Equal Excess Norm by Komorita and Kravitz (1979).

to opt out if the gain from their alternative is higher than their agreement outcome. If the opponent offers an amount slightly higher than the outside option the player should not "leave the negotiation table". Binmore et al. (1989) report that their model predicted the outcomes "overwhelmingly" better than the Equal-Excess-model. However, the authors point out that the existing bargaining theories do not at all predict disagreements which they, however, find in their experiments. Considering the conflicts, their data do not support any of these theories. In our experiment conflicts also occurred, and in Section 7.6 we will explain break offs in a motivational framework allowing for other than fully rational behavior of subjects which was displayed by the videotapes.

The infinite horizon model by Rubinstein (1982) was tested by Rapoport, Weg, and Felsenthal (1990) using fixed cost factors. The infinite character of the game was induced by the experimenter in telling the subjects that bargaining would be terminated after "too many" rounds. In fact, 6 of 162 sessions were terminated by a random mechanism. The authors point out that players cannot solve the bargaining problem by backward induction when the number of proposals is infinite, and thus they may employ decision heuristics to achieve a solution. Subjects may ignore the strategic aspects of the game, and they may even ignore the difference in costs of the two participants involved. Considerations of equity and equality may become important, and, as we have briefly indicated already, did become important.

Selten (1981) presented a noncooperative model of characteristic function bargaining in order to be able to run experiments in characteristic function form where interaction and communication are anonymous and highly formalized. He points out that a game in characteristic function form is an insufficient description of real game situations because no specification is made how the proposals can be made and how agreements can be reached. The model Selten proposes allows for an infinite horizon as well as outside options, but no bargaining costs are assumed. The bargaining procedure suggested in this "allocation proposal" model was applied to the computer experiment by Uhlich (1988, 1990) and Kuon and Uhlich (1993) as well as to our videoexperiment the rules of which have been described in Chapter 2.

The data of the experiments by Uhlich and Kuon and Uhlich motivated a descriptive aspiration level based area theory, the Negotiation Agreement Area (NAA), which was introduced in Uhlich (1988) and further tested and refined in Kuon and Uhlich.

Before we describe the Negotiation Agreement Area in detail we want to mention an experiment by Klemisch-Ahlert (1996) which is methodologically similar to ours in that it directly observes subjects in decision situations. Groups of two players negotiated on the distribution of a certain amount of money in a variety of treatments their discussions having been audiotaped. In contrast to the experiment by Kuon and Uhlich the sum of payoffs for the two groups is not constant but depends on the agreements of the parties. The goal of Klemisch-Ahlert's study is to evaluate the distributive principles the subjects apply in order to reformulate normative bargaining theories based on these observations. Klemisch-Ahlert only uses certain aspects of the whole data set provided by the transcripts and does not investigate the protocols as extensively as we did.

The basic idea of the Negotiation Agreement Area is that players start their negotiation process from an initial aspiration level which they reveal by their first demand. Each opponent proceeds by making concessions in the same proportion as his counterpart did in the round before. The model predicts an area of final outcomes, the Negotiation Agreement Area, and proved to be most successful in comparison to a number of other theories including the solution concepts of Split the Difference and the outside option principle.

The Negotiation Agreement Area is based on the concept of aspiration levels. Four kinds of aspiration levels are derived which are crucial for constructing the NAA.

(i) The *minimal aspiration level* of a player is defined by his outside option $A_i^{\min} := v(i),\ i = 1, 2.$

(ii) The *maximal aspiration level* of a player equals his contribution to the grand coalition $A_i^{\max} := v(12) - v(j),\ i, j = 1, 2,\ i \neq j.$

(iii) The *attainable aspiration level* of a player, A_i^{att}, is assumed to be the worst case a player will receive if justice norms are taken into account. Kuon and Uhlich assume this amount to be the Equal Split for player 1 and Split the Difference for player 2.

(iv) The *tactical aspiration level* of a player is defined as his initial demand and is the only aspiration level which is observable. For player 1 it is assumed to be close to the maximal aspiration level; the tactical aspiration level for player 2 is assumed to lie in the range between the maximal and the attainable aspiration level.

The lower bounds for the players' payoffs predicted by the Negotiation Agreement Area result from assumptions on these aspiration levels. x_1, the lower bound for the payoff for the player with the higher alternative is reached if both players demand their maximal aspiration levels initially:

$$x_1 := \frac{A_1^{\max}}{A_1^{\max} + A_2^{\max}} v(12). \tag{5.1}$$

The lower bound x_2 for the payoff of the player with the lower alternative results from the W-player claiming his attainable aspiration level as first demand:

$$x_2 := \frac{A_2^{\text{att}}}{A_1^{\max} + A_2^{\text{att}}} v(12). \tag{5.2}$$

If both players' alternatives are equal, they both demand their maximal aspiration levels. In this case, the Negotiation Agreement Area predicts an equal division of the coalition value.[30]

Since our experiment followed the same procedure as the experiment by Kuon and Uhlich and was selected from the same game base we will make an intensive comparison of our results with the Negotiation Agreement Area in Section 6.5 after we have analyzed payoffs, proposals, and aspiration levels in our experimental setup.

5.2 Payoffs

Payoffs in I- and E-sessions are shown in Figure 5.1 as well as in Table 5.1. 16 of the 20 sessions ended by agreement, 4 sessions were terminated by break off being the ones where $P_S < 160$. Break offs in sessions 5, 6, and 17 were induced by W-groups, in session 12 by the S-group. All but 2 final agreement payoffs are divisible by 5, 9 are divisible by 10. In case of agreement all S-groups received 160 or more. $P_S = 160$ were caused by a group that was an S-group in I- and E-sessions, and was satisfied with the Equal Split.

In L-sessions as well as in H-sessions, P_S are concentrated in a range between 160 and 185, $P_S > 185$ occurring only twice in E-groups. Payoffs in L- and H-sessions obviously do not differ essentially. This is remarkable since it seems to be intuitively plausible that SH-groups who are 'stronger' in terms of their alternative in comparison to SL-groups should be able to enforce a much higher payoff. As was mentioned before, theories do exist that propose solution concepts which explicitly refer to alternatives and predict different payoffs for different threat points[31].

---

[30] The graphical representation of the Negotiation Agreement Area is to be found in Section 6.5.

[31] See for instance the Nash bargaining solution (Nash, 1950), Split the Difference (Schelling, 1960) or the Negotiation Agreement Area (Kuon and Uhlich, 1993)

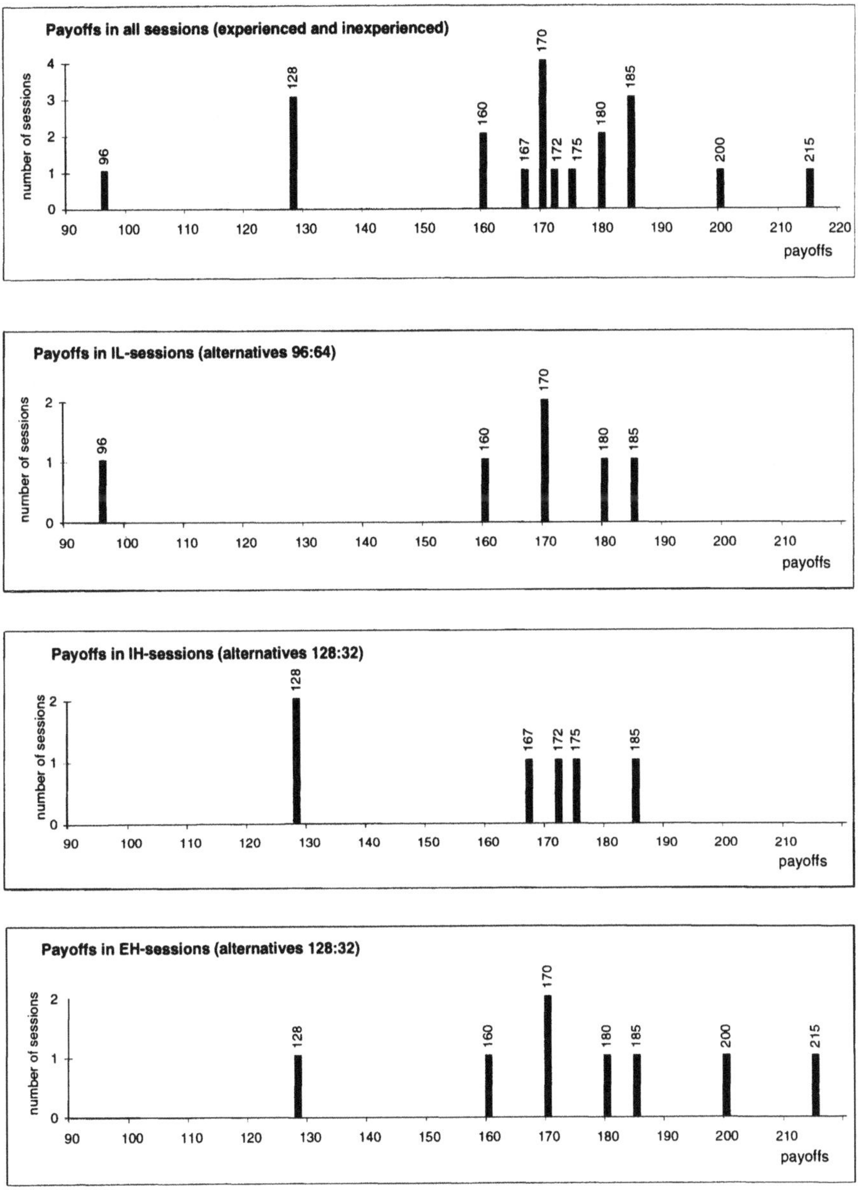

Figure 5.1: Distribution of outcomes in terms of payoffs for S-groups

Table 5.1: Payoffs in different treatments

Game Type	Experience of Groups			
	Inexperienced (I)		Experienced (E)	
	Session Number	Payoff	Session Number	Payoff
Low (L)	1	170		
	2	160		
	3	170		
	10	185		
	11	180		
	12	96 (Break off)		
High (H)	4	167	13	170
	5	128 (Break off)	14	160
	6	128 (Break off)	15	170
	7	172	16	200
	8	185	17	128 (Break off)
	9	175	18	215
			19	185
			20	180

5.2.1 Inexperienced Groups

In order to check whether the payoffs differ significantly between H- and L-groups we conducted the Mann-Whitney-U-Test for independent random samples for ISH- and ISL-groups.[32] H_0 is the hypothesis that the payoffs do not differ, H_1 is the hypothesis that the payoffs for ISH-groups are larger than for ISL-groups. The one-sided test gives $p = 0.531$. This means that for a nominal significance level of even 0.10 we cannot reject H_0 since $p \gg 0.10$. We did not find significance in the data that the payoffs for ISH-groups are larger than for ISL-groups.

Our impression from the protocols that most IW-groups are not impressed by the difference between the alternatives $v(1)$ and $v(2)$[33], even not in H-sessions[34], complies with this finding. All IW-groups do present themselves as self-confident, their first offers to S-groups amounting to 160 or less. Their general view is that alternatives are important when breaking off negotiation. But since the assumption predominates that S-groups' decisions will

[32] We do not describe the tests used in this study. See Gibbons (1985), Siegel (1956), Siegel and Castellan (1988) for a detailed description.

[33] For instance in 1.2.1, 1.2.3; 2.2.4; 3.2.1, 3.2.3, 3.2.3; 10.2.27, 10.2.29; 11.2.6, 11.2.8, 11.2.10, 11.2.13, 11.2.17, 12.2.4, 12.2.17.

[34] For instance in 4.2.1, 4.2.3, 4.2.6, 4.2.11, 4.2.15, 4.2.29, 4.2.45; 6.2.1; 7.2.2, 7.2.15, 7.2.19, 7.2.25, 7.2.35; 8.2.19; 9.2.1, 9.2.31.

be payoff-oriented[35], alternatives are not relevant in situations where offers are larger than the outside option, and thus an agreement is expected to be reached[36]. Even some IS-groups conclude that differences between $v(1)$ and $v(2)$ should not matter[37] or lose importance when negotiations drag on[38].

5.2.2 Experienced Groups

It does not seem unplausible to expect payoffs in E-sessions nearer to the Equal Split than in I-sessions taking into account that demands of IS-groups considerably higher than the Equal Split had not been accepted by IW-groups. To the contrary these demands resulted in extensive negotiations, and most ES-groups had experienced this having been IW-groups. On the other hand one could argue in the spirit of Binmore et al. (1985) that only experience enables players to fully acknowledge the strategic features of the game and therefore payoffs further away from the Equal Split are to be expected. Looking at Figure 5.1 we see that payoffs in E-sessions apparently do not differ essentially from those of all I-sessions. Again we find a concentration of outcomes in a range between 160 and 185. However, $P_S > 185$ occurs twice in E-sessions.

We checked the payoffs for ES-groups against all IS-groups by the Wilcoxon Signed Ranks Test[39]. H_0 is the hypothesis that the payoffs do not differ, H_1 is the hypothesis that the payoffs for ES-groups do differ. However, payoffs in E-sessions are not independent observations since in some E-sessions groups were combined which had played already against other groups in I-sessions (c.f. Table 5.2). We calculated the average payoffs in I- and E-sessions for those classes of groups who may have influenced each other by playing in different combinations in I- and E-sessions. We thus got averages for 5 classes of

---

[35]i.e. subjects will not break off bargaining if they are offered an amount of money that is larger than their outside option. See Section 7.2 for a detailed analysis of decisions with prevailing monetary and nonmonetary motivations.

[36]This was discussed in IW-groups 1.2.1; 2.2.5; 3.2.1, 3.2.2, 3.2.3, 3.2.5; 4.2.1, 4.2.3, 4.2.6, 4.2.39; 5.2.1, 5.2.4, 5.2.9; 7.2.25, 7.2.29; 8.2.2, 8.2.5, 8.2.13, 8.2.19; 9.2.2, 9.2.4, 9.2.8, 9.2.12, 9.2.22, 9.2.27, 9.2.29, 9.2.31, 9.2.35; 10.2.3, 10.2.6, 10.2.9, 10.2.28, 10.2.31, 10.2.57; 11.2.3, 11.2.6, 11.2.10, 11.2.17; 12.2.3, 12.2.4, 12.2.5, 12.2.7, 12.2.17.
This was also discussed in IS-groups 1.1.3; 2.1.6; 3.1.6; 4.1.9, 4.1.33; 5.1.3, 5.1.7, 5.1.22, 5.1.24, 5.1.26; 6.1.8, 6.1.11, 6.1.14, 6.1.18, 6.1.22, 6.1.24; 7.1.1, 7.1.2, 7.1.16, 7.1.25, 7.1.32; 8.1.1, 8.1.3; 9.1.1, 9.1.3, 9.1.10, 9.1.16, 9.1.22, 9.1.26, 9.1.30, 9.1.33; 10.1.6, 10.1.9, 10.1.10, 10.1.34; 11.1.1, 11.1.4, 11.1.7, 11.1.12; 12.1.1, 12.1.7.
Discussions on this point are also found in E-groups, 13.2.1; 16.2.15, 16.2.20; 17.2.4, 19.2.27, 19.2.29; 17.1.14; 19.1.9, 19.1.12, 19.1.25, 19.1.26, 20.1.5, 20.1.10.

[37]Groups 1.1.7; 2.1.1 (2.1 is quoted also in 16.2.15); 3.1.3, 3.1.9, 3.1.11.

[38]Groups 7.1.19, 7.1.34, 10.2.27, 10.2.29, 10.2.31, 10.2.37.

[39]Cf. Gibbons (1985), Siegel (1956), Siegel and Castellan (1988).

groups that are independent against the other classes (c.f. Table 5.3). These averages we tested by the Wilcoxon Signed Ranks Test. The two-sided test gives p = 0.438. This means that for a nominal significance level of even 0.10 we cannot reject H_0 since $p \gg 0.10$. We found no significance in the data that the payoffs of ES-groups differ from those of all IS-groups.

Table 5.2: Total and average payoffs in I- and E-sessions

Sessions	Group No.	E-group was I-group No.	P_S and P_W in E-Sessions	P_S and P_W in I-Sessions	Average Payoff	Rank of Average Payoff
ESH	13.1	4.2	170	153	161,50	5
	14.1	2.1	160	160	160,00	7
	15.1	10. 2	170	135	152,50	10
	16.1	8.2	200	135	167,50	2
	17.1	10.1	128 (Break off)	135	156,50	9
	18.1	5.2	215	32 (Break off)	123,50	14
	19.1	12.2	185	64 (Break off)	124,50	13
	20.1	3.2	180	150	165,00	3
EWH	13.2	7.1	150	172	161,00	6
	14.2	8.1	160	185	172,50	1
	15.2	9.1	150	175	162,50	4
	16.2	2.2	120	160	140,00	12
	17.2	6.1	32 (Break off)	128 (Break off)	80,00	16
	18.2	12.1	105	96 (Break off)	100,50	15
	19.2	1.1	135	170	152,50	10
	20.2	11.1	140	180	160,00	7

Table 5.3: Average payoffs for classes of groups playing against each other in I- and E-sessions

Classes of groups in I-sessions	Average payoff	Classes of groups in E-sessions	Average payoff
4 ; 7	169,5	13	170
2 ; 8	172,5	14 ; 16	180
6 ; 9 ; 10	162,7	15 ; 17	149
1; 5 ; 12	131,3	18 ; 19	200
3 ; 11	175	20	180

How can this finding be explained? Groups obviously did not behave as hypothesized above. On the one hand groups carry over their experience from I- to E-sessions, and each group refers to experience in I-sessions.[40] On the other hand we found that groups show a typical behavior that is maintained in E-sessions. They behave according to the ***status*** they have: S-groups bargain for high payoffs, W-groups try to keep the payoff as near as possible to the Equal Split. There are several groups that would not have come to an agreement had they played against themselves[41]. Five of the eight ES-groups demanded and received more than they conceded in their IW-sessions (13.1, 16.1, 18.1, 19.1, 20.1). Group 17.1, having been an ISL-group before, demanded even more than in the I-session, and was not willing to concede any substantial amount. The session ended by a break off of their opponent group. Finally there is one group that received less than they conceded in their IW-session: group 15.1 showed the most modest behavior among ES-groups. During a substantial part of the negotiation they discussed to accept the Equal Split[42] and negotiated a moderate surcharge on this amount. Groups are aware of the fact that they argue differently in I- and E-sessions pointing out that the view changes with the position[43].

The situation explained above may be reinforced by the effects of a change from an IH- or IL-group to an EH-group: ISL- and IWL-groups who become ESH-groups may feel more powerful, and ISL- and IWL-groups who become EWH-groups may feel weaker than in I-sessions. Groups 17.1 and 19.1 have been ISL-groups, became ESH-groups, and felt very powerful. Groups 16.2 and 18.2 felt very weak, and were willing to concede the highest payoffs in the experiment: group 16.2 was the only IW-group staying an EW-group, group 18.2 was an ISL-group having broken off bargaining, and became an EWH-group.

It is interesting to note that groups 16.2, 18.2, 19.2, 20.2 had been L-groups in I-sessions, and conceded payoffs being the four highest ones in E-sessions. Groups 13.2, 14.2, 15.2, and 17.2 had been H-groups in I-sessions. They conceded payoffs that are the four lowest ones in E-sessions, group 17.2 even initiating a break off.

[40]For instance in 13.1.4, 13.1.10; 14.1.1, 14.1.2; 15.1.2; 16.1.1, 16.1.8, 16.1.19; 17.1.2, 17.2.7, 17.1.9; 18.1.1, 18.1.14, 18.1.5; 19.1.4, 19.1.30; 13.2.1, 13.2.4, 13.2.5; 14.2.1; 15.2.2; 16.2.2ff.; 17.2.1, 17.2.7, 17.2.8, 17.2.14; 18.2.7, 18.2.17; 19.2.7; 20.2.2.

[41]13.1.4; 16.1.1ff., 16.1.8, 16.1.19; 18.1.2ff., 18.1.18; 19.1.4, 19.1.6, 19.1.12; 20.1.2ff., 20.1.15; 19.2.5, 19.2.15, 19.2.25, 19.2.37

[42]15.1.6 - 15.1.14

[43]For instance in 13.1.4; 18.1.19; 19.1.6, 19.1.12; 19.2.15, 19.2.25, 19.2.37. Two members of group 19.2 stated that they would not have been satisfied with the "symbolic bonus" they were willing to yield to their opponent group. They would not have been as tolerant as group 19.1, had they been the S-group.

Finally we will analyze the success of groups in I- and E-sessions measured by the average amount of money they received[44] (c.f. Table 5.2). One might suspect that those IS-groups who remained S-groups in E-sessions come up with the best results, and that the only IW-group remaining a W-group in their E-session came off worst. However, this is not the case. Of course, the behavior of the group to whom one is matched does play a very important role for the final outcome, and thus the most successful groups 14.2 and 16.1 took advantage of a favourable matching: Group 14.1 accepted the Equal Split proposed by 14.2, and the opponent of group 16.1 was the only IW-group being an EW-group again. Going for the Equal Split as an S-group in I- and E-sessions was not the best strategy in our experiment[45]. Half of the groups on average achieved at least the Equal Split. Groups who had been too hard a negotiator risked a break off and came off badly[46].

5.2.3 Group Effects

A factor that is likely to influence people's behavior and thus should be analyzed is a "group effect" that certainly is prevalent in our experiment. Subjects have been acting in groups and have been requested by the experimenter to intensely discuss their choices.[47] They readily argued on pro's and con's of different allocations, possible reactions of opponent groups, fairness concepts etc. Often group members brought contrasting views and deviating concepts to bear in the discussion. By getting familiar with ideas subjects had not been aware of before, the spectrum of decision alternatives available to them was enlarged even though the compulsion to find a joint decision might have reduced the set of choices actually being at disposal.[48]

[44]Here, we do not take into account the time groups devoted to their negotiations since subjects had different bargaining goals. Some tried to maximize their absolute money payoff. Some stated that they have been "broke" (pleite) and needed the absolute amount of money (5.1.9; 9.1.4; 10.1.42, 10.1.70ff.), for instance to buy a ticket for a concert. Others aimed at a high payoff in relation to the time spent.

[45]However, group 14.1 succeeded to achieve this amount in an average length of only 13.5 minutes (c.f. Table 5.5).

[46]17.1/10.1, 17.2/6.1, 18.2/12.1, 19.1/12.2.

[47]Even though the relations between group members in our experiment are certainly different from those in face-to-face coalition bargaining experiments where subjects negotiate with each other and have to form coalitions, a "socio-psychological field" is created (Selten and Schuster, 1970, p. 100) and the behavior of subjects is influenced by socio-emotional factors (Ostmann, 1992a,b).

[48]See also Lamm and Myers (1978) and Herkner (1988) for the effects of decision rules applied by group members. In this context it may be interesting which rules have been chosen in our experiment to aggregate the individual positions within the groups. In 7 of the 30 groups consisting of 3 persons the question on the group decision rule was posed at the beginning of the negotiation. The rule chosen was the majority rule. 5 out of these 7 groups found a compromise without applying this

The low payoffs in our experiment, e.g. in comparison to the experiment by Kuon and Uhlich[49] may be explained by the fact that group discussions often result in a behavioral and attitudinal polarization of the groups. Group decisions tend to be more extreme than individual choices[50], in the direction of a "risky shift" as well as towards more conservatism, c.f. Lamm and Myers (1978), Gergen and Gergen (1986, pp. 326) and Herkner (1988, pp. 513).

Yet, we have to explain why this polarization operates to the advantage of W-groups rather than of S-groups.[51] The transcripts clearly reveal that arguments influence choices.[52] The Equal Split proves to be a focal point that strongly influences the reasoning of participants. Even though S-groups want to achieve *more* than the Equal Split, this norm is the reference point determining the dividing line between allocations acceptable resp. inacceptable to S-groups.[53] Thus the Equal Split is a concept mentioned frequently. Moreover, also members of S-groups often specify this norm as one of several possible fairness concepts[54]. Burnstein, Vinokur, and Trope (1973) as well as Gergen and Gergen (1986, p. 327) point out that the number of arguments that are used in a discussion may influence the choice finally taken. This effect, the Equal Split being "in the back of S-group members' minds", may have (unconsciously) induced S-groups to make relatively high concessions, and thus may have caused the shift of final outcomes towards equality in our experiment.

---

rule. The remaining 23 groups did not discuss a decision rule at the beginning of the session. 6 of these practiced a majority vote later, 4 only discussed this rule in a subsequent phase of the negotiation. The compromise in one of the latter groups was found in that the person who best could get along with a deviating decision agreed to the allocation different from his proposal.
In 2 of the 10 groups consisting of 2 persons the impossibility of aggregating divergent positions by the majority rule was discussed and the necessity to come to a compromise was emphasized. Decision rules to overcome the problem were not proposed.

[49] C.f. session 6.5 for a detailed comparison of both experiments.

[50] Even though there are subjects who would have been more extreme had they played on their own, e.g. in groups 4.1, 7.1, 8.1, 20.2

[51] Note that only 3 of the 20 W-groups receive less than 50% of the surplus defined by Split the Difference, 6 of them receiving even more than 70%.

[52] For instance, individual aspiration levels that have been brought up in an early stage of the negotiation have been taken up later without subjects' explicitly pointing out that these have already been stated previously. Groups 7.1; 8.1; 9.1, 15.1; 18.1; 19.1; 4.2; 10.2; 11.2; 13.2; 15.2; 18.2; 19.2.

[53] See also Sections 5.2.2, 7.3.2 and 7.4.2.

[54] Groups 1.1.3, 1.1.5, 1.1.7; 2.1.3, 2.1.4; 3.1.2; 4.4.1, 4.1.11, 4.1.13; 5.1.5; 6.1.4, 6.1.6; 7.1.1, 7.1.12, 7.1.34; 8.1.5; 9.1.3, 9.1.7; 10.1.56, 10.1.72; 20.1.2, 20.1.3.

5.3 Proposals

In the sequel we will investigate proposals, i.e.the negotiation process during the sessions. The diagrams of the bargaining processes of all sessions are to be found in Appendix B.

In this section we are interested in the following characteristics of the bargaining process: number of proposal rounds, bargaining time, initial demands, and prominence level of the data set. Other features as the importance of threats and special bargaining patterns will be investigated in Sections 5.4 and 5.5.

5.3.1 Inexperienced Groups

Even though we found that payoffs in IL- and IH-sessions do not differ significantly it may be possible that IH-groups who are stronger in terms of their alternative try to resist outcomes perceived as disadvantageous. Thus, it may take more rounds and more time to end negotiations in IH-sessions.

In order to check whether in IH-sessions bargaining takes more rounds than in IL-sessions we conducted the Mann-Whitney-U-Test. H_0 is the hypothesis that the number of proposal rounds does not differ, H_1 is the hypothesis that the number of proposal rounds in IH-sessions is larger than in IL-sessions. The one-sided test gives $p = 0.047$. This means that we can reject H_0 on a nominal significance level of 0.05. There is significance in the data that the number of proposal rounds in IH-sessions is larger than in IL-sessions.

Analyzing the time spent on the negotiation by the Mann-Whitney-U-Test shows, however, that on a significance level of 0.05 we cannot reject H_0 that bargaining in IH-sessions does not take more time than in IL-sessions ($p = 0.066$, one-sided).

We conclude that obviously IH-groups resist terminating the negotiation to their disadvantage by delaying an agreement. However, the time they need for such a delay does not significantly take longer than in IL-sessions.

Groups who have to make the first proposal, i.e. the first-moving player group, have a difficult task. Their first demand has an influence on the final payoff in two respects. Not only does it determine the upper or lower bound[55] of the range of possible outcomes[56], it also has positive or negative psychological effects on bargaining. The initial demand is the first observable action and creates the atmosphere which is decisive for a cooperative or noncoop-

[55] Dependent on whether group 1 or 2 is the first moving group.

[56] There have been groups in our experiment that did raise their demands after their first proposals, but if an agreement was found, the final payoff was always lower than the first demand and not higher than the lowest previous claim.

erative attitude of the opponent party. The question posed by Rabin (1993) whether a first mover can do something that will compel a second player to regard him positively (p. 1296) or unfriendly is in line with our interest in opening demands of participants.[57]

According to which principles players find their first proposal will be analyzed in detail in Section 6.4. In this section we will concentrate on possible differences between IS- and IW-groups, and first and second movers.

Since alternatives of ISH-groups as well as of IWH-groups are higher than those of ISL-groups and IWL-groups one might expect that also the initial demands of these groups are higher. We conducted the Mann-Whitney-U-Test and we did not find significance in the data that the initial demands of ISH-(IWH-)groups are larger than of ISL-(IWL-)groups . The one-sided test gives $p = 0.197(0.294)$. Even on a nominal significance level of 0.10 we cannot reject H_0 since $p > 0.10$.

We conclude that all characteristics of the bargaining process we tested up to now except the number of proposal rounds do not differ significantly in the aspects analyzed above.

5.3.2 Experienced Groups

In this section we will look for behavioral features of E-groups that may be distinct from those of I-groups.

A first point of interest is the number of proposal rounds in I- and E-sessions. Appendix B conveys the impression that the length of negotiation decreases with experience. The Wilcoxon Signed Ranks Test shows, however, that there is no significance in the data that the number of proposal rounds in I-sessions is lower than in E-sessions. We cannot reject H_0 that there is no difference between I- and E-sessions in this respect ($p = 0.219$).

The second point of interest refers to bargaining time in I- and E-sessions. Even though the number of proposal rounds does not differ significantly the bargaining time may be shorter in E-sessions (c.f. Table 5.5). For instance, groups do not have to discuss general aspects of bargaining again since they have done this already in I-sessions, the group is familiar with the experimental setting, they have bargaining experience etc. The Wilcoxon Signed Ranks Test shows that in this respect there is significance in the data, negotiations in E-sessions take less time than in I-sessions. We can reject H_0 that bargaining time is not shorter in E- than in I-sessions ($p = 0.031$).

A last point of interest are initial demands. Does experience result in bargaining behavior starting from a more moderate first claim? We conducted

[57]See also the concept of tactical aspiration levels in the Negotiation Agreement Area.

the Wilcoxon Signed Ranks Test and found no significance in the data that neither S-groups nor W-groups require less as first demand in E-sessions than in I-sessions ($p = 0.406$ resp. $p = 0.312$).

Obviously in our experiment experience causes players to negotiate more economically in that they need less time. All other features which we tested are not affected by experience.

5.3.3 Prominence Level of Proposals

The phenomenon that subjects tend to choose "round" numbers can easily be seen from Figures 5.2 and 5.3 showing the distributions of relative frequencies of S- and W-groups' proposals. Frequencies are labeled for proposals that possess a structural prominence like alternatives or equitable allocations as well as for those that are divisible by 5 without remainder. Frequencies for proposals divisible by other integers are aggregated.

In the following the determination of the prominence level of our data set, i.e. proposals of S- and W-groups, will be described according to Selten (1987, pp. 83 -91, 1997).[58]

A data set in which the observations are numbers in the set X of all integer multiples of a smallest money unit $\gamma > 0$ can be thought of as a frequency distribution. Formally, a *frequency distribution over* X is a function k that assigns a positive integer $k(x)$ to every x in a nonempty finite subset Y of X and $k(x) = 0$ to every $x \in X \backslash Y$. The set Y is the *support* of k. The number $k(x)$ is interpreted as the frequency with which the value x occurs in the data set. The *number of all observations* is given by

$$H = \sum_{x \in X} k(x) \tag{5.3}$$

For every prominence level Δ let $m(\Delta)$ be the number of values x in Y at the respective prominence level Δ, $m(\Delta)$ being called the *number of values on the prominence level* Δ. For every prominence level Δ let $h(\Delta)$ be the sum of all $k(x)$ at the respective prominence level Δ, $h(\Delta)$ being called the *number of observations* on the prominence level Δ.

For every prominence level Δ, $M(\Delta)$ is the sum of all $m(\Delta')$ with $\Delta' \geq \Delta$, $M(\Delta)$ being called the *number of values at least on the prominence level* Δ. The number of all elements of Y is denoted by M. The *number* $H(\Delta)$ *of observations* at least on the prominence level Δ is the sum of all $h(\Delta')$ with $\Delta' \geq \Delta$.

The difference between the relative cumulative number of values $\frac{M(\Delta)}{M}$ and the relative cumulative number of observations $\frac{H(\Delta)}{H}$ is called the relative

[58] The computation of the prominence level will be illustrated by Table 5.4.

cumulative occupation surplus, resp. occupation surplus

$$D(\Delta) = \frac{H(\Delta)}{H} - \frac{M(\Delta)}{M}. \tag{5.4}$$

The prominence level Δ of a data set is defined as the greatest maximizer of the occupation surplus $D(\Delta)$.

Table 5.4 shows that the prominence level of all S-groups' proposals in our experiment is 5. The same is true if we calculate the prominence level for all proposals. The prominence level of all W-groups' proposals in terms of payoffs for group 1 is 10.

Table 5.4: Determination of the prominence level of all S-groups' proposals

	Number of		Cumulative number of		Cumulative distributions		
Prominence level Δ	Values $m(\Delta)$	Observations $h(\Delta)$	Values $M(\Delta)$	Observations $H(\Delta)$	$\frac{M(\Delta)}{M}$	$\frac{H(\Delta)}{H}$	Surplus $D(\Delta)$
250	1	19	1	19	0,019	0,092	0,073
200	1	21	2	40	0,037	0,193	0,156
25	2	7	4	47	0,074	0,227	0,153
20	7	28	11	75	0,204	0,362	0,159
10	6	34	17	109	0,315	0,527	0,212
5	7	39	24	148	0,444	0,715	**0,271**
2	18	44	42	192	0,778	0,928	0,150
1	12	15	54	207	1,000	1,000	0,000

It seems to be important, however, that the procedure proposed by Selten (1987) to determine the prominence level is applied to a sufficiently large data set. Separate calculations of the prominence level for proposals in IH-, IL- and E-sessions resulted in an unplausibly high prominence level of 200 for IHS- and ES-groups.

It is obvious from the transcripts that subjects are aware of the phenomenon of prominence which is explicitly discussed. "Non-round" numbers (krumme Zahlen) are seen as a means to send messages to the other group. Participants believe that these numbers should induce the other party to reason about the meaning of the proposed allocation, for instance Split the Difference. One group points out that deliberately making nonprominent

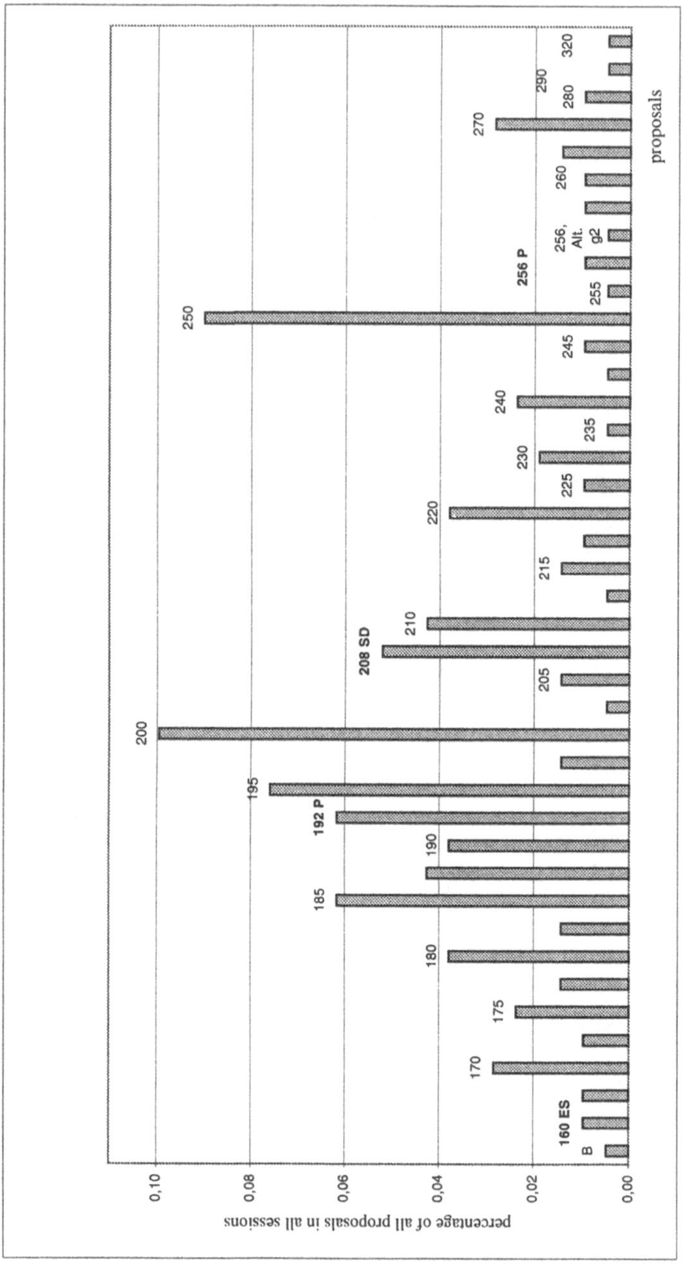

Figure 5.2: Proposed allocations of S-groups

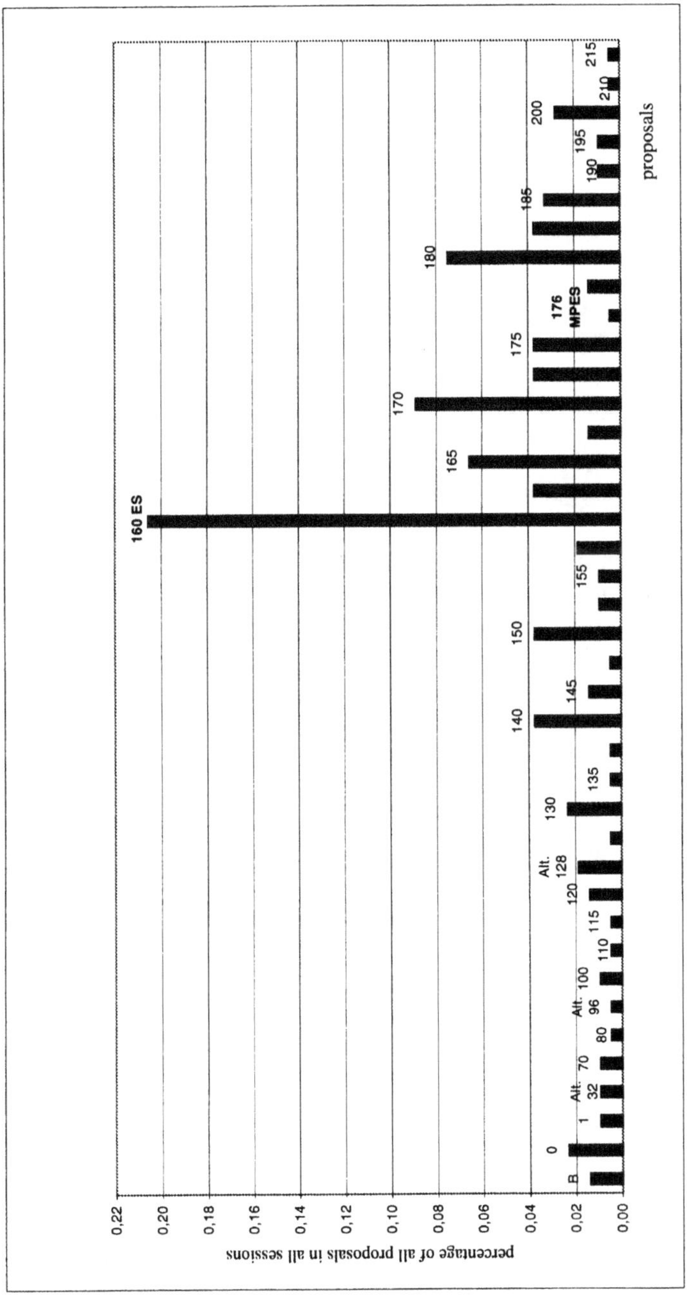

Figure 5.3: Proposed allocations of W-groups

proposals may cause the other group to think that "some mathematical strategy is persued". In some groups there is a dispute between group members whether round or non-round numbers are to be chosen.[59]

5.4 Threats

In the following sections we more closely will investigate the negotiation process, i.e. the sequence of proposals that were alternately made by S- and W-groups.

The shapes of proposal curves especially in I-sessions differ considerably. Two kinds of differences can be distinguished:

1. There are monotone and nonmonotone negotiation processes.
2. Different patterns in behavior seem to exist that reflect particular ideas of how bargaining goals are to be achieved.

Bargaining processes are not necessarily monotone (see Appendix B and Table 5.5). This is an astonishing fact since in general bargaining is understood as lowering demands by both opponents to achieve an agreement[60] or as Bartos (1970) put it: Negotiation is a process whereby parties who disagree to start with reach an agreement by a sequence of ever decreasing demands (p. 46, 48). However, we have to take into consideration the design of our experiment in which groups could not bargain directly with each other. They could not exchange verbal messages, and had to transmit via their proposals what they wanted to express. Nonmonotone proposals are a possibility of showing disagreement.[61] Yet, 21 out of 40 groups did not behave in this way.

[59]Nonprominent allocations have been discussed in 3.1.4, 3.1.10, 3.1.12; 4.1.6, 4.1.14, 4.1.16, 4.1.24, 4.1.36; 5.1.4, 5.1.5, 5.1.7, 5.1.9, 5.1.12, 5.1.13, 5.1.19; 6.1.7, 6.1.16, 6.1.19; 7.1.1, 7.1.3, 7.1.7; 8.1.7, 8.1.8, 8.1.10; 9.1.7; 10.1.2, 10.1.3, 10.1.4, 10.1.5, 10.1.6, 10.1.9, , 10.1.10, 10.1.20, 10.1.81; 11.1.11; 3.2.11, 3.2.13; 4.2.17; 7.2.27; 8.2.5, 8.2.8, 8.2.9, 8.2.13; 9.2.6, 9.2.7, 9.2.8, 9.2.9, 9.2.18; 10.2.14; 11.2.19; 13.2.4.

[60]This was discussed in several groups, for instance 1.1.4; 1.1.5; 1.1.11; 9.1.1; 12.1.1; 18.1.1, 18.1.18, 18.1.19; 19.1.19, 19.1.26. 5.2.1, 5.2.3, 5.2.9, 5.2.12; 5.2.16; 6.2.15; 7.2.2, 7.2.3, 7.2.8, 7.2.11, 7.2.14; 9.2.3; 11.2.5, 11.2.9; 12.2.11, 12.2.13; 15.2.4; 18.2.7. C.f. also the motivation for the Negotiation Agreement Area (Kuon and Uhlich (1993), Uhlich (1990), Kuon (1994)).

[61]This has been discussed in 3.1.10; 9.1.3., 9.1.22ff.; 3.2.5; 4.2.3; 4.2.19; 9.2.16, 9.2.18, 9.2.30; 10.2.18, 10.2.28, 10.2.34; 11.2.12

Table 5.5: Monotone proposals, threats, bargaining time and fictitious payoffs per hour

Session Number	Monotone Proposals (No Threats)	Non-monotone Proposals (Threats)	Success-ful Threats	Unsuc-cessful Threats	Counter-threats by Opponent Group	Bargaining Time in Minutes (1st Proposer)	Payoffs	Ficti-tious Payoffs per Hour
1.1	•					35	170	291
1.2	•							
2.1	•					22	160	436
2.2	•							
3.1		•		•	•	60	170	170
3.2		•		•	•			
4.1		•		•	•	115	167	87
4.2		•		•				
5.1		•	•	•	•	87	128	88
5.2		•		•			Break off	
6.1		•		•	•	75	128	102
6.2		•		•			Break off	
7.1		•		•		118	172	87
7.2	•							
8.1	•					52	185	213
8.2	•							
9.1		•	•			122	175	86
9.2		•		•				
10.1		•		•	•	149	185	74
10.2		•	•	•	•			
11.1	•					74	180	146
11.2		•		•				
12.1		•		•		39	96	148
12.2	•						Break off	
No. of Sessions	9	15	3	14	7			
13.1	•					29	170	352
13.2	•							
14.1	•					5	160	1920
14.2	•							
15.1	•					46	170	222
15.2	•							
16.1		•		•		46	200	261
16.2	•							
17.1	•					26	128	295
17.2		•		•			Break off	
18.1	•					20	215	645
18.2	•							
19.1	•					57	185	195
19.2		•		•				
20.1		•		•		28	180	386
20.2	•							
No. of Sessions	12	4		4				

We learn from the transcripts that groups try to assert their demands by lowering offers to their opponents. They *threaten*[62]. Therefore a proposal is said to be a threat when a group is offering less than in the previous round.[63] If the opponent group raises their offer above their highest level immediately after the threat we call it *successful* since this is what groups want to achieve. We call it *unsuccessful* if the opponent group does not raise their offer in the same way as described before. A *counterthreat* is a threat by the opponent group that immediately follows the threat.

In I-sessions groups obviously make extensive use of the rules that do not prohibit raising demands (resp. reducing offers) the purpose of these threats being to transmit the message that groups do not at all agree with their opponent's offer.[64] Moreover, all groups initiating a break off lowered their offers dramatically to signal that a conflict was impending.

Since threatening is intensely used, we will analyze in the sections to come whether groups by their threats achieve what they hope to achieve.

5.4.1 Are Threats Successful?

Table 5.5 shows that only 3 out of 15 threatening I-groups are successful at least once. In 14 out of 15 I-groups unsuccessful threats occur, 4 I-groups make both kinds of threats. Threats are answered by counterthreats in 7 I-groups.

From analyzing the proposals alone, it seems as if in 5 groups threats had been successful since the opponent group raises their offer in the round immediately following the threat. However, taking into account the transcripts we found that only 3 groups remain who, due to the threat, increase their proposals to a level that they did not want to offer before which therefore

[62]According to Webster's New International Dictionary (1966) a threat is "an expression of an intention to inflict evil, injury or damage on another usually as retribution or punishment for something done or left undone". This is exactly what groups have in mind when they merely discuss or actually make nonmonotone proposals. "Nonmonotone" and "threat" are used synonymously.
This was discussed in 1.1.7; 3.1.4 ff., 3.1.10; 4.1.16, 4.1.28, 4.1.31; 5.1.6, 5.1.8, 5.1.9, 5.1.10, 5.1.12, 5.1.15; 7.1.1, 7.1.2, 7.1.8, 7.1.16, 7.1.19, 7.1.21, 7.1.23, 7.1.25, 7.1.27, 7.1.29; 8.1.1, 8.1.10, 8.1.12; 9.1.3, 9.1.6, 9.1.16, 9.1.20, 9.1.21, 9.1.22; 10.1.2, 10.1.6, 10.1.12, 10.1.13, 10.1.17, 10.1.44, 10.1.65, 10.1.66, 10.1.73; 12.1.8, 12.1.9, 12.1.10. 5.2.9, 5.2.10, 5.2.15, 5.2.24; 6.2.14, 6.2.17, 6.2.18, 6.2.22; 9.2.16; 10.2.18, 10.2.32, 10.2.49; 11.2.6.
Sometimes even 'Shift' has been already interpreted as a threat, e.g. in 4.1.3, 4.1.4, 4.1.5, 4.1.11, 4.1.12; 4.1.19, 4.1.28; 7.1.19; 10.1.21; 15.1.7, 15.1.8. 9.2.19; 12.2.6.

[63]If a group intensifies their threat in the next round(s) by the same low offer or by "Shift" this is also regarded as a threat.

[64]See also Section 7.4.2 on reciprocity.

can be called successful threats.[65] All other concessions after threats concern proposals below the Equal Split which are thought off as not being acceptable for S-groups anyway. It is remarkable that successful threats happen only once in a session if they occur at all.

Thus, we can state that only 3 out of 24 I-groups make threats that can be called successful. Threats obviously are not an efficacious means of intimidating opponents, and making them raise their offers immediately. However, even though an immediate concession after threats is seen rarely, it is not impossible that threatening conveys an impression of firmness in bargaining, and thus has a favourable impact on the final payoff. This is certainly true for groups 3.2, 7.2, 9.2 and 10.2. Their opponent groups would not have reduced their demands had these groups not been so firm, and taken the risk of a break off.

We saw that the purpose of a threat to achieve a desired behavior of the opponent group is reached only in 3 cases. Threats do cause defiance, and create an atmosphere of toughness and noncooperation. Break offs are seriously taken into consideration[66] even if groups realize that in monetary terms this decision does not pay. As mentioned before, all groups initiating a break off lowered their offers dramatically signaling that a conflict was seriously taken into account. But this did not induce their opponent to make concessions to prevent an impending break off. Threats obviously achieve the contrary of what they are intended for.

These results comply with a study of Gumpert reported by Raven and Kruglanski (1970). Threats might be seen as a potentially useful bargaining tool. However, such behavior ignores the negative psychological effects on the threatened party, especially "humiliation and hurt feeling which are likely to instigate a resentful counterthreat" (pp. 90). Sending threatening messages may have a deleterious effect on conflict resolution and may reduce the chance to reach a mutually advantageous agreement.

5.4.2 Does Threatening Pay in Monetary Terms?

Even though threats do not immediately achieve what they are meant for it might still be that they result in increased final payoffs. Therefore we checked whether in I-sessions with threats payoffs are higher than in those without. We conducted the Mann-Whitney-U-Test, and we found no evidence in the data that the payoffs of groups with nonmonotone bargaining behavior tend to be greater than those with monotone bargaining behavior ($p = 0.3936$ in the one-sided test).

[65] They occur in 5.2.9, 9.1.26, 10.1.59.

[66] In 4.1.4, 4.1.21; 3.2.6; 5.2.2ff; 6.2.3, 6.2.13ff.; 12.2.12, 12.2.13.

5.4.3 Do Threats Reduce the Bargaining Time?

We saw that threats are neither very successful nor do they pay in final payoffs. Do they at least reduce the bargaining time? From Table 5.5 we see that the bargaining time varies considerably. However, the 3 I-sessions without threats belong to the 4 shortest inexperienced ones. We conducted the Mann-Whitney-U-Test and found clear evidence in the data that the bargaining time in nonmonotone sessions is significantly higher than in monotone ones ($p = 0.0104$ in the one-sided test).

Connected to bargaining time is the fictitious payoff per hour. How do threats affect this variable? All I-groups calculate their possible payoff per hour. Nearly all groups make the point that it might (have) be(en) better to receive a slightly lower amount in a reasonable time than to bargain hard, and achieve only a negligible gain[67]. Despite these considerations most groups did not put these ideas into action. The Mann-Whitney-U-Test shows that the payoff per hour is significantly higher in monotone sessions than in nonmonotone ones ($p = 0.0064$ in the one-sided test). Group 2.1 behaves logically in this respect. They are satisfied with the Equal Split, and offer this amount after 6 rounds (22 minutes). They maximize their fictitious payoff per hour to 436 points, resp. DM 43,60 (c.f. Table 5.5).

Most E-groups seem to have learned their lessons in I-sessions (c.f. Table 5.5), yet for a few the temptation remains to use nonmonotone proposals as a means of influencing the bargaining process[68]. However, all these threats are unsuccessful[69], i.e. successful threats don't occur any more. The same is true for counterthreats.

From our findings in the previous sections we conclude that threats have no positive effects on negotiations. They induce the intended reactions by the opponent group only in very few cases. There is no significance in the data that final payoffs are higher in nonmonotone sessions, and moreover, they cause delays, and thus worsen the relation between time spent and monetary outcome.

---

[67]This was discussed in 1.1.3, 1.1.7; 2.1.3, 2.1.4, 2.1.5; 3.1.15; 4.1.2, 4.1.16, 4.1.23, 4.1.33; 7.1.1, 7.1.16, 7.1.25, 7.1.32; 8.1.14, 8.1.16; 9.1.1, 9.1.5, 9.1.36; 10.1.22, 10.1.72, 10.1.88, 10.1.100; 12.1.1, 12.1.8; 1.2.1; 3.2.5, 3.2.10, 3.2.15; 5.2.2; 6.2.1, 6.2.4, 6.2.5, 6.2.14; 7.2.4, 7.2.5, 7.2.15 7.2.27; 8.2.7; 9.2.3, 9.2.27; 10.2.5; 10.2.10, 10.2.39; 11.2.5, 11.2.6, 11.2.9, 11.2.13; 12.2.15.

[68]Groups 16.1.3, 16.1.4; 17.1.1; 19.1.12, 19.1.32; 20.1.7ff.; 17.2.8, 17.2.9; 19.2.11, 19.2.13, 19.2.14, 19.2.22. See also the discussions on threats in groups 13.1.5; 14.1.1; 15.1.2; 17.1.9; 13.2.1ff; 14.2.1; 15.2.1.

[69]And moreover in 19.1.15, 19.1.33; 16.2.5 break offs are seriously taken into consideration.

5.5 Strategic Ideas

In game theory a strategy is a complete and exact behavioral plan that assigns a decision to every situation that may arise (Selten, 1967, p. 137). In real decision situations such complete and exact plans do not exist, and therefore it cannot be expected that subjects behave according to such plans. Subjects in our experiment only occasionally vaguely formulate what to do in special situations, and how to proceed[70]. If they plan their own behavior by exactly specifying what to do they do not think ahead more than three own proposals[71]. Planning their reactions to anticipated opponent's actions in even the next round, and anticipating their opponent's reaction to their own action proved too complicated. Groups tend to wait for the proposal and decide afterwards, they experiment their opponent's reaction[72]. In some cases, even though they plan ahead, they do not realize their plans.[73]

Yet, subjects do have general ideas how to achieve their bargaining goals. It is the realization of these ideas via their proposals that they call "strategy"[74]. To distinguish these ideas from the game theoretic concept we use

[70]For instance in 4.1.6; 5.1.3, 5.1.13; 6.1.4; 7.1.8, 7.1.10; 8.1.7, 8.1.8; 9.1.3, 9.1.7, 9.1.10, 9.1.12, 9.1.22, 9.1.23, 9.1.30, 9.1.35; 10.1.4, 10.1.8, 10.1.10, 10.1.17, 10.1.27, 10.1.44, 10.1.83; 11.1.1, 11.1.12, 11.1.15, 11.1.16; 12.1.1; 13.1.5; 15.1.1, 15.1.6, 18.1.7, 18.1.8, 18.1.14; 19.1.3, 19.1.13, 19.1.17, 19.1.21, 20.1.1; 2.2.3; 3.2.4; 4.2.19, 4.2.22, 4.2.45; 6.2.1; 8.2.1, 8.2.7. 8.2.14; 9.2.3, 9.2.12, 9.2.18, 9.1.11, 9.1.34; 10.2.9, 10.2.12, 10.2.90; 11.2.11, 11.2.16, 11.2.17; 12.2.15; 13.2.1;15.2.2, 15.2.4, 15.2.6, 15.2.14;17.2.12; 18.2.4, 18.2.11

[71]For instance in 3.1.7; 4.1.8, 4.1.21, 4.1.28; 6.1.4, 6.1.12; 7.1.11; 8.1.16, 8.1.12; 9.1.6,9.1.12, 9.1.18. 9.1.20; 10.1.4, 10.1.6,10.1.44, 10.1.90; 11.1.17; 12.1.7, 12.1.12,12.1.13, 12.1.14; 13.1.4, 13.1.5, 13.1.6, 13.1.8, 14.1.1; 15.1.4, 15.1.6, 16.1.17; 18.1.5, 18.1.7, 18.1.14; 19,1,9, 19.1.14, 19.1.21; 20.1.10; 3.2.3, 3.2.4, 3.2.12; 5.2.9, 5.2.12, 5.2.16, 5.2.22; 6.2.6, 6.2.15, 6.2.18; 8.2.4; 9.2.23, 9.2.32, 9.2.34; 10.2.7; 11.2.11, 11.2.18, 11.2.20; 12.2.15; 17.2.4.

It is interesting to note that in the experiment by Selten, Mitzkewitz, and Uhlich (1997) the memory depth of the typical strategies is 2, i.e. if specifications of strategies depend on previous periods they never depend on periods earlier than the last two (Selten, 1998). This finding shows that subjects do not only tend to simplicity in the planning procedure but also to simplicity properties when including past experience into their strategies.

[72]For instance in 1.1.3; 2.1.2, 2.1.3; 3.1.3, 3.1.5, 3.1.7, 3.1.10; 4.1.31; 5.1.6,5.1.9, 5.1.15, 5.1.16; 6.1.7; 7.1.14; 8.1.1, 8.1.3, 8.1.4; 9.1.1, 9.1.8, 9.1.10, 9.1.16, 9.1.22, 9.1.28, 9.1.29, 9.1.30; 10.1.2, 10.1.20, 10.1.21, 10.1.86; 11.1.1; 12.1.1; 19.1.8, 19.1.24; 2.2.4; 4.2.1; 5.2.3; 6.2.1; 7.2.2, 7.2.32; 9.2.3, 9.2.9, 9.2.13, 9.2.29; 10.2.6, 10.2.24, 10.2.34, 10.2.35; 11.2.2, 11.2.3, 11.2.6, 112.7, 11.2 9; 12.2.2, 12.2.3, 12.2.7, 16.2.19; 19.2.3, 19.2.11; 20.2.3, 20.2.13.

[73]For instance in 9.1.16; 11.2.12.

[74]Groups 3.1.15; 4.1.1, 4.1.2, 4.1.6, 4.1.10, 4.1.22; 5.1.9, 5.1.24; 6.1.4, 6.1.7, 6.1.8,

the term ***strategic ideas***[75].

Participants in our experiment pointed out that bargainers face a dilemma in the course of the negotiation: If they are willing to make concessions the opponent group might expect even more compromises, and if they want to induce an impression of firmness they run the risk of a break off. A different evaluation of the possible choices in this dilemma may lead to different negotiation styles. In the following we will describe the strategic ideas which result in distinguishable negotiation patterns (c.f. the diagrams in Appendix B). We start with the aggressive one, and proceed to the ones that are guided by more cooperation.

5.5.1 Constant Demand

In groups 5.1, 6.1, 12.1, 12.2, 17.1 a bargaining behavior is seen that does not show any cooperation, their negotiation style being characterized by maintaining their bargaining demands. They are "tough" negotiators (Bartos, 1970, p. 48) starting with a high demand and making concessions only hesitantly, if at all. Even though the patterns of these groups are not exactly the same the main feature is that the proposals are in a close relation or correspond to the bargaining goal which is fixed in a very early stage of the negotiation at a very high level. Considerable and lasting concessions are not made except possibly in the first round. The goals correspond to or are induced by the equity principle[76].

The strategic idea that lies behind this pattern is the following[77]: if the opponent group receives an offer that is "considerably" higher than their alternative[78] they will behave payoff-oriented, and rather take the offer than the outside option. Therefore no considerable concessions have to be made.[79] These ideas are realized by demands that are (nearly) constant over time.

6.1.10; 7.1.1., 7.1.36; 9.1.22, 9.1.26, 9.1.28, 11.1.13; 18.1.7; 20.1.11; 1.2.4; 4.2.45; 9.2.2, 9.2.6, 9.2.12, 9.2.13, 9.2.35; 15.2.4.

[75]In psychology the notion of strategy is used also in the sense it was termed by our participants: Gruder (1970, p. 130) points out that a strategy refers to specific behavior, the intention of which is some relatively immediate effect on the opponent's actions. The strategies employed characterize the negotiator's style, and they are techniques used to increase usable power in bargaining. See Section 7.3.2 for an analysis of power and the power motivation.

[76]Equal Split: 12.2.4; Split the Difference: 5.1.2; Proportional Split: 6.1.1f; 12.1.1, 12.1.4;. 17.1.5

[77]For example in 5.1.9, 5.1.24; 6.1.4, 6.1.7, 6.1.8, 6.1.10; 12.1.7; 12.2.7; 17.1.14.

[78]For instance at least 2 times their alternative, i.e. the Proportional Split (6.1.4f), or at least 100 (5.1.9).

[79]Similar considerations are also formulated by other groups (4.1.9, 4.1.33; 7.2.25, 7.2.29). But these groups in principle are willing to make concessions and finally lower their demands.

It is remarkable that all those sessions ended by a break off in which at least one group showed a negotiation pattern as described above. These groups have been the most unsuccessful ones by not reaching an agreement. Making (practically) no concessions "violates negotiation mores" (Gruder, 1970, p. 131), giving their opponent group a feeling of "dictatorship"[80] and "a loss of face"[81]. They were not willing to accept these offers and broke off negotiation at last after considerable length of bargaining.

5.5.2 "Jumping" between a Minimal Demand and a "Punishment Value"

There is only one group (7.1) showing this behavior very clearly. Other groups had the same ideas[82], but did not realize them at all (5.1, 9.1, 10.1, 7.2, 9.2, 11.2) or not as consequently (4.1) as group 7.1.

The strategic idea that lies behind this behavior is similar to the one described in Section 5.5.1: since group 7.1 believes in the payoff-orientation of their opponent group[83], they are not afraid that the latter will break off. They want to achieve a rather high amount that they specify very early in the negotiation process. This amount is the minimal value they demand for themselves and is also motivated by the equity principle[84]. If the opponent group does not react in the desired way they reduce their offer to an amount being higher than $v(2)$, but considerably lower than their maximal offer. By jumping between these two values the group clearly shows which amount they want to achieve as final payoff. Contrary to the groups in Section 5.5.1 group 7.1 reacts to behavior of their opponent group in certain phases of the bargaining process. They "reward" their opponents if they behave in the desired way by offering more, and they "punish" behavior that they consider unsatisfactory by offering less.[85]

Another difference to the groups described in the previous section is that in principle they are cooperative even though they pretend to be the opposite. In addition, group 7.1 has respect for the consequent bargaining behavior of their opponent group.[86] This is a completely different attitude.

---

[80] 5.2.12, 5.2.24, 5.2.27, 5.2.34, 5.2.36; 12.2.13, 12.2.17. Other groups not being involved in a break off stated that they understand such a behavior as dictatorship or capitulation if they give in, c.f. 2.1.5; 9.1.25; 7.2.33; 12.2.13

[81] For instance in 5.2.2, 5.2.7, 5.2.12, 5.2.13; 6.2.7ff; 12.2.17; 17.2.10, 17.2.14. See also the argumentation in 9.1.3.

[82] 4.1.14, 4.1.16, 4.1.31; 5.1.12; 9.1.6, 9.1.8, 9.1.12, 9.1.21; 10.1.13, 10.1.25; 7.2.17; 9.2.16; 11.2.6.

[83] 7.1.1, 7.1.2, 7.1.16, 7.1.25, 7.1.32.

[84] Split the Difference: 7.1.1

[85] See also Section 7.4 on reciprocity.

[86] 7.1.22, 7.1.29, 7.1.34

5.5.3 Concessions to Reach an Agreement

Groups in this category show cooperative bargaining behavior in the whole or in parts of the bargaining process. Here we find groups with monotone bargaining behavior as well as groups with only minor threats (4.2; 9.1; 19.2). Also groups 5.2, 6.2, 17.2 show a highly cooperative behavior over large parts of their negotiation processes, even though they ended the session by a break off.

Since we include groups with monotone bargaining processes into this category, also those groups are found here that show constant proposals over a considerable part of the negotiation (c.f. 1.1, 19.1, 1.2, 7.2, 8.2, 20.2). The strategic idea behind these constant proposals is one answer to the dilemma mentioned above: insisting on an offer rather than steady concessions will induce the opponent to lower demands[87]. Finally, however, cooperative behavior prevails resulting in concessions so that an agreement could be reached.

Even though the plots show quite nonhomogeneous curves as compared to Section 5.5.1 a categorization as above seems to be justified since groups finally behave according to the idea that the notion of bargaining corresponds to both opponents' lowering their demands in order to achieve an agreement.

5.5.4 Proposal of Equal Split by an S-group

The most cooperative behavior is shown by one S-group proposing, resp. accepting, an Equal Split after a few rounds. This group acted as an S-group in I- and E-sessions (2.1, 14.1), and both times realized the same strategic idea, namely to maximize payoff per hour by making or agreeing to an acceptable offer very early in the negotiation process.[88] Their considerations, and their experience from another bargaining experiment, were that their opponent W-group would immediately accept an Equal Split. Their expectations came true, and they reached the highest fictitious payoffs per hour in I- and E-sessions. Other groups discussed these ideas, too, but they did not put them into action[89], even not in E-sessions in spite of their experience in I-sessions.

5.5.5 Combinations of Behavior in 5.5.2 and 5.5.3

Several groups behave in a way that can be seen as a combination of the behavior described in Sections 5.5.2 and 5.5.3 (3.1, 3.2, 4.1, 9.2, 10.1, 10.2, 11.2, 16,1, 20.1). We see no clear pattern. In some phases of the negotiation

[87] 1.1.3; 19.1.11, 19.1.27; 7.2.11, 7.2.14, 7.2.18, 7.2.28, 7.2.32; 8.2.3, 8.2.6ff., 8.2.14, 8.2.16; 20.2.12.

[88] 2.1.4; 14.1.1, 14.1.2.

[89] 3.1.2, 3.1.3, 3.1.5, 3.1.9, 3.1.10; 4.1.1, 4.1.2, 4.1.7, 4.1.13, 4.1.15, 4.1.27, 4.1.33, 4.1.45; 7.1.1, 7.1.2, 7.1.11, 7.1.25; 8.1.2, 8.1.6; 9.1.1, 9.1.2, 9.1.4, 9.1.22; 10.1.88, 10.1.100; 11.1.1, 11.1.3, 11.1.4, 11.1.7; 15.1.2, 15.1.6, 15.1.7, 15.1.9, 15.1.11.

process groups stick to their previous proposals, while in others they raise their demands considerably. They threaten, resp. "punish" their opponents for not reacting according to their ideas. At the end of the sessions, however, cooperative behavior is predominant.

5.6 Conclusion

In this chapter we analyzed payoffs and proposals as well as negotiation processes interpreting our results on the basis of the observed behavior of subjects as revealed by the transcripts. We found that payoffs in IL- and IH-sessions as well as in I- and E-sessions did not differ significantly. We identified as reasons for such a behavior that W-groups are not impressed by the difference in alternatives, and that S- and W-groups in I- and E-sessions behave according to the status they have. A group polarization effect and an inclination of S-groups to regard the Equal Split as one of several possible fairness concepts may explain the shift in final outcomes towards equality.

Investigating the bargaining process we found that subjects behave according to strategic ideas as how to achieve their bargaining goal. Threats did not prove to be a successful means to induce opponent groups to behave in the desired way. We pointed out the importance of taking into account the tendency of subjects to choose round numbers when solving a problem, and calculated the prominence level of the data set consisting of proposals of S- and W-groups.

Chapter 6

Equity and Prominence in Aspiration Levels and Proposals

6.1 The Equity Principle and Fairness

In Section 4.3 we pointed out that participants of our experiment discussed a variety of solutions to the equity principle due to different standards of distribution and comparison. The concepts have been the following:

Equal Split (ES) The coalition value is divided into two equal amounts. Both groups receive the same absolute payoff, i.e. $P_S = P_W = \frac{1}{2}v(12) = 160$ in H- and L-games.

Proportional Split (P) The coalition value is divided proportionally to alternatives. In H-games $P_S = 256$ and $P_W = 64$, in L-games $P_S = 192$ and $P_W = 128$.

Split the Difference (SD) The difference between the sum of alternatives and the coalition value is split equally, and is added to the guaranteed payoff. Thus in H-games $P_S = 208$ and $P_W = 112$, and in L-games $P_S = 176$ and $P_W = 144$.

Middle between Proportional and Equal Split (MPES) The coalition value is split such that both groups receive a payoff according to the middle between Proportional and Equal Split. In our experiment the values for MPES and SD are the same.

Middle between Split the Difference and Equal Split (MSDES) This allocation gives both groups a payoff according to the middle between Split the Difference and Equal Split which amounts to $P_S = 184$ and $P_W = 136$ in H-games. MSDES was discussed in group 5.1 only[90]

[90] 5.1.5, 5.1.12, 5.1.19.

In the following we present the arguments which are brought forward by group members to characterize allocations as fair that correspond to the equity principle:

Equal Split (ES)

For members of W-groups equality seems to be the natural definition for equity, and thus in many W-groups the Equal Split is characterized as the fair allocation.[91] A division of the coalition value is regarded as fair if each of the two player groups receives half of it. S-groups also discuss that the Equal Split might be regarded as a fair allocation.[92]

Proportional Split (P)

Groups interpret the amounts that are guaranteed to them in case of a break off as reflecting their bargaining power[93]. A division of the coalition value proportional to alternatives leaves the initial relation unchanged, and is therefore considered as a fair proposal.[94]

Split the Difference (SD)

The essential argument behind Split the Difference is the following: half of the coalition value is distributed already by the guaranteed payoffs. If the surplus is split equally each group in addition to their alternative receives the same amount as a reward for not breaking off the negotiation, or loses the same amount if they initiate a conflict. Again the point is made that splitting an amount equally is considered as a fair principle of distribution.[95] In S-groups this argument is used as a justification for an allocation according to Split the Difference[96], only three W-groups accept this argument, and would have been satisfied with this amount.[97]

---

[91] 1.2.1, 1.2.3; 2.2.4, 2.2.5; 3.2.1, 3.2.9, 3.2.10, 3.2.15; 4.2.1; 5.2.1; 7.2.2, 7.2.3; 8.2.1; 9.2.1, 9.2.2; 10.2.10, 10.2.29; 11.2.1, 11.2.3, 11.2.6, 11.2.11; 13.2.1; 15.2.1, 15.2.22; 16.2.1; 19.2.1, 19.2.37.

[92] 1.1.3, 1.1.5, 1.1.7; 2.1.3, 2.1.4; 3.1.2, 3.1.3; 4.1.1, 4.1.11, 4.1.13; 5.1.5, 5.1.9; 6.1.4, 6.1.6; 7.1.1, 7.1.12, 7.1.34; 8.1.5; 9.1.1, 9.1.3, 9.1.7, 10.1.56, 10.1.72; 11.1.1; 15.1.2; 20.1.2, 20.1.3.

[93] See Section7.3.2 for a detailed analysis of the power motivation.

[94] Group 3.2 made the point that the Proportional Split might be the "equal split" for group 3.1 as the Equal Split is the "equal split" for group 3.2 (rounds 3.2.3 and 3.2.10). This was also discussed in 4.1.3, 5.1.9, 10.1.2,10.1.34, 10.1.40, 10.1.50, 10.1.56, 10.1.73, 10.1.82; 11.1.9, 17.1.5; 11.2.10.

[95] For instance in 6.1.4: "The remaining 160 we brotherly divide totally fair 80/80."

[96] 4.1.6, 4.1.43; 5.1.2, 5.1.4, 5.1.5, 5.1.7, 5.1.9; 6.1.4; 7.1.1, 7.1.4, 7.1.12; 8.1.3, 8.1.6, 8.1.7, 8.1.8.

[97] 1.2.1, 1.2.3, 1.2.7, 1.2.9; 8.2.12, 8.2.13; 17.2.3. Group 5.2 discusses Split the Difference, but does not accept the allocation (5.2.3, 5.2.9, 5.2.10).

Middle between Proportional and Equal Split (MPES)

The middle between the two equitable allocations Proportional and Equal Split is regarded as a fair compromise. Since in our experiment the values for Middle between Proportional and Equal Split and Split the Difference are the same, from the proposals alone we would not have been able to draw the correct conclusion on the underlying reasoning for the proposed allocation. Only the analysis of the transcripts enabled us to find out that a different fairness concept was applied.[98]

Middle between Split the Difference and Equal Split (MSDES)

This allocation is discussed as the least acceptable compromise also being seen as fair since it is based on an equitable distribution.[99] Without having been able to analyze the transcripts we would not have considered this allocation to be a result of fairness considerations.

All fairness criteria except Equal Split are particularly suitable if a group needs a well-founded justification for the argument that it deserves more than half of the coalition value.[100]

Group 5.1 is very eloquent in discussing several possible fairness concepts even though they are guided by the principle of Split the Difference. "From our opponent group's point of view the Equal Split is a fair allocation, we, however, divided the surplus equally and fair. For me one definition of fairness is the Equal Split, the other is the equal division of the surplus. Yet, our opponents' idea of fairness obviously is different from ours. A Proportional Split is also to be seen as just. However, one would have to explain to the other group how this division has been calculated and how it is to be justified. An allocation in the middle between the outcomes perceived as fair by us and by our opponents is also a fair result"[101].

Our findings on fairness are in line with observations of several studies in social psychology. McClintock, Kramer, and Keil (1984) report that multiplicity of fairness rules may induce subjects to select those which correspond most with self-interest. Bargainers with less inputs or power may select equality as the fair distribution mechanism. Negotiators with larger inputs or power, however, will recommend equity as a fair allocation scheme.

---

[98] 3.2.10ff.; 11.2.11, 11.2.17, 11.2.18; Middle between Proportional and Equal Split is also discussed in 10.1.84, 10.1.88.

[99] 5.1.5, 5.1.12, 5.1.19.

[100] 5.1.4, 5.1.5, 5.1.7, 5.1.9. This was also discussed in 7.1.12, 7.1.34; 8.1.1, 8.1.3, 8.1.4, 8.1.5, 8.1.7; 10.1.1, 10.1.2; 10.1.40, 10.1.50, 10.1.56, 10.1.73, 11.1.9, 11.1.10; 12.1.1; 17.1.5.

[101] 5.1.4, 5.1.5, 5.1.7, 5.1.9, 5.1.12, 5.1.19.

Kelley and Thibaut (1978, pp. 279) point out if arguments of equity and equality are brought up by the parties involved in the negotiation, final outcomes are to be expected that are a compromise between these two kinds of reasoning. Middle between Proportional and Equal Split would be a compromise according to this prediction. Middle between Split the Difference and Equal Split would be a compromise between the two equality arguments Split the Difference and Equal Split.

Komorita and Kravitz (1979) have investigated whether different alternatives and different fairness concepts may effect the outcome of bargaining. Experimental subjects repeatedly bargained in face-to-face negotiations in groups of two, three, and four persons. Komorita and Kravitz suggested that the three fairness concepts Equal Split, Equal Excess, i.e. Split the Difference, and Proportional Split might guide the outcomes of bargaining. They found that reward division was not a simple function of alternatives and that all three of the fairness principles have been used depending on the treatments which combined different sizes of rewards, different "power ratios" between alternatives and different group sizes.

As could be seen from Figure 5.1 the final payoffs in our experiment are not in accordance with the above mentioned fairness principles. Yet, we will demonstrate the importance of the equity principle in forming and adapting aspiration levels as well as in posing the first demand and adjusting proposals during the bargaining process (c.f. Sections 6.3 and 6.4).

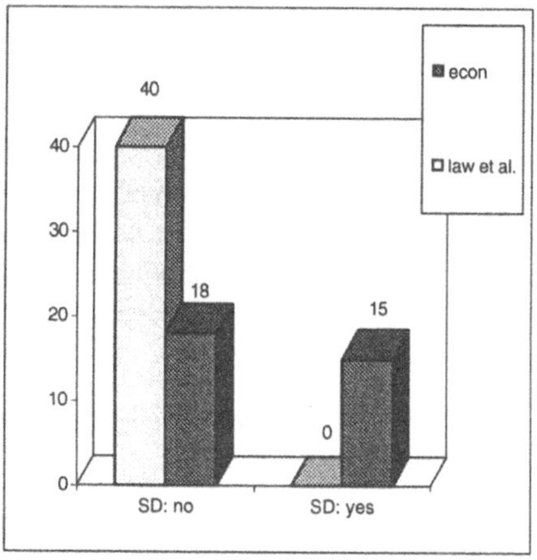

Figure 6.1: Group members mentioning or recognizing SD

An astonishing finding is that the concept of Split the Difference that corresponds mainly to game theoretic solution concepts, in our experiment is known only by economists. This result is highly significant (F-Test, one-sided, $p < 0.01$). Split the Difference is never mentioned or recognized by students of other subjects[102], and more than half of the economists do not discuss it (c.f. Figure 6.1).[103] Although some of these students, even economists, calculate and compare the amount that each group would receive in addition to their guaranteed payoff[104] they obviously do not make the further step to divide the surplus equally.[105]

Equal Split and Proportional Split may be more natural or more familiar principles of allocation than Split the Difference which, moreover, involves several computational steps which are not as easy as one might think. Even calculating the Proportional Split proved to be a rather difficult task which some groups did not succeed to manage. Theorists who would have observed the difficulty of some persons, students of economics as well as of other subjects, to solve these easy exercises may be induced to rethink the concept of full rationality of agents.

According to a reference by Kuon and Uhlich (1993, p. 337) Aristotle said that "equality and justice are always sought by the weaker party, but those who have the upper hand pay no attention to them". As we saw, people in our experiment who have the upper hand do pay attention to equality and justice in defining equality in the sense of equity, the definition and interpretation of S-groups being different from that of W-groups. They use the concept(s) that promise(s) a higher payoff.

[102] A noneconomist in group 8.1. for instance stated: "I would not be able to understand the meaning (of Split the Difference) and, moreover, perceive that this should be good for me because you think it is fair. This is not at all my opinion" (8.1.7).

[103] Yet, in seven of the nine groups where at least one group member knew this concept the group aspiration level was determined by Split the Difference (4.1, 5.1, 7.1, 8.1; 1.2, 8.2, 17.2).

[104] 3.2.2, 3.2.10; 9.1.3, 9.1.8, 9.1.16, 9.2.12, 9.2.29, 10.1.1, 10.1.6, 10.1.9; 10.2.57; 12.2.1, 12.2.2, 12.2.4, 12.2.12, 12.2.17, 12.2.18; 15.2.18, 16.2.17, 16.2.22; 19.1.6, 19.1.9, 19.1.11, 19.1.12, 19.1.21, 19.1.23, 19.1.26, 19.1.28, 19.1.32, 19.1.33, 19.1.36; 19.2.6, 19.2.7, 19.2.11, 19.2.12, 19.2.19, 19.2.21, 19.2.22, 19.2.25, 19.2.27, 19.2.29, 19.2.33, 19.2.35, 19.2.36, 19.2.37.

[105] A member in group 19.1 even states that the additional gain for both groups could not exactly be the same (19.1.12).

6.2 Prominence

The tendency of subjects to choose round numbers was stressed in Sections 4.2 and 5.3.3. Therefore it is important to calculate the prominence level of a particular data set if the only information on the behavior of subjects are payoffs and proposals. If, however, one is able to draw conclusions from the direct observation of persons and if one has, as we had, access to the discussions within groups a more exact description of the way prominence influences behavior may be possible. We will see that the following aspects other than the prominence level of the whole data set determine the behavior of subjects in our experiment: prominence when fixing first demands and adjusting proposals as well as prominence in formation and adaptation of aspiration levels (see Sections 6.3 and 6.4).

6.3 Aspiration Levels

When applying the theory of aspiration levels we have to specify how an aspiration level is to be defined in our experiment. Experimental subjects have not been asked to state the goals they wanted to achieve[106] but made spontaneous remarks. They either explicitly asked which goal the group should try to achieve, or the discussion within the group made clear that they aimed at a certain division of the coalition value. We had to decide from the transcripts which payoffs they were striving for. We used the following definition:

- *An aspiration level is the amount of money that a member in one of the groups is striving for as final payoff or would be willing to accept for at least one round.*
- *If several values are discussed, and if it is not clear which one is the actual aspiration level the lowest level is chosen.*
- *The aspiration level is valid as long as the transcripts do not indicate that a person aims at another one.*
- *An aspiration level for the group is defined as above if it is mentioned by at least two group members during one round.*[107]

[106] In an experiment by Tietz (1972) and Ostmann (1992a) subjects have been explicitly asked for various aspiration levels, c.f. Section 6.6.

[107] If group members do not want to accept an upper or a lower bound this is understood in our analysis as a separate aspiration level, even though it does not exactly correspond to the notion of a level. However, the formulations in the transcripts were unambiguous that the value taken as a reference point should not be accepted even though a concrete goal was not yet mentioned. We wanted to show

Aspiration levels formulated by the subjects have been plotted (c.f. Appendix E) in order to get a visual impression which aspiration levels are formed, and how they are adapted during the bargaining process.[108] From the diagrams we see that aspiration levels change during the negotiation process (see for instance Session No. 7 in Figure 6.2)[109]. The adaptation, however, need not be monotone; this is true for 17 out of 40 groups (c.f. Tables 6.1 and 6.2). These findings correspond to the observation by Sauermann and Selten (1962, p. 597) that aspiration levels are raised when satisfying solutions are found easily. They are lowered when their realization is difficult.

6.3.1 Formation and Adaptation of Aspiration Levels

How are aspiration levels formed, and how are they adapted? Are there any principles that guide their formation and adaptation?

Aspiration levels that are mentioned during the sessions are found in Figures 6.3 and 6.4 which show the percentage of sessions in which the plotted aspiration levels have been mentioned at least once. The figures show clearly that those numbers seem to attract the attention of subjects

(i) that correspond to social norms;

(ii) that are considered to be round numbers in the decimal system.

6.3.2 Finding the First Aspiration Level

How do subjects form the first aspiration level in the negotiation? From Tables 6.1, 6.2, 6.3 and 6.4 we see that, with the exception of three cases, subjects are oriented towards social norms. The equity principle, so to speak, serves as a means for constructing the first aspiration level. As we see from the tables, exact aspiration levels are not always mentioned. In many cases a reference point that has been found according to the equity principle is not seen as realizable or should not be accepted[110]. In Tables 6.1 and 6.2

---

clearly that it is not appropriate to take the reference point as aspiration level or the concrete value that was formulated later. Nor did we want to neglect these upper or lower bounds at all. Therefore, in figures and tables aspiration levels will be found that are not a concrete value, but are greater or smaller than a reference point.

[108]From the transcripts we get the aspiration levels for each group member. If not stated otherwise, in the sequel, however, we consider aspiration levels for the whole group since the proposals on the allocation of the coalition value also are group decisions.

[109]For an interpretation of Figure 6.2 and diagrams of all sessions c.f. Appendix E.

[110]C.f. Fn. 107, p. 66.

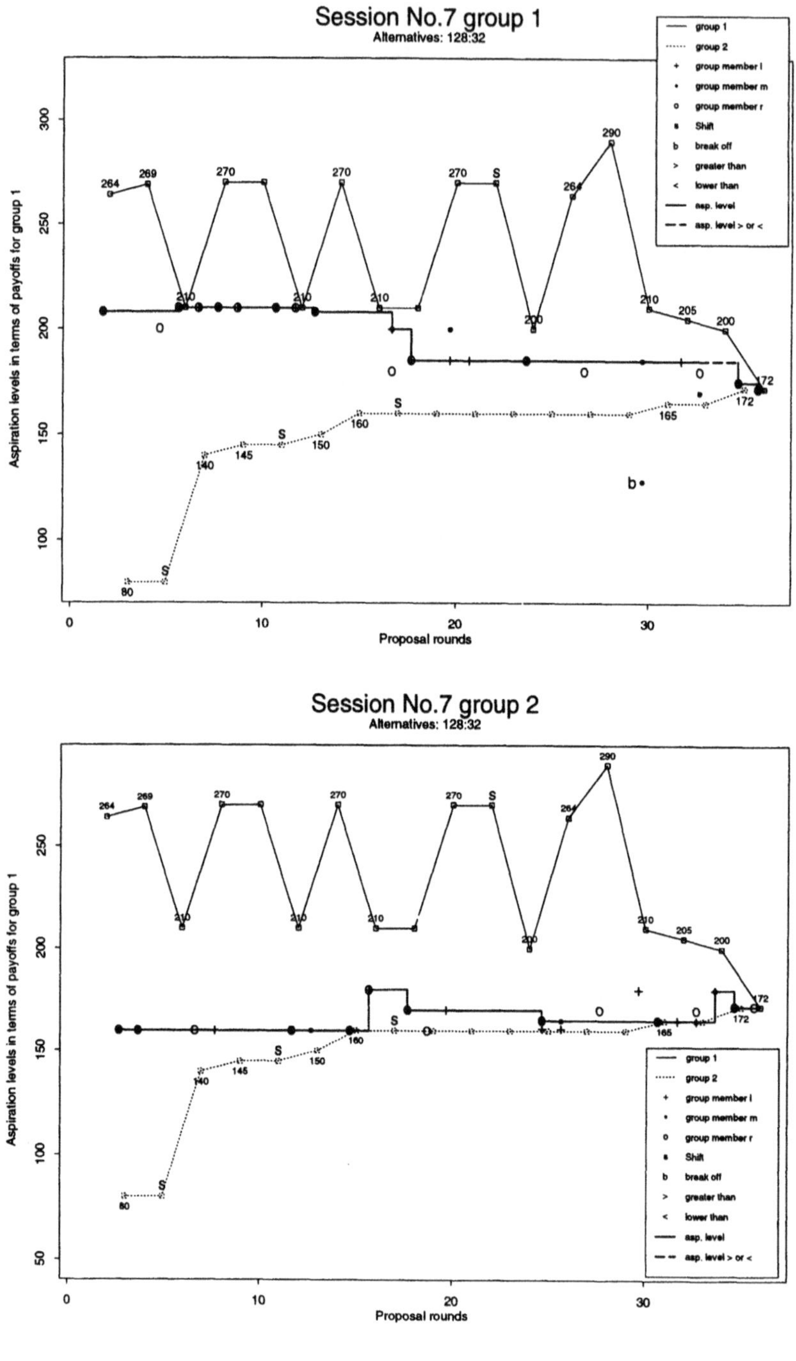

Figure 6.2: Formation and adaptation of aspiration levels in Session No. 7

Table 6.1: Formation and adaptation of aspiration levels in S-groups

Sessions	Group Nr.	Payoff in Terms of Group 1	Aspiration Level in Round No. 1	Reason	Adaption of Aspiration Levels During the Negotiation Process (Group Level)
ISL	1.1	170	[>160]	[l: $v(1) > v(2)$; better starting value]	*180,>160(ES),161, 170*
	2.1	160	[160(ES)]	[l: $v(12)/2$; accept ES]	160(ES)
	3.1	170	>160(ES)[a)]	strive for more than $v(12)/2$ that has been offered	>160(ES),170
	10.1	185	192 (P)	P: divide $v(12)$ proportionally to alternatives	*192(P),190,185,186,185*
	11.1	180	[>160(ES)]	[r: >160 (ES); after 2 hours accept 160 (ES)]	*>160(ES),192(P),<192(P),190,188,>160(ES),>162,180*
	12.1	break off	200 (P)	Miscalculation: $v(1)$ is 30% > v(2)(!)	200, either 200 or B(96), B(96)
ISH	4.1	167	[160(ES)]	[r: each group receives ES and is satisfied]	>160(ES),208(SD),200,180,174,170,168,167
	5.1	break off	208 (SD)	SD: better starting value	208(SD),200
	6.1	break off	[250(P)][a)]	[m: next decimal < P: 2*$v(1)$]	*240,230,240*
	7.1	172	208 (SD)	each group gets half of the surplus more and is satisfied	*208(SD),210,208,200,185,<185,175,172*
	8.1	185	>160(ES)	$v(1) > v(2)$; better bargaining position	>160(ES),208(SD),198,188,180
	9.1	175	>160(ES)	$v(1) > v(2)$; better starting position when B	>160(ES),180,178,175
ESH	13.1	170	>160(ES)[a)]	$v(1) > v(2)$; g1 should receive a symbolically larger amount	>160(ES),180,170
	14.1	160	[160 ES;>160]	[l: >160; r: 160, fifty/fifty]	160(ES)
	15.1	170	>160(ES)[a)]	$v(1) > v(2)$; g1 is in a more comfortable position	*>160(ES),160,170*
	16.1	200	220	100 points to g2	220,200
	17.1	break off	256(P)[b)]	P: divide $v(12)$ proportionally to alternatives	*256(P),240,250*
	18.1	215	>160(ES)[a)]	$v(12)/2$ is too much for g2	>160(ES),200,210
	19.1	185	[190]	[r: spontaneous 200; -10, i.e. g1 is satisfied with approx. 190]	190,185,<185
	20.1	180	[160 ES;>160(ES)]	[l: $v(12)/2$; r: >160, since g1 is in a stronger position]	*180,170,>170,170*

ES: Equal Split
P: Proportional Split
SD: Split the Difference
MPES: Middle between Proportional and Equal Split
B: Break off

italics: non monotone adaptation of aspiration levels
bold face: first moving player group
[ ]: individual aspiration level
a): proposal round 2
b): proposal round 5
l, m, r: group members
g1: S-group
g2: W-group

Table 6.2: Formation and adaptation of aspiration levels in W-groups

Sessions	Group Nr.	Payoff in Terms of Group 1	Aspiration Level in Round No. 1	Reason	Adaption of Aspiration Levels During the Negotiation Process (Group Level)
IWL	**1.2**	170	< 192(P)	r: P is a reasonable allocation for both groups; m,l: don't want to give that much to g1	<192(P),176(SD),175
	2.2	160	180	140 for g2 would be adequate	180,160(ES)
	3.2	170	[160(ES);170]	[l: ES: Fifty/fifty is the most reasonable solution; r: ES +10, since $v(1) > v(2)$]	170,176(MPES)
	10.2	185	[160(ES)]	[m: propose equal division which hopefully is accepted by g1]	160(ES),180,>180,>181,185
	11.2	180	160(ES)	ES: equal is always the fairest thing	*160(ES),170,180,170,176(MPES),180*
	12.2	break off	[165][b]	[r: ES + 5]	>160(ES)
IWH	**4.2**	167	160(ES)	ES: It is better for g1to accept ES than to break off	*160(ES),170,165,170,167*
	5.2	break off	160(ES)	ES: 160 is the best proposal, no long bargaining is needed	*160(ES),180,<180,180,190,180,>180,B(128)*
	6.2	break off	>160(ES)	g1 wants to receive more than g2	*>160(ES),180,190,200,B(128)*
	7.2	172	160(ES)	ES: Fifty/fifty is the only just division	*160(ES),180,170,165,180,172*
	8.2	185	160(ES)	ES: Fifty-fifty is always a good thing	*160(ES),190,170,180,208(SD),180,188,185*
	9.2	175	160(ES)	[r: ES is a just division]	160(ES),170,175
EWH	**13.2**	170	160(ES)	ES: moral decision	160(ES),163,165,170
	14.2	160	[135;>160(ES)]	[l: 135, like payoff of g2 in I-session; r:>160, to reach the goal fast]	
	15.2	170	[160;>160]	[l:160, to come to an end fast; r: >160, since $v(1) > v(2)$]	161,170
	16.2	200	[160(ES)]	[m: 160 is just]	>160(ES),200
	17.2	break off	208(SD)	SD: half of the surplus is the "absolute optimum"	*208(SD),200,208,B(128)*
	18.2	215	[220(P)]	[m: proportional division; miscalculation:1/4(!) $v(12)$=8,-; 10,- for g2 is o.k.	*220,210,215*
	19.2	185	[160(ES)]	[ES: g1 will not receive more than ES; no proportional division of $v(12)$ (by 4!)]	*160(ES),>160,165,170,175,180,185,180,185*
	20.2	180	[160(ES)][a]	[r: propose fifty-fifty division]	180

ES: **Equal Split**
P: **Proportional Split**
SD: **Split the Difference**
MPES: **Middle between Proportional and Equal Split**
B: **Break off**

italics: non monotone adaptation of aspiration levels
bold face: first moving player group
[ ] individual aspiration level
a) proposal round 2
b) proposal round 4
l, m, r: group members
g1: S-group
g2: W-group

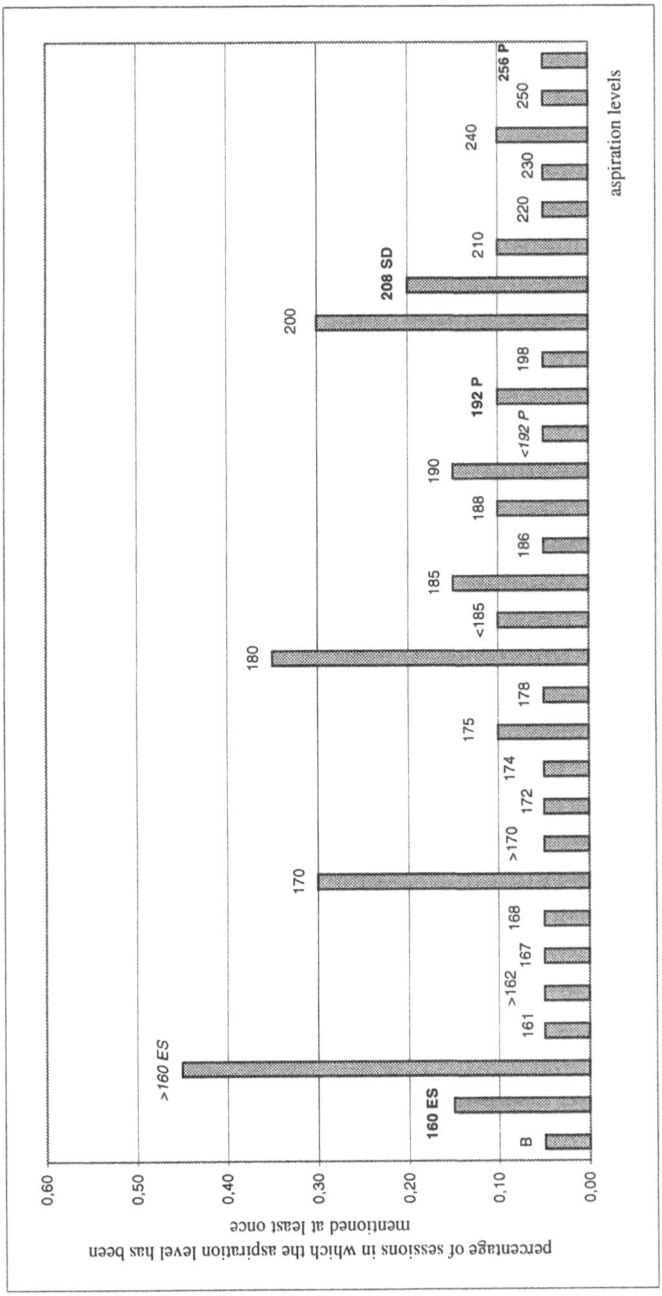

Figure 6.3: Aspiration levels of S-groups

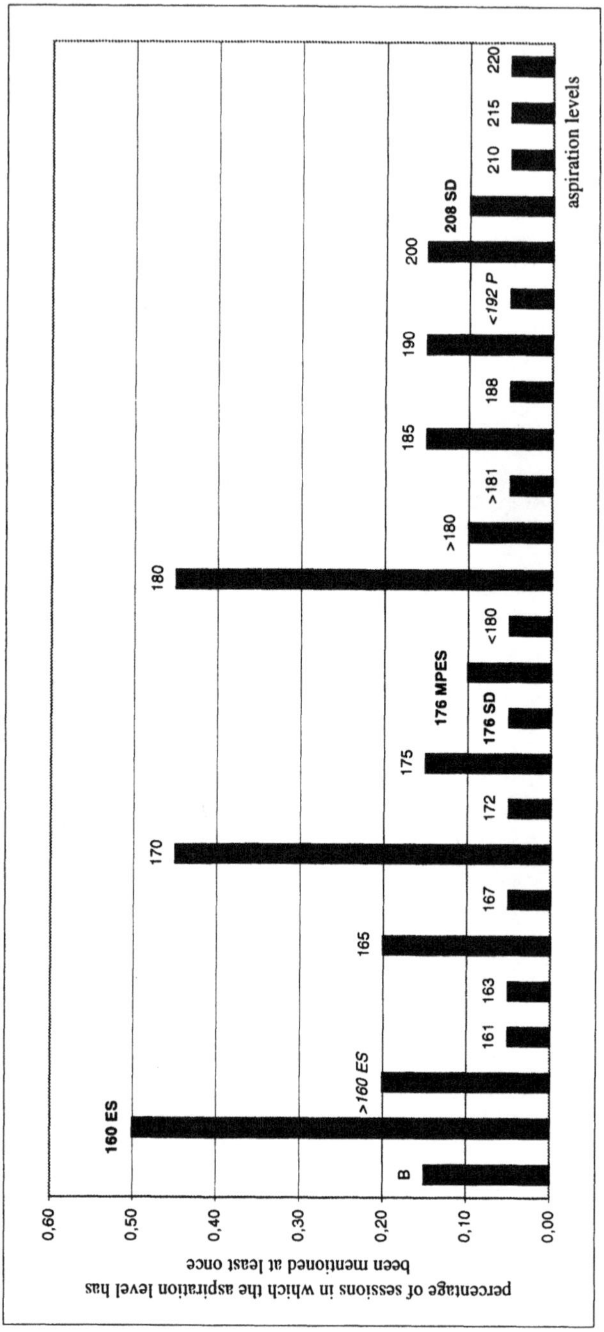

Figure 6.4: Aspiration levels of W-groups

we quote the reasons for the decisions the subjects discussed in the first round(s). Equity considerations being the basis of the equity principle play a very important role.

When forming the first aspiration level, also the prominence principle is valid (c.f. Tables 6.1, 6.2, as well as Tables 6.3 and 6.4) The numbers 200, 180 (140 respectively) and 100 are mentioned spontaneously. Subjects round aspiration levels to the next (second lower) integer multiple of 10 below or above a previously mentioned value regardless whether this value had been found according to the equity or the prominence principle. In session 14.2 an aspiration level has been mentioned which was not found according to these two principles: one participant wanted to achieve at least as much as the opponent group received in the I-session.[111]

We can state as a result that the formation of the first aspiration level in nearly all groups is characterized by equity resp. fairness considerations resulting in the application of the equity principle.

6.3.3 Adaptation of Aspiration Levels

When forming the first aspiration levels, prominence played only a minor role. Whereas regarding the adaptation of aspiration levels, this principle becomes much more important. Yet, the equity principle keeps significance. The adaptation of aspiration levels during the negotiation process can be seen in Tables 6.1 and 6.2.

The following forms of adaptations result from the *equity principle*:

- Adaptation to another social norm.
- Adaptation to a value that corresponds to the middle between aspiration levels or demands of both groups.
- The reduction of the aspiration level equals the concession of the other group in a previous round.

Two effects of the *prominence principle* can be distinguished:

- Subjects adapt to prominent aspiration levels.
  The amount of adaptation, however, need not to be prominent.
- The aspiration level is adapted by a prominent amount
  resulting sometimes in an aspiration level that is not prominent
  in the decimal system.

[111]This aspiration level could also be regarded as a prominent one in that it equalled the agreement of the previous negotiation, c.f. Schelling (1957), p. 28.

Table 6.3: Principles of formation and adaptation of aspirations levels for I-groups

Aspiration Levels	IS-groups												IW-groups											
Formation of aspiration levels	1.1	2.1	3.1	4.1	5.1	6.1	7.1	8.1	9.1	10.1	11.1	12.1	1.2	2.2	3.2	4.2	5.2	6.2	7.2	8.2	9.2	10.2	11.2	12.2
Equity Principle	●	●	●	●	●		●	●	●	●	●		●		●	●	●	●	●	●	●	●	●	●
Equal Split		●		a)											a)	●	●		●	●	●	●	●	
> Equal Split	a)		●	●				●	●		●							●						●
Split the Difference					●		●																	
Proportional Split (P); < P										●			●											
Middle between demands	●																							
Prominence Principle														●										
Spontan.: 140 for group 2														●										
Equity *and* Prominence Principle						●						●			●									●
Equal Split +10; +5															●									a)
Prop.Split: next integer mult. 10; -10						●						●												
Adaptation of aspiration levels	1.1	2.1	3.1	4.1	5.1	6.1	7.1	8.1	9.1	10.1	11.1	12.1	1.2	2.2	3.2	4.2	5.2	6.2	7.2	8.2	9.2	10.2	11.2	12.2
Equity Principle	●			●			●	●	●	●	●		●	●	●	●	●		●	●	●	●	●	
Adaptation to (another) social norm																								
Equal Split (ES); > ES	●													●					a)					
Split the Difference				●				●					●							●				
Proportional Split (P)											●											a)		
Middle between ES and P (MPES)															●								●	
Adaptation to previous social norm				a)			●				●													
Adaptation to the middle between aspiration levels of both groups				●				a)									●							
Adaptation to the middle between demands of both groups				●			●		●	●	●					●					●			
Adaptation to the middle between proposals (ingroup)																			●					
Reduction equals concession of gr. 2								●																

(shaded) group initiating a break off ● Group level a) Individual level

Table 6.3 continued

Aspiration Levels	**IS-groups**												**IW-groups**											
Adaptation of aspiration levels	1.1	2.1	3.1	4.1	5.1	6.1	7.1	8.1	9.1	10.1	11.1	12.1	1.2	2.2	3.2	4.2	5.2	6.2	7.2	8.2	9.2	10.2	11.2	12.2
Prominence Principle	●		●	●		●	●	●	●	●	●		●			●	●	●	●	●	●	●	●	●
Adaptation to prominent aspiration level																								
Spontaneously: 180; 200; 200 - 10				●			●	a)	●	a)										●				
Spontaneously: 140; 150 for group 2																	●	●	●	●		●		
Adaptation to previous aspir. level						●										●	●		●	●			●	
Next integer mult. 10 to pr. asp. lev.	●			●																●				
Next integer mult. 5 to prev. asp. lev.									●													●		
Offer of opponent group; +10							●	●					●							●				
Accept offer of opponent group										●										●			●	
Adaptation by prominent amount																								
+/-20																		a)	a)					
+/-10			●			●			a)							●	a)	●	●	●		a)	●	a)
+/-5							a)		a)							●	a)		●		●	a)		
+/-2									●		●													a)
+/-1			a)						a)								a)					●		a)
Accept offer of opponent group				●												a)								a)
Equity *and* Prominence Principle	●			●	●		●			●	●								●				●	
Equal Split +/-1	●																		a)					
Split the Diff.: next integer mult. 10				●	●		●																	
Prop. Split: next integer mult. 10				a)						●	●													
MPES: next integer mult. 10																							a)	
Other							●			●	●													
> offer of opponent group											●													
Accept offer of opponent group							●			a)														

group initiating a break off ● Group level a) Individual level

Table 6.4: Principles of formation and adaptation of aspirations levels for E-groups

Aspiration Levels	**ES-groups**								**EW-groups**							
Formation of aspiration levels	13.1	14.1	15.1	16.1	17.1	18.1	19.1	20.1	13.2	14.2	15.2	16.2	17.2	18.2	19.2	20.2
Equity Principle	•	•	•		•	•		•	•	•	•	•	•		•	•
Equal Split		a)						a)	•		a)	a)			•	a)
> Equal Split	•	a)	•			•		a)		a)	a)	•				
Split the Difference													•			
Proportional Split					•											
Middle between proposal (ingroup)								•								
Prominence Principle				•			•							•		•
Spontaneously: 200 - 10							•									
Spontan.: 100 for group 2				•										•		
Previous offer opponent group: 180																•
Equity and Prominence Principle											•			•		
Equal Split +1											•					
Proport. Split: next integer mult. 10														•		
Other										•						
Payoff as in I-session										a)						
Adaptation of aspiration levels	13.1	14.1	15.1	16.1	17.1	18.1	19.1	20.1	13.2	14.2	15.2	16.2	17.2	18.2	19.2	20.2
Equity Principle		•	•	•		•	•		•		•		•	•	•	
Adaptation to ES; > ES			•												•	
Adaptation to previous social norm													•			
Adaptation to the middle between demands of both groups				•		•	a)		a)		a)			•		
Reduction equals concession of gr. 2							a)									
Accept offer of opponent group		•														

(shaded) group initiating a break off • Group level a) Individual level

Table 6.4 continued

Aspiration Levels	ES-groups								EW-groups							
Adaptation of aspiration levels	13.1	14.1	15.1	16.1	17.1	18.1	19.1	20.1	13.2	14.2	15.2	16.2	17.2	18.2	19.2	20.2
Prominence Principle	•		•	•	•		•	•	•			•	•	•	•	•
Adaptation to prominent aspiration level																
Spontaneously: 180; 200	•			a)												
Spontaneously: 100+20; 120 for gr. 2												•	•			
Next integer mult. 5 to prev. asp. level									•							
Accept offer of opponent group							a)	a)	a)					•	•	a)
Adaptation by prominent amount																
+/-10	•		•		•			•								
+/-5							•		•						•	
Equity and Prominence Principle					•	•					•				•	•
Equal Split +10; +20											•				a)	a)
Prop. Split: next integer mult. 10 - 10					•											
Adaptation to the middle between demands of both groups -10						•										
Other								•	•							
> offer of opponent group								a)								
+ 3									•							

(shaded column) group initiating a break off • Group level a) Individual level

The effects of the equity and the prominence principle are to be seen in Tables 6.3 and 6.4.

We found that aspiration levels are adapted in amounts divisible by 10 and 5 without remainder, and in amounts of 2 and 1. These amounts become the smaller, the less groups are willing to make concessions. Aspiration levels are also adapted in other amounts. Except in one case these amounts occur, however, because subjects switch from the equity principle to the prominence principle and vice versa, or because the aspiration level was (nearly) reduced to the offer of the opponent group.

6.3.4 Test of the Predictive Success of the Principles Guiding Aspiration Level Formation and Adaptation

In this section we will test the predictive success of the principles which we found to guide aspiration level formation and adaptation, i.e. the equity and/or the prominence principle. For this purpose we calculate the *measure of predictive success* which has been developed by Selten and Krischker (1983), and Selten (1991). This success measure, M, is the difference between the relative frequency R of correct predictions (hits) of an area theory and the average size of the predicted area A, where

$$A = \frac{1}{n}\sum_{i=1}^{n} a_i, \quad R = \frac{c}{n} \quad \text{and} \quad M = R - A\,.$$

We use the following notation:

L_i lower bound of predicted area for aspiration level i, $i = 1, \ldots, n$

U_i upper bound of predicted area for aspiration level i, $i = 1, \ldots, n$

I_i length of interval $U_i - L_i$

P_i number of predicted points within I_i at aspiration level i

$a_1 = \frac{P_1}{I_1+1}$ relative size of predicted area for formation of aspiration level

$a_i = \frac{P_i}{I_i}$ for $i = 2, \ldots, n$ relative size of predicted area for adaptation of aspiration level

n number of observed aspiration levels

c number of correct predictions

The success measure M will be in the range of -1 to $+1$. The higher M, the better is the predictive power of the area theory.

To calculate A we, as a pre-theory, have to make assumptions on a reasonable area of possible predictions for aspiration level formations and adaptations. As was clearly shown by the transcripts, S-groups will not accept an allocation that gives them less than the Equal Split, and their highest expected value for aspiration levels is the contribution to the grand coalition, $v(12) - v(2)$. They cannot reasonably strive for more than this amount because their opponents will decline an allocation that gives them less than their alternative. W-groups will reduce their aspiration levels at most to their alternative; so the highest amount S-players will be offered is $v(12) - v(2)$. If groups are offered higher amounts than these minimal values, they at most adjust their aspiration levels to the best offer / lowest demand previously given by their opponent. This amount is seen as the value to be guaranteed as lowest final payoff, since groups assume and experience that their opponent finally returns to this offer even if they increase their demand(s) afterwards.

Table 6.5 shows the upper and lower bounds of the predicted area for S- and W-groups. Note, that aspiration levels are stated in terms of payoffs for S-groups.

Table 6.5: Upper and lower bounds of S- and W-groups' aspiration levels

<table>
<tr><th colspan="2"></th><th>Lower bound: L_i</th><th>Upper bound: U_i</th></tr>
<tr><td rowspan="2">W-groups</td><td>Aspiration level formation</td><td>Equal Split</td><td>- $v(12) - v(2)$ if formation prior to S-groups' first demand
- lowest previous demand if demand $< v(12) - v(2)$</td></tr>
<tr><td>Aspiration level adaptation</td><td>Equal Split</td><td>lowest previous demand $\geq$ ES</td></tr>
<tr><td rowspan="2">S-groups</td><td>Aspiration level formation</td><td>- Equal Split (ES) if offer $\leq$ ES
- best previous offer if offer $>$ ES</td><td>$v(12) - v(2)$</td></tr>
<tr><td>Aspiration level adaptation</td><td>best previous offer</td><td>$v(12) - v(2)$</td></tr>
</table>

We calculated A, R and M making the following restrictions:

- We always use the values of group aspiration levels. Decisions to break off are not counted.
- Whenever an upper or a lower bound should not be accepted (c.f. Tables 6.1 and 6.2) we in the calculation of A use the value of the reference point.
- Since aspiration levels of S- and W-groups might be influenced by the bargaining behavior and thus by aspiration levels of the opponent group we cannot assume the observed aspiration levels to be independent observations. We therefore will calculate and test M for sessions.
- We will test also E-sessions bearing in mind that they are not independent observations.

Table 6.6 shows A, R and M for all 20 sessions.

Table 6.6: A, R and M for all 20 sessions

Sessions	A	R	M
1	0.2096	1.0000	0.7904
2	0.1883	1.0000	0.8117
3	0.1866	1.0000	0.8134
4	0.2766	1.0000	0.7234
5	0.1431	1.0000	0.8569
6	0.1445	1.0000	0.8555
7	0.2084	0.9231	0.7147
8	0.2341	1.0000	0.7659
9	0.2253	1.0000	0.7747
10	0.2246	1.0000	0.7754
11	0.2458	0.9231	0.6773
12	0.0906	1.0000	0.9094
13	0.1348	0.8571	0.7224
14	0.0620	1.0000	0.9380
15	0.1453	1.0000	0.8547
16	0.0872	1.0000	0.9128
17	0.1043	1.0000	0.8957
18	0.0963	1.0000	0.9037
19	0.2006	1.0000	0.7994
20	0.0852	1.0000	0.9148

We are now able to test the predictive success of our results that the different forms of the equity and/or the prominence principle guide aspiration level formation and adaptation. By the Binomial Test we check whether more frequently than randomly expected $M > 0$, i.e., the relative frequency R of correct predictions is larger than the average size of the predicted area A of aspiration levels. H_0 is the hypothesis that $M > 0$ does not occur more often than randomly expected, H_1 is the hypothesis that $M > 0$ does occur more frequently than randomly expected. The one-sided test gives $p < 0.003$ for all I-sessions and $p = 0.004$ for all E-sessions. For a nominal significance level of even 0.01 we thus can reject H_0 since $p < 0.01$. We conclude that the different forms of the equity and/or the prominence principle guide aspiration level formation and adaptation since in a significantly higher number of cases than randomly expected $M > 0$.

6.4 Proposals

When each of two players envolved in a negotiation is assigned the same standard of comparison, i.e a weight of $\frac{1}{2}$, the equity principle proposes a solution which seems to be a common principle in bargaining, namely, to expect an agreement just in the middle between two demands[112]. And if the standard of distribution is such that it comprises the bargaining range being bounded by the initial demands of both players the equity principle should predict an outcome in the middle between first proposals. And indeed, in Sessions 7 and 9 the groups agreed upon a payoff exactly in the middle of the groups' opening demands[113]. However, the groups were not aware of this fact and proposed the payoff which was finally agreed upon because of quite different considerations.

Groups do not relate the decision on their final agreement to the mid-payoff between initial demands even though they often calculate the mid-payoff between actual proposals. Yet, they might have an intuitive rough estimate of this midpoint and thus some kind of a reference point for perceiving an outcome as fair. Therefore it might be interesting to see whether

[112]This was discussed for instance in 1.1.3; 2.1.1; 3.1.2; 4.1.36, 4.1.45; 5.1.3, 5.1.5, 5.1.10, 5.1.12, 5.1.15, 5.1.16, 5.1.19; 6.1.17, 6.1.22; 7.1.7, 7.1.8, 7.1.14, 7.1.17, 7.1.19, 7.1.23, 7.1.29, 7.1.31; 8.1.13; 9.1.1, 9.1.29, 9.1.35; 10.1.53, 10.1.84, 10.1.88; 11.1.19; 16.1.17; 18.1.5, 18.1.8; 20.1.1, 20.1.3. 1.2.9; 2.1.2; 2.2.4; 3.2.1, 3.2.11, 3.2.13; 5.2.1, 5.2.5, 5.2.7, 5.2.9, 5.2.10, 5.2.13; 7.2.2, 7.2.8, 7.2.11, 7.2.30, 7.2.32; 9.2.3, 9.2.7, 9.2.23, 9.2.28, 9.2.33; 10.2.5, 10.2.15; 11.2.9, 11.2.10, 11.2.12, 11.2.17; 13.2.5; 15.2.2; 16.2.2; 18.2.7; 19.2.14;

[113]First demand 7.1: 264; first demand 7.2: 80, agreement: 172. First demand 9.1: 220; first demand 9.2: 130, agreement: 175

there is any systematic deviation from this appearance of the equity principle which might be used as an additional characterization of bargaining behavior.

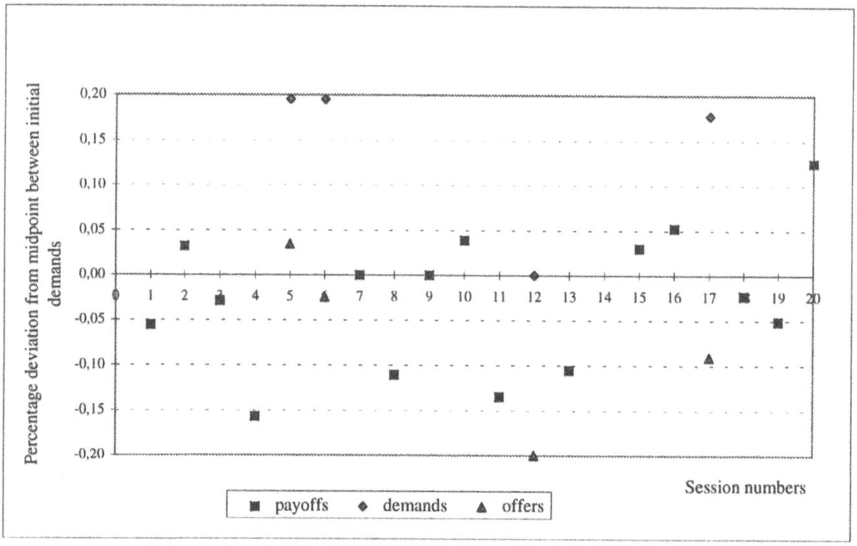

Figure 6.5: Percentage deviations of final outcomes for S-groups from mid-payoffs between initial demands

Figure 6.5 shows the relative deviations of final payoffs for S-groups from mid-payoffs between initial demands. In sessions ending by conflict the computations have been based on the last demands of S-groups and the last offers of W-groups. We see that with one exception, agreement outcomes in I- and E-sessions only deviate about 5% from the mid-payoff in favour of S-groups. It seems as if W-groups do not tolerate an outcome which gives S-groups much more than this mid-payoff, whereas S-groups do tolerate a much larger deviation in favour of W-groups. In sessions ending by disagreement opponents of conflict initiating groups obviously violate the above mentioned bargaining principle by *perseveringly* demanding amounts that are around 20% higher than the middle between their initial proposals. There are other groups that also persist in demanding resp. offering a constant amount but on a much lower level. Without overestimating the percentage numbers, it seems as if groups tend to punish those opponents who reveal themselves as being too greedy.

6.4.1 First Demands and Adjustments of Proposals

What are the determinants for first demands/offers and how are they adjusted? Are choices guided by the same principles as with aspiration levels?

Proposals made by S- and W-groups have been shown in Figures 5.2 and 5.3 The figures show clearly that those allocations are proposed which correspond to social norms or which are prominent in the decimal system.

6.4.2 First Demands/Offers

The criteria according to which subjects chose first demands/offers to open the negotiation are found in Tables 6.7 and 6.8. We see that subjects are guided by the equity *and* the prominence principle when opening the negotiation by first proposals. Proposing an allocation which conforms to a social norm does not necessarily mean that this norm determines the aspiration level (c.f. groups 4.1, 8.1, 1.2, 17.2). Again, the equity principle serves as a means to find a justifiable first demand, to determine the upper resp. lower bound of the negotiation area.

In contrast to the formation of aspiration levels, with opening proposals the prominence principle is much more important. Again, prominent numbers are mentioned spontaneously (Tables 6.7 and 6.8). Another clue for determining the first offer is the opponent group's alternative. There is one group offering only the outside option and one group offering an additional ε of 1 point (10.1, 11.1). 6 groups offer an amount corresponding to the next integer multiple of 10 larger than the alternative, thus offering an allocation which gives their opponents between 2 and 8 points in addition to their outside option (6.1, 17.1, 6.2, 9.2, 10.2, 15.2). Two W-groups offer less than the alternative as a reaction showing anger over their opponent's high first demand (7.2, 20.2). Nearly all groups start with a very low offer. W-groups present themselves as self-confident, there is only one group that starts with an opening offer larger than the Equal Split (18.2).

We can conclude that subjects behave according to the same principles when making initial demands/offers as they did when forming the first aspiration level. Yet, prominence is more important.

6.4.3 Adjustments of Proposals

When regarding the adjustments of proposals both principles keep significance (c.f. Tables 6.7 and 6.8).

Table 6.7: Principles of chosing first demands and adjusting proposals by I-groups

Proposals	**IS-groups**												**IW-groups**											
Initial demand/offer	1.1	2.1	3.1	4.1	5.1	6.1	7.1	8.1	9.1	10.1	11.1	12.1 (shaded)	1.2	2.2	3.2	4.2	5.2 (shaded)	6.2 (shaded)	7.2	8.2	9.2	10.2	11.2	12.2
Equity Principle				●	●		●	●					●		●					●			●	●
Equal Split													●		●					●			●	●
Split the Difference					●																			
Proportional Split				●				●																
Arithmetic mean (ingroup proposals)							●																	
Prominence Principle	●		●			●			●	●	●	●		●		●	●	●	●		●	●		
Spontan.: 200; 200 - 10; 80	●		●						●										●					
Alternative (+/-1)										●	●													
next integer multiple of 10						●												●			●	●		
next integer multiple of 10 +/-10												●		●		●	●							
Equity and Prominence Principle		●																						
Same offer to opponent as opponent to group +10		●																						
Adjustment of demands/offers	1.1	2.1	3.1	4.1	5.1	6.1	7.1	8.1	9.1	10.1	11.1	12.1 (shaded)	1.2	2.2	3.2	4.2	5.2 (shaded)	6.2 (shaded)	7.2	8.2	9.2	10.2	11.2	12.2
Equity Principle	●	●		●	●		●	●	●	●	●		●	●	●		●	●	●		●	●	●	●
Adjustment to (another) social norm																								
Equal Split (ES)		●															●	●	●		●	●		●
Split the Difference				●				●																
Proportional Split (P)										●	●													
Middle between ES and P																							●	
Previous social norm				●	●										●							●	●	
Adjustment to the middle between proposals of both groups				●					●				●		●									
Adjustment to the middle between proposals (ingroup)	●			●					●										●					
Same offer to opponent as opponent to group															●			●					●	
Concession equals concession of opponent group							●	●														●	●	
Accept offer of opponent group														●										

(shaded) group initiating a break off

Table 6.7 continued

Proposals	IS-groups												IW-groups											
Adjustment of demands/offers	1.1	2.1	3.1	4.1	5.1	6.1	7.1	8.1	9.1	10.1	11.1	12.1	1.2	2.2	3.2	4.2	5.2	6.2	7.2	8.2	9.2	10.2	11.2	12.2
Prominence Principle	●		●	●	●	●	●	●	●	●	●	●	●	●	●	●	●	●	●	●	●	●	●	
Adjustment to prominent proposal																								
Spontaneously: 200 for group 2																●							●	
0 or 1												●			●							●		
Alternative; +/-1; next integer mult. 10							●										●				●	●		
Prominent proposal; +/-1			●	●				●									●							
Previous prominent proposal				●		●	●			●		●				●					●	●		
Previous proposal							●			●											●	●		
Next integer mult. 10 to prev. proposal				●			●		●	●	●						●				●			
Next integer mult. 5 to prev. proposal								●	●	●	●													
Deliberately non-prominent proposal										●											●			
Accept offer of opponent group	●		●							●				●						●	●		●	
Adjustment by prominent amount																								
+/-20									●									●						
+/-10				●			●		●	●		●					●	●		●	●		●	
-10+2																						●		
+/-5						●	●	●		●			●			●	●	●	●			●		
5-1			●																					
+/-2									●	●	●					●					●			
+/-1					●				●	●						●	●				●	●		
Accept offer of opponent group				●																				
Equity and Prominence Principle						●	●					●		●		●			●		●			
Equal Split +/-1; +/- 2; +/-20																●			●		●			
Split the Diff.: next integer mult. 10							●																	
Proportional Split: next integer mult. 10						●						●												
Same offer to opponent as opponent to group +10														●										
Other							●														●			
Accept offer of opponent group							●																	
-3-2							●																	
+4																					●			

(shaded) group initiating a break off

Table 6.8: Principles of chosing first demands and adjusting proposals by E-groups

Proposals	**ES-groups**								**EW-groups**							
Initial demand/offer	13.1	14.1	15.1	16.1	17.1	18.1	19.1	20.1	13.2	14.2	15.2	16.2	17.2	18.2	19.2	20.2
Equity Principle		•							•	•			•		•	•
Equal Split		•							•	•			•		•	
Same offer to opponent as opponent to group																•
Prominence Principle	•			•	•	•	•	•			•	•		•		
Spontaneously: 250								•								
Spont. 150; 100; 100-10, -20 for gr. 2	•			•			•							•		
Alternative																
next integer multiple of 10					•						•					
next integer multiple of 10 +/-10						•						•				
Equity *and* Prominence Principle			•													
Same offer to opponent as opponent to group +10			•													
Adjustment of demands/offers	13.1	14.1	15.1	16.1	17.1	18.1	19.1	20.1	13.2	14.2	15.2	16.2	17.2	18.2	19.2	20.2
Equity Principle						•		•			•	•		•		
Adjustment to Equal Split											•	•				
Adjustment to middle between proposals (ingroup)								•								
Concession equals concession of opponent group						•								•		

(shaded) group initiating a break off

Table 6.8 continued

Proposals	ES-groups								EW-groups							
Adjustment of demands/offers	13.1	14.1	15.1	16.1	17.1	18.1	19.1	20.1	13.2	14.2	15.2	16.2	17.2	18.2	19.2	20.2
Prominence Principle	•		•	•	•	•	•	•	•		•	•	•	•	•	•
Adjustment to prominent proposal																
Spontaneously: 180, 200	•			•									•			
Spontaneously: 50 group 2				•												
Alternative													•			
Previous prominent proposal				•	•			•					•		•	
Next integer mult. 5 to prev. proposal											•					
Accept offer of opponent group	•		•									•		•	•	•
Adjustment by prominent amount																
+/-20					•	•										
+/-10				•			•	•				•	•	•	•	
+/-5	•		•			•	•		•		•	•		•	•	
+/-1					•				·		•					
Equity *and* Prominence Principle																•
Equal Split +10																•

(shaded) group initiating a break off

The following forms of adjustments result from the *equity principle*:

- Adjustment to another social norm.
- Adjustment to a value that corresponds to the middle between demands of both groups or between ingroup proposals.
- The concession equals the concession of the other group in a previous round.
- Groups offer the same amount as their opponent.

The following effects of the *prominence principle* can be distinguished, the first two being the same as with aspiration levels:

- Subjects adjust to prominent proposals. The amount of adjustment, however, need not to be prominent.
- Proposals are adjusted by a prominent amount resulting sometimes in proposals that are not prominent in the decimal system.
- Proposals are adjusted by amounts being composed of prominent numbers resulting in a nonprominent amount of adjustment.

Proposals are adjusted in amounts divisible by 10 and 5 without remainder, and in amounts of 2 and 1. Adjustments become the smaller, the less groups are willing to make concessions. Proposals are also adjusted in other amounts. Except in two cases these amounts occur, however, because subjects switch from the equity principle to the prominence principle and vice versa, or because the proposal was reduced to the offer of the opponent group.

The analysis of the transcripts showed that by the two very simple principles equity principle and prominence as well as combinations of both of them, all aspiration levels are formed and all but one adaptations are carried out. Moreover, also the proposals on the allocation of the coalition value and their adjustments are based on these principles with two exceptions. We think that this result is remarkable. A first evaluation of the transcripts conveyed already the impression that equitable divisions and prominence played an important role in our experiment. But it was a surprising result that nearly all proposals and aspiration levels were guided by these principles.

6.5 The Negotiation Agreement Area - Comparison of Results

After having analyzed payoffs, proposals, negotiation processes and aspiration levels in our experiment we are able to compare our results with those of Kuon and Uhlich (1993) (in this section quoted as KU) who proposed the Negotiation Agreement Area (NAA) as a descriptive solution concept for experimental two-person characteristic function games the KU- and our (in this section quoted as HSch-) experiment are based on. Since both experiments follow the same design it is natural to ask how well the Negotiation Agreement Area fits to our data even though there had been the (possibly substantial) methodological difference that subjects in the KU-setup participated in a computer experiment playing totally on their own, whereas subjects in the HSch-experiment not only played together in groups but, moreover, have been observed by being videotaped.

Before comparing the results in detail we want to stress that the approach taken by KU has the major advantage that it incorporates aspiration level based behavior and that it explicitly models the negotiation process. Yet, KU have no information on aspiration levels since subjects have not been interviewed in this respect. They infer from first demands on players' tactical aspiration levels[114] which are one of the Negotiation Agreement Area's two basic components besides assumptions on the shape of the negotiation process. Even though the NAA fits the data better than other theories it may not be a good description of actual decision processes. This is the major drawback of the "indirect" method inferring from outcomes on factors, e.g. motivations, that might influence people's behavior but about which one has no direct knowledge.

Table 6.9 presents the payoffs for the treatments identical in the KU- and HSch-experiment. Figures 6.6 and 6.7 show the Negotiation Agreement Area-Hits in both experiments. We see that in L-sessions only two out of 6, and more markedly in H-sessions only 2 out of 14 payoffs hit the Negotiation Agreement Area[115] which obviously does not describe the outcomes of the HSch-experiment very well. On average the payoffs in the HSch-experiment are by 8 to 10% lower than those in the KU-experiment.

As a first test of whether it is justified to apply the Negotiation Agreement Area to our data set we calculate the *measure of predictive success*, M, as in

[114]The term tactical aspiration level may be misleading in that it suggests that subjects' first demands coincide with their initial aspiration levels. We found, however, that only in 1 out of 20 S-groups and in 4 out of 20 W-groups both variables coincide.

[115]Since KU did not differentiate between inexperienced and experienced players we aggregated the final payoffs of IH- and E-sessions.

Table 6.9: Payoffs in the KU- and HSch-experiment

Kuon-Uhlich (KU)		Hennig-Schmidt (HSch)	
L-sessions	H-sessions	L-session	H-sessions
96(B)	172	96(B)	128(B)
180*	190	160	128(B)
187*	202*	170	128(B)
192*	208*	170	160
200*	210*	180*	167
208		185*	170
			170
			172
			175
			180
			185
			185
			200*
			215*
∅ 193,4	196,4	173,0	179,9

* NAA-Hits

KU. Computing M for all groups together and counting break offs as failures gives a hit rate $R = 0.2$ and an area, A, of 0.1157, i.e. $M = 0.0843$ for the HSch-experiment. The values for the KU-experiment are $R = 0.6363$ and $A = 0.1157$, i.e. $M = 0.5206$.[116] According to M the predictive success of the Negotiation Agreement Area is very poor when applied to our data.

The Negotiation Agreement Area rests on two main behavioral assumptions: initial demands and the shape of the negotiation process. It is assumed that players 1 open the negotiation with a proposal close to their maximal aspiration level $v(12) - v(2)$ which amounts to 288 in H-sessions and 256 in L-sessions. Looking at first demands in both experiments we see that they are much lower than assumed by KU. In the HSch-experiment 6 out of 20 sessions are opened by a first proposal that is, what we would call, "near" to the maximal aspiration level of S-groups, i.e. not lower than the second lower integer multiple of 10 to this level (270 in L-sessions and 240 in H-sessions). In the KU-experiment only two out of 12 sessions correspond to the amount assumed, the average initial demand of players 1 being 238 in H- and 223 in L-sessions (HSch), and 216.8 in H- and even 219.5 in L-sessions (KU).

[116] KU report an $M = 0.6099$ for all treatments including a correction according to the prominence level.

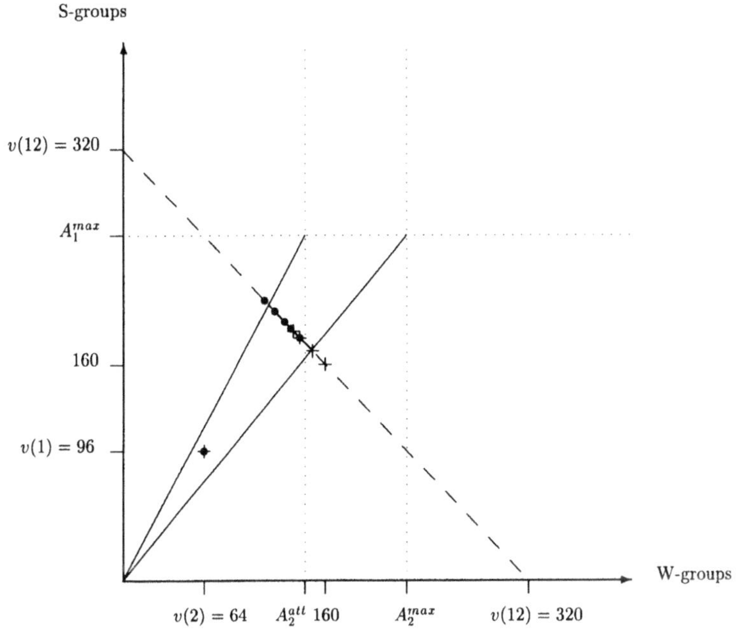

Figure 6.6: Negotiation Agreement Area-Hits in KU (•)- and HSch (+)-experiments (L-sessions)

Taking into account these figures the assumption on initial demands does not seem to be a good description of the observed behavior of players 1. However, we analyzed only a small subsample of the KU-data set, and it is possible that in the treatments we chose in our experiment players 1 refrain from demanding their maximal aspiration level. It may depend on player 2's alternative whether player 1 will take the risk to ask for a share which does amount to $A_1^{\max}$. Yet, Figure 8 in KU shows that the initial demands of about 62% of players 1 deviate by at least 10%, i.e. by at least 29 (26) points, from their maximal aspiration level. This suggests that factors other than those assumed by KU may influence opening demands.

In the HSch-experiment we see that S-groups' first demands *are* motivated by different considerations than supposed by the Negotiation Agreement Area. We stated in Sections 5.3.1 and 5.3.2 that a significant difference could not be found between first demands of IH- and IL-groups which should be the case if the assumption of KU were right. From the transcripts we learn that only four IS- and two ES-groups relate their first demands to the maximally achievable payoff (c.f. Tables 6.7 and 6.8).[117] Note that the formation

[117]If they deviate and relate their demand to their $A_1^{\max}$ this demand is guided

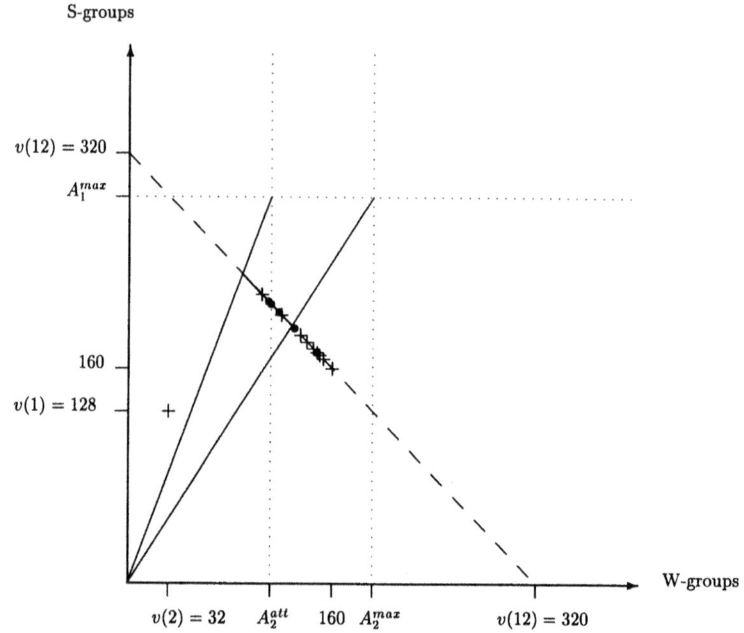

Figure 6.7: Negotiation Agreement Area-Hits in KU (•)- and HSch (+)-experiments (H-sessions)

of aspiration levels has been guided by principles of equity and prominence but never by the maximally achievable share of the coalition value (c.f. Tables 6.3 and 6.4).

The assumption on players 2's tactical aspiration levels seems to be in correspondence with observed behavior. Only one first demand in the KU-experiment does not fall into the range bounded by the attainable and the maximal aspiration level.

To overcome the above mentioned deficiency of the Negotiation Agreement Area it may be reasonable to change the assumption on players 1's tactical aspiration levels by lowering the amount demanded as first proposal. This would change the range of outcomes predicted by the NAA such that it may comprise more of the observed payoffs in both experiments. Yet, to decide which factors determine the specific value(s) of these new tactical aspiration levels will be a crucial step if the concept of the Negotiation Agreement Area should be changed in this respect.

---

by the prominence principle and the payoff requested is not lower than the second lower integer multiple of 10, the deviation amounting to only 5% from the maximal aspiration level.

The second component of the Negotiation Agreement Area is the modelling of the negotiation process. It is assumed that a bargainer changes his last demand in proportion to the opponent's relative change from the initial demand. We did not find any indication that subjects ever made such a calculation. Adjustments of proposals and adaptations of aspiration level have been influenced by equity and prominence aspects. Moreover, the diagrams of the bargaining processes in Appendix B and C show that there are many sessions that show a totally different negotiation behavior. Yet, it may be possible that modelling the bargaining process as done by KU grasps an essential tendency of outcomes even if subjects' decisions are motivated by other considerations. Calculating the concession process from too high an initial demand drives the range of predicted outcomes to be higher than subjects in our experiment were willing to accept. W-groups did not agree in conceding payoffs that deviate as much from the Equal Split as the Negotiation Agreement Area predicts. This is particularly evident in H-sessions. The impact of such a behavior on final outcomes is not accounted for if it is player 2's alternative that influences player 1's first demand as assumed by the NAA.

Since the Negotiation Agreement Area does not perform well in predicting the outcomes of the HSch-experiment and since the experimental setup differs as described above we presume that both samples do not have the same distribution and that the differences in outcomes of both experiments may be due to the difference in the procedures applied in both experiments (one-person computerized versus group videotaped). We tested this assumption by the Mann-Whitney-U-Test for independent samples. H_0 is the hypothesis that the agreement payoffs do not differ, H_1 is the hypothesis that the payoffs in the KU-experiment are larger than in the HSch-experiment. The one-sided test gives $p = 0.001$. This means that we can reject H_0 since $p \ll 0.05$. There is significance in the data that the "KU-payoffs" are larger than the "HSch-payoffs". The same is true if we compare all outcomes including break offs or if we test payoffs in L- and H-sessions separately.

What may be the reasons that subjects behave significantly differently in both experiments? One could argue since subjects in the KU-experiment played several games in one session whereas in the HSch-experiment they played only once, W-groups in the latter experiment may have taken the task more seriously because they had only one opportunity to gain money. Yet, this reasoning does not explain why the "one-shot-effect" should only be in favor of W-groups, i.e. why W-groups should have bargained harder than S-groups, since W-groups in the HSch-experiment gain more than in the KU-experiment.

Another argument for the difference in outcomes may be that subjects who played the computerized game totally on their own are not forced to argue as people might be induced to do in groups and therefore behave differently. Instead of reasoning about possible allocations and their effects on opponents' actions they might be temptated to use the gambling facility which the computer readily provides and by trial and "learning by doing" experience the opponent's reactions. This behavior would imply a larger number of proposal rounds in the computerized than in the group experiment. However, we did not find evidence in the data that the number of rounds in the KU-experiment is significantly higher than in the videotaped experiment (Mann-Whitney-U-Test, $p = 0.2358$, one-sided).

What we think distinguishes both experiments most is the "group effect" that certainly is prevalent in the HSch-experiment and which we analyzed in Section 5.2.3. Discussing divergent arguments and especially the Equal Split as a reference point for S- as well as for W-groups might have caused a shift of outcomes in favour of W-groups.

We conclude our discussion on the Negotiation Agreement Area by stating that this model incorporates important features of bargaining behavior: aspiration levels, tactical aspects when opening negotiations and the form of the bargaining process. One of the major reasons why its predictions are very poor when applied to our data set may be that subjects behave differently when acting in groups. However, if changing the NAA's basic concept of maximal aspiration levels by a different method of determining initial demands which certainly is a major component of tactical aspects in bargaining[118], the predictive success of the Negotiation Agreement Area may be improved also in experiments different from the KU-setup[119].

6.6 Other Aspiration Level Based Approaches Explaining Outcomes of Bargaining

In Section 4.1 it has been mentioned that aspiration based theory obviously attracted more interest among German than among American authors from the late Sixties onwards. The volume "Aspiration Levels in Bargaining and Economic Decision Making" edited by Tietz in 1983 gives a good overview on the situation in the early Eighties and shows that the issue was still under discussion. Aspiration levels as a determinant of subjects' behavior have continued to attract attention, and models of aspiration guided behavior have been developed, restated, or refined[120]. Authors who take into account as-

[118] C.f. Section 5.3.1 and 5.3.2

[119] C.f. e.g Kuon (1994).

[120] See e.g Selten (1987), Tietz, Daus, Lautsch, and Lotz (1988), Selten, Mitzkewitz, and Uhlich (1988, 1997), Bolle (1989), Uhlich (1990), Ostmann (1992a), Kuon and Uhlich (1993), Klemisch-Ahlert (1996), Selten (1996a), Ostmann and Leopold-Wildburger (1997).

piration levels being defined as the level of achievement a subject is satisfied with have consciously or unconsciously been motivated to allow for *psychological* factors like feelings of satisfaction, dissatisfaction or disappointment, and thus develop models of decision making agents that are more realistic. This tendency can also be seen in theoretical aspiration based models of bounded rationality (for instance on repeated Prisoner's Dilemma games) not having been directly motivated by divergent experimental findings[121].

In the last section we extensively described the Negotiation Agreement Area model; in the rest of this section we will give a short overview on the aspiration based theories developed by Tietz as well as by Tietz and Weber[122] since these models involve bargaining as did our experiment and since they correctly predict outcomes and negotiation processes of different experimental setups in an impressingly high percentage.[123]

The aspiration level based models of Tietz and Weber have been developed in the context of a decision game where decisions were embedded in a complex macroeconomic model. This model was motivated by the fact that most economic decisions are not made isolated from each other but are results from bargaining. By a process of mutual adaptation of aspiration levels the plans of the decision units are coordinated. In this experiment students had to play the roles of an employers' association, a workers' union and a central bank. In several repeated face-to-face bargaining sessions they had to negotiate over wage, working hours, and the period of notice for the employment contracts.

In a pre-bargaining phase, both parties, employers' association and workers' union, had to fill in a planning form intended to yield information about players' reflections. The most important variables in the context considered here are the following:

- D, first demand,
- P, the planned bargaining result,
- A, the result regarded at least attainable,
- T, the planned conflict threat,
- L, the conflict limit,
- E, the expected first demand of the opponent.

[121] Karandikar, Mookherjee, Ray, and Vega-Redondo (1998), Palomino and Vega-Redondo (1997)

[122] Tietz (1972), Tietz (1975), Tietz (1976), Weber (1976), Tietz et al. (1988), Tietz (1997)

[123] C.f. Selten (1997) for an evaluation of these theories.

These levels form an ordinal scale of potential aspiration levels.

In negotiations over one bargaining variable, the wage, the static *aspiration balancing principle*[124] predicts an agreement value or a range of values at which both partners reach equally high aspiration levels, i.e. a comparison of the aspiration grids of both opponents yields a final outcome that corresponds to the highest common level.

The semi-dynamic *planning difference theory*[125] determines the degree of toughness of a negotiation by means of the difference between the planned goals P_1 and P_2 of the workers' union and the employers' association. If the planning difference $P_1 - P_2 > 0$ the plans cannot be realized. In this case the theory predicts that the player with the larger *concession reserve* $D - A$ makes the first concession. In easy bargaining situations where $P_1 - P_2 \leq 0$, i.e. concessions below P_1 are not necessary, the player with the smaller *tacit concession* (the difference between E and D) concedes first. If a higher first demand than the actual one was expected then this can be regarded as if a concession had already been made.

The *dynamic aspiration balance theory*[126] is designed to predict the whole bargaining process. It is a highly complex theory assuming additional components being decisive for predicting the concession behavior. The *aspiration securing principle* is added which compares the aspiration levels secured by the opponent's last bid being measured on a refined aspiration scale. This principle serves as a decision filter (rule) to predict the first concession maker. The partner with the higher secured aspiration level should concede first because he has an aspiration securing advantage. If this first filter does not lead to a decision the same filters as in the planning difference theory (concession reserve and tacit concession) are applied. Moreover, the statements of the filters determine the relative strength of the players which in turn determines the size of the first concession. From now on the players alternate in making concessions if the concessions are seen as "true sacrifices" (Tietz 1975, p. 68).

This theory completely determines the bargaining process. It predicted the final agreement correctly in 93% of the sample and the total bargaining process in 60% of all cases. Yet, its crucial conditions are the pre-bargaining statement of the five aspiration levels and the expected first demand of the opponent as well as the assumption of (nearly) full information on the other party's aspiration levels. These conditions obviously are satisfied in an experimental setup with repeated face-to-face bargaining as the one reported here. If subjects are in an environment where they react spontaneously because they had no time and knowledge to plan ahead and where communication

[124] Tietz (1972)
[125] Tietz (1972)
[126] Tietz (1975), Tietz (1976)

is anonymous (as in our experiment for reasons of learning about motivations) the conditions of the Tietz-Weber models are not met. Tietz (1975, p. 56) states that the variables planned before bargaining started, obviously gained such a high "commitment power" that parties bargained along these previously stated levels. We, to the contrary, did not want to predispose our subjects. We looked for the *principles* which might have guided their behavior and which are possibly different from what we think could have been their guidelines. Principles of equity and prominence which we found essential for subjects' decision behavior might also have led subjects' determination of the different aspiration levels in the Tietz-experiment but we have no information about that.

We did not analyze our data in order to check which of the concepts of the Tietz-models might apply in our experiment, and it could be an interesting though time-consuming task to read the transcripts again in the light of the different theories mentioned above. Our impression, however, is that the reflections concerning filters, order and size of concessions are too complicated to be carried out. Some of the five aspiration levels have been mentioned, and groups have expectations on first demands and goals of their opponents. But they are certainly not as determinant for their bargaining behavior as in the Tietz-experiment. Only occasionally subjects really fix their own or their opponent group's conflict limit even though they discuss possible own and opponent's break offs[127]. Those groups who are engaged in thinking about the value of their counterpart's conflict limit because they persue a tough bargaining strategy are those who finally have been confronted with a break off. As to the full information aspect, there are groups who are eager to make their counterpart know their own aspiration level, but there are others who do not want to reveal their true goals since they fear that they otherwise would be beaten down and wanted to have a concession reserve.

6.7 Conclusion

Subjects in our experiment behave goal-oriented. They form aspiration levels which are adapted during the negotiation. The formation and adaptation of aspiration levels is guided by two simple principles of boundedly rational behavior: the equity and the prominence principle. But not only aspiration levels also the choice of proposals is determined by these principles. Up to a negligible number of proposed allocations (2 out of 409) all first demands and all adjustments of proposals have been chosen according to the equity and/or the prominence principle.

[127]C.f. the analysis in Chapter 7.

We think it a very remarkable finding that principles exist which so continually and generally have been employed by our experimental subjects on different bargaining determinants: aspiration levels and proposed divisions of the coalition values. These results could only be obtained since we were able to observe experimental subjects directly during their decision processes and also between choices.

Chapter 7

Break Offs

Our aim in this Chapter is to study break off behavior, i.e. potential or actual conflicts stemming from the incompatibility in goals by the two parties involved in the bargaining process. Gruder (1970) describes the dilemma which arises from the conflicting motives guiding the behavior of bargainers as follows: By cooperating with their opponents, groups have a relatively good chance of reaching an agreement. By competing with them for a greater share of the total, they endanger a conflict. As mentioned before, participants in our experiment also pointed out the dilemma they face in the course of negotiations: If they are willing to make concessions the opponent group might expect even more compromises, and if they want to induce an impression of firmness they run the risk of a conflict.

Break offs are a nonnegligible phenomenon in bargaining, in field studies as well as in experiments. Roth devotes a substantial part of his survey article on "Bargaining Experiments" in the Handbook of Experimental Economics (Roth, 1995a) to the discussion of disagreements and delays. The interest in disagreements in ultimatum and dictator games is due to the fact that their outcomes deviate considerably and systematically from the equilibrium results game theory predicts: since it is assumed that bargainers' utility is measured by their monetary payoffs a receiver should agree to accept an allocation of a given amount of money proposed by a first mover that gives him the smallest monetary unit allowed, and break offs should not occur.

However, there is a number of studies showing frequent conflicts (c.f. the examples in Table 7.1).

The situation in our experiment is similar to the other studies cited in Table 7.1: a nonnegligible percentage (20 %) of all sessions actually ended by conflict. Some other features of the sessions ending by a break off are described in Table 7.2.

Moreover, also in those sessions *not* ending by disagreement potential break offs play a very important role. Even if a resolution to the conflicting

Table 7.1: Frequency of break offs in selected studies

STUDY	FREQUENCY OF BREAK-OFFS (%)
Ultimatum Games)*	
Güth, Schmittberger, Schwarze (1982)	19
Binmore, Shaked, Sutton (1985)	15
Neelin, Sonnenschein, and Spiegel (1988)	14
Ochs and Roth (1989)	16
Bargaining (alternating offer) games with full information and infinite number of rounds	
Kuon and Uhlich (1993)	10**)
Hennig-Schmidt (1996b)	20

*) *Source:* Roth 1995a
**)Only games with a positive threat point and sessions in which at least one offer was greater than the alternative of either player

interests has been found which, however, might not necessarily be to the mutual satisfaction of the bargainers subjects discuss potential break offs. The evaluation of the transcripts shows that break offs are intensely discussed in all I-sessions, and in more than 70 % of E-sessions finally ending by agreement (c.f. Table 7.3). Realized conflicts and the discussion of potential break offs obviously are important characteristics of bargaining behavior. Therefore in this chapter we will analyze the phenomena that proved to be relevant in the context of disagreements.

Table 7.2: Features of sessions ending by a break off

Game Type	Break offs		Break offs caused by		Break offs caused by		Maximal offer to conflict initiating group
	# sessions	percentages	S-group	W-group	1st mover	2nd mover	
IL	1	0.17	1		1		160 (ES)
IH	2	0.33		2	2		112 (SD) 75: (P) + 11
EH	1	0.13		1	1		61: (P) - 3
Sum	4	0.20	1	3	4	-	

Before going on in our analysis we have to specify when a discussion is counted as a break off discussion. In all groups break offs as a decision alternative given by the rules of the game are not only discussed in a general and vague manner by e.g. using the passive voice. Subjects rather point out that the own group or the opponent group has the possibility and the power of initiating a break off. This is counted as a break off discussion. Therefore

any mentioning of the own or the opponent group by at least one group member when arguing on the possibility of a break off is defined as break off discussion (BOD).

Discussing break offs does not mean that all or at least two members of the group have to come out against or in favour for a break off, or that group members give the same view on the evaluation of their opponent group's break off. Since we aim at analyzing not only the finally realized break offs, but all references to and motivations for conflicts we registered every single comment on break offs and thus the spontaneous remarks of each individual participating in the experiment. Discussing break offs does not mean either that group members only discuss that they want to break off. To the contrary, in many sessions they decided that a break off does not pay.

Table 7.3: Break off discussions, inexperienced and experienced groups

Break off discussions	**IS-groups**												
	#	1.1	2.1	3.1	4.1	5.1	6.1	7.1	8.1	9.1	10.1	11.1	12.1
Sessions	**12**	•	•	•	•	•	•	•	•	•	•	•	•
% of rounds in session		36	33	40	53	38	38	33	26	31	13	19	72
	IW-groups												
	#	1.2	2.2	3.2	4.2	5.2	6.2	7.2	8.2	9.2	10.2	11.2	12.2
Sessions	**12**	•	•	•	•	•	•	•	•	•	•	•	•
% of rounds in session		27	33	27	30	69	42	17	42	56	13	38	61

Break off discussions	**ES-groups**								
	#	13.1	14.1	15.1	16.1	17.1	18.1	19.1	20.1
Sessions	**6**	•		•		•	•	•	•
% of rounds in session		9	0	30	0	14	11	59	27
	EW-groups								
	#	13.2	14.2	15.2	16.2	17.2	18.2	19.2	20.2
Sessions	**6**	•		•	•	•	•	•	
% of rounds in session		18	0	9	26	43	26	41	0

(shaded) group initiating a break off
• BOD occurring in at least one round
0 - 72 percentage of rounds with BOD in relation to total rounds in session

In order to quantify break off discussions we use the number of proposal rounds in which subjects discuss break offs as a counting unit for the frequency of BOD. Thus we move from a qualitative characteristic (break off discussions occur or not) to a quantitative measure, the number resp. the percentage of proposal rounds in which break offs are discussed. Table 7.3 shows that these percentages differ considerably among groups.

7.1 Correlates of Break Off Discussions

In this section we will investigate some features of rounds that are more frequent in rounds with break off discussions than in rounds without. Reading the transcripts suggested that features of rounds exist which are connected to break off discussions indicating situations that may become dangerous in the sense that they eventually lead to actual break offs. We call such features correlates of break off discussions. We now explain more precisely what we mean by saying that a feature is a "correlate of break off discussions". For every group we determine the percentage of rounds of break off discussions with the feature and compare it with the percentage of rounds without break off discussions.[128] If the former percentage is greater than the latter, we say that for this group the feature is *positively connected* to break off discussions. The feature is a *correlate of break off discussions*, if it is positively connected to break off discussions either for a majority of all S-groups or for a majority of all W-groups. We call it a *significant* correlate if the Wilcoxon Signed Ranks Test indicates that it is more frequent than randomly expected on a significance level of $p \leq 0.10$, one-sided.

In order to address this task systematically all rounds in which the issue of break offs was brought up by any subject have been marked in the graphs showing the alternating proposals as well as the aspiration levels. As an example, Figure 7.1 presents the resulting picture for groups 6.1 and 6.2. The diagrams of all groups are to be found in Appendix F.

We pointed out in the last section that every comment by any single person on break offs was counted as break off discussion since we want to analyze all references to and motivations for break offs. For the same reason we count a round as having a feature involving aspiration levels if this is expressed by at least one individual in the group.

The following four features are correlates in the sense defined above.

Correlate 1: Formation of aspiration level

A round has this feature if the first aspiration level in the bargaining process is formed by at least one member of the group.

[128] In Table 7.4 a denotes the percentage of rounds with break off discussions which have the concerning feature, and b stands for the percentage of rounds without break off discussions which have the concerning feature.

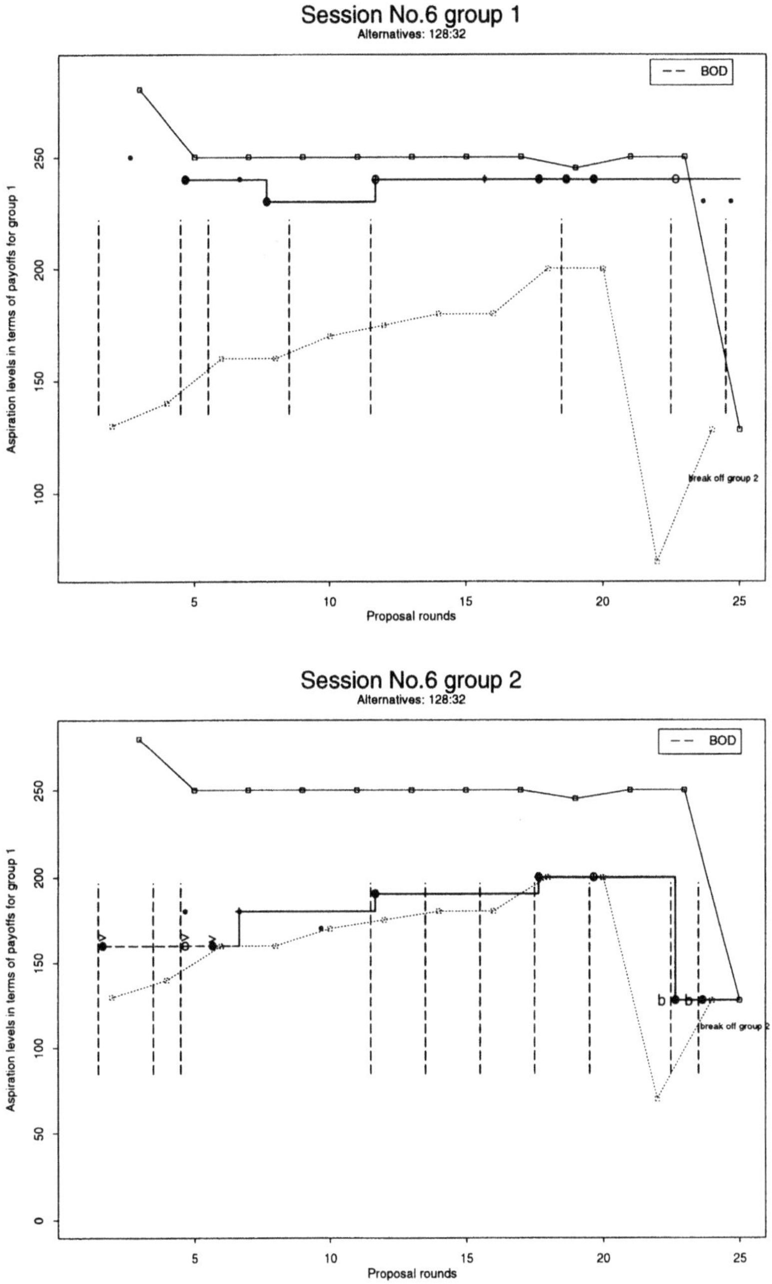

Figure 7.1: Break off discussions (BOD) in Session 6.

Correlate 2: Adaptation of aspiration level

A round has this feature if group members adapt their aspiration levels, i.e. it becomes clear from the discussion within the group that group members change their aspiration level by reducing or increasing the amount of money they are trying to achieve.

Correlate 3: W-group concedes not more than Equal Split

A round has this feature if with their last proposal W-groups did not concede more to S-groups than the Equal Split.

Correlate 4: No concession

A round has this feature if the opponent group's last demand was at least as high as their second last demand.

We found Correlates 1, 2, 3 and 4 in S-groups, and Correlates 1, 2, and 3 in W-groups (see Table 7.4).

In order to test which of the correlates are significant correlates we apply the Wilcoxon Signed Ranks Test[129] to the difference $(a-b)$ shown in Table 7.4 H_0 is the hypothesis that the percentages do not differ, H_1 is the hypothesis that the percentages in rounds with break off discussions are higher than in rounds without BOD. According to our definition above, Correlates 1, 2, and 3 proved to be significant for S-groups, and Correlates 1 and 2 are significant for W-groups (see Table 7.4).

In S-groups Correlate 1 "Formation of aspiration level" is the one that is most typical in terms of the highest significance level ($p = 0.021$, one sided). Obviously it is typical for participants in S-groups to discuss break offs when the first aspiration level is formulated, thus already very early in the negotiation. On average aspirations in S-groups have been formed in the second round. Subjects in S-groups stress their own strong position in case of a conflict and deny the willingness of W-groups to only take the outside option. Persons in 9 of the 10 S-groups with Correlate 1 lay great emphasis on the point that they are the ones to terminate the negotiation. If the willingness of W-groups to initiate a conflict is discussed when aspiration levels are formed (8 out of the 10 S-groups), subjects in all these S-groups conclude that W-groups would not take the risk of breaking off. From the beginning of the negotiation they present themselves as self-confident and emphasize their strong bargaining position.

Correlate 2 "Adaptation of aspiration level" is another significant correlate of break off discussions in S-groups, ($p = 0.042$, one sided). Obviously subjects typically tend to think about their own or their opponent group's

[129] Cf. Gibbons (1985), Siegel (1956), Siegel and Castellan (1988).

Table 7.4: Correlates of break off discussions, IS- and IW-groups

Correlates of break off discussions		# of groups in which (a - b) > 0		IS-groups 1.1	2.1	3.1	4.1	5.1	6.1	7.1	8.1	9.1	10.1	11.1	12.1
(1) Formation of aspiration level	rounds **with** BOD		a	25	0	17	8	0	13	8	20	8	8	25	8
	rounds **without** BOD		b	14	25	0	4	6	6	0	0	0	0	0	0
		10***	a - b	11	-25	17	4	-6	7	8	20	8	8	25	8
(2) Adaptation of aspiration level	rounds **with** BOD		a	50	0	50	44	10	25	50	40	25	0	0	31
	rounds **without** BOD		b	14	0	0	13	0	13	21	21	30	10	41	0
		8**	a - b	36	0	50	31	10	12	29	19	-5	-10	-41	31
(3) W-group concedes not more than Equal Split	rounds **with** BOD		a	75	100	83	64	30	50	67	80	67	62	50	85
	rounds **without** BOD		b	43	75	78	74	31	31	83	50	74	31	35	100
		7*	a - b	32	25	5	-10	-1	19	-16	30	-7	31	15	-15
(4) No concession in *opponent's last* proposal	rounds **with** BOD		a	50	0	67	44	60	25	67	60	33	46	50	77
	rounds **without** BOD		b	29	0	56	43	56	31	46	50	56	74	47	80
		7	a - b	21	0	11	1	4	-6	21	10	-23	-28	3	-3
				IW-groups 1.2	2.2	3.2	4.2	5.2	6.2	7.2	8.2	9.2	10.2	11.2	12.2
(1) Formation of aspiration level	rounds **with** BOD		a	33	0	25	7	6	10	20	0	9	15	0	9
	rounds **without** BOD		b	0	25	9	0	0	0	0	9	0	1	8	13
		8§	a - b	33	-25	16	7	6	10	20	-9	9	14	-8	-4
(2) Adaptation of aspiration level	rounds **with** BOD		a	33	50	25	14	33	40	60	63	5	31	50	45
	rounds **without** BOD		b	13	0	0	12	0	13	23	18	6	3	31	25
		11§§	a - b	20	50	25	2	33	27	37	45	-1	28	19	20
(3) W-group concedes not more than Equal Split	rounds **with** BOD		a	67	100	75	57	44	40	80	50	82	69	63	82
	rounds **without** BOD		b	100	50	82	61	38	33	77	55	53	25	46	88
		7	a - b	-33	50	-7	-4	6	7	3	-5	29	44	17	-6

BOD Break off discussions

(shaded) group initiating a break off

a # of BOD-rounds with the feature as percentage of number of rounds in which break offs **are** discussed in a group

b # of **Non-BOD**-rounds with the feature as percentage of number of rounds in which break offs **are not** discussed in a group

*** p = 0.021 one-sided, Wilcoxon Signed Ranks Test

** p = 0.042 one-sided, Wilcoxon Signed Ranks Test

* p = 0.076 one-sided, Wilcoxon Signed Ranks Test

§§ p = 0.001, one-sided, Wilcoxon Signed Ranks Test

§ p = 0.088, one-sided, Wilcoxon Signed Ranks Test

break off if they decide to strive for a higher goal than before or if they are forced to reduce their preferred outcome. Striving for a higher aspiration level may induce discussions on whether W-groups will tolerate this claim or not. It also may cause reactions of defiance in the sense that if W-groups do not accept the higher claim, S-groups could easily break off because of their higher alternatives.

Having to lower one's aspiration level caused by the fear that the opponents might not be willing to accept the higher demand causes an uneasy feeling of being induced to do something which one actually does not want to do. This uneasiness becomes even more important since S-groups are endowed with the high alternative and therefore consider themselves the stronger bargaining partner. In addition, subjects have been encouraged in the introduction to the experiment "to maximize their own profit", and they conformed to the experimenter's request if they fix their aspiration at a high level. The uneasy feeling of being "forced to give in" is likely to be reduced if punishment by breaking off is stressed as a possibility of retaliation if W-groups will not accept the lowered goal.

Correlate 3 "W-group concedes not more than Equal Split" is also a significant correlate, even though at a low significance level ($p = 0.076$, one sided). For all S-groups the equal share of the coalition value is a clear lower bound for the aspiration levels of S-groups and an upper bound for those of W-groups. For all but one S-groups an allocation is acceptable only if they get *more* than the Equal Split, and they try to reinforce this claim if necessary at the cost of a break off. W-groups in 50% of all sessions and in many of the sessions in a considerable part of the negotiation strive for a final payoff amounting to the Equal Split. This results in 49% of their proposals being less or equal to half of the coalition value. This behavior induces discussions on S-groups' own possible break offs as well as on W-groups' inclination for conflicts. S-groups argue on the question whether they themselves would rather take the outside option than to accept an allocation that gives them only the Equal Split. Moreover, they consider it worthwhile and necessary to discuss whether W-groups would rather take the outside option than to accept an allocation that gives them *less* than the Equal Split which they are obviously striving for because in substantial parts of the negotiation they firmly do not offer more than half of the coalition value.

In W-groups Correlate 2 "Adaptation of aspiration level" is the most typical one in terms of the highest significance level according to the Wilcoxon Signed Ranks Test ($p = 0.001$, one sided). W-groups are not willing to concede much more than half of the coalition value. But if they reduce their aspiration level, and this is the case in 83% of all aspiration level adaptations, this may be caused by realizing that S-groups could think about a break off. On the other hand they themselves take a conflict into consideration if their decreased goal on final payoffs will not be accepted by their opponent group. Defiance may arise in the sense that if S-groups do not concede the reduced claim, W-groups also are able to break off despite their lower alternative. Moreover, they, too, have been encouraged by the experimenter to strive for a maximal profit and may also have an uneasy feeling of being "forced to give in" which is likely to be reduced by discussing a break off as a retaliative action.

Correlate 1 "Formation of aspiration level" is another significant correlate of break off discussions in W-groups, however, at a low significance level ($p = 0.088$, one sided). Participants in W-groups, too, formulate aspiration levels on average also in the second round; yet, there is an important difference. Subjects in W-groups give priority to the danger of their opponent's breaking off in relation to their own willingness to risk a conflict. Persons in 5 of the 8 W-groups with Correlate 1 only mention the possibility that their opponent S-group might break off when formulating their first aspiration level. In 2 W-groups also own break offs are discussed, but opponent's break off are accentuated; in 1 W-group own break offs are discussed only.

Obviously correlates of break off discussions which involve aspiration levels (formation and adaptation) are the ones that proved to be most significant with S- and W-groups.

7.2 Monetary and Nonmonetary Motives

Thinking about a break off in bargaining when being offered more than the outside option comprises an element that can hardly be induced by prevailing monetary motives.[130] We will see that behavior can be motivated also by nonmonetary factors and can result in decisions taking the outside option instead of the higher offer.

In the transcripts we could distinguish break off discussions that were induced by prevailing monetary and nonmonetary motives since subjects argue in a corresponding way:

If subjects are induced by *prevailing monetary motives* in discussions on break offs of their own group and/or assume prevailing monetary motives in the break off behavior of their opponent group (break off discussions of the *own* group will be abbreviated *BOW* in the following, break off discussions of the *opponent* group *BOP* accordingly) they discuss BOW and BOP, but they take the conclusion that it does not pay to break off bargaining since the offer is higher than the alternative, and therefore it will not pay for themselves or for their opponent group to take the outside option.

If subjects are induced by *prevailing nonmonetary motives* in discussions on break offs in BOW, and/or assume prevailing nonmonetary motives in BOP they discuss arguments that take into account that they themselves or their opponent group might break off even if the amount offered is greater than their alternative.

[130] As said before we do not want to characterize such decisions as irrational since subjects had motives which are not unreasonable, see Section 7.3.2, p.115 and Section 7.4, p.122.

In game theory nonmonetary motives are assumed not to be present as a factor influencing the behavior of economic agents and are therefore not taken into account. Thus in many situations actual behavior of experimental subjects, for instance in ultimatum games, cannot be explained. Table 7.5, however, shows that the number of groups and the percentage of rounds in which nonmonetary motives guide break off discussions are considerably large. Moreover, groups 5.2, 6.2, 12.1, 17.2 finally broke off even though the amount offered was much higher than their outside option (cf. Table 7.2).

Table 7.5: Break off discussions, induced by prevailing monetary and nonmonetary motivations, I-sessions

Break off discussions	**IS-groups**												
	#	1.1	2.1	3.1	4.1	5.1	6.1	7.1	8.1	9.1	10.1	11.1	12.1 ░
Prevailing Monetary Motivation													
own group	**12**	•	•	•	•	•	•	•	•	•	•	•	•
% of rounds		9	33	33	30	12	4	17	16	15	1	10	17
opponent group	**12**	•	•	•	•	•	•	•	•	•	•	•	•
% of rounds		9	17	7	15	19	29	11	16	21	9	19	11
Prevailing Nonmonetary Motivation													
own group	**11**	•		•	•	•	•	•	•	•	•	•	•
% of rounds		27	0	13	38	15	4	28	11	10	2	5	67
opponent group	**9**				•	•	•	•	•	•	•	•	•
% of rounds		0	0	0	11	15	21	6	11	13	7	5	6
	IW-groups												
	#	1.2	2.2	3.2	4.2	5.2 ░	6.2 ░	7.2	8.2	9.2	10.2	11.2	12.2
Prevailing Monetary Motivation													
own group	**8**			•		•	•		•	•	•	•	•
% of rounds		0	0	13	0	19	13	0	16	8	1	33	17
opponent group	**11**	•	•	•	•	•		•	•	•	•	•	•
% of rounds		27	17	20	19	23	0	11	26	44	11	33	28
Prevailing Nonmonetary Motivation													
own group	**9**			•	•	•	•		•	•	•	•	•
% of rounds		0	0	7	6	50	33	0	5	5	5	19	17
opponent group	**12**	•	•	•	•	•	•	•	•	•	•	•	•
% of rounds		18	17	20	21	35	13	6	37	31	3	14	33

░ group initiating a break off

• BOD occurring in at least one round

0 - 67 percentage of rounds with BOD in relation to total rounds in session

Since we found from the transcripts that prevailing nonmonetary motives are not to be neglected in getting insight into the determinants of peoples' behavior we will focus on the analysis of these motives in the sections to follow. Behavior induced by prevailing monetary and nonmonetary motives is analyzed later on, but we can state that for non-payoff-oriented decisions the monetary aspect, i.e. the economic motivation, completely loses importance.

7.3 Motivations

Arguments are used in break off discussions which indicate that also noneconomic motivations may guide subjects' behavior. From the transcripts we evaluated arguments and actions, and from these we inferred onto the underlying motives and motivating forces if subjects did not verbalize them themselves.

Since nonmonetary factors haven't been the subject of neoclassical microeconomic and game theory we will refer to concepts having been developed in psychology[131].

Subjects' behavior is indeed guided by the following economic (i) and noneconomic motivating forces (ii), (iii):

(i) economic efficiency
(ii) power
(iii) reciprocity.

Tables 7.6 and 7.7 show the groups mentioning one of these *at least once* in the bargaining process. Since our concern is to explain potential and actual break offs we concentrate on those motivations, norms and emotions that call forth a corresponding behavior.

7.3.1 Economic Efficiency

The *economic* motivation assumed in game theory to guide economic agents influences subjects' behavior in our experiment, yet besides others. This motivation we call *economic efficiency.*

In all groups in which payoff-oriented BOW or BOP occurred (c.f. Table 7.6) the motivation for not breaking off or the assumption on the opponent group's motivation for not breaking off is *economic efficiency.* Typical statements by participants of our experiment are:

- You harm/punish yourself.
  (Du schädigst/bestrafst Dich selbst.)

- You will cut your nose to spite your face.
  (Sich ins eigene Fleisch schneiden.)

- It doesn't pay to be a dogged person.
  (Ein sturer Typ zu sein, bringt nichts.)

[131] C.f. Simon (1963) and Camerer (1997b) for a discussion of the mutual relationship between psychology and economics.

- The opponent will punish himself.
  (Der Gegner bestraft sich selbst.)

Economic efficiency, however, is a motivation guiding also primarily non-payoff-oriented break off discussions (c.f. Table 7.7). After having bargained already for some rounds it was argued that S-groups could have broken off immediately because of their larger alternative, thus having been able to realize a very high fictitious payoff per hour. This argument is only valid for first moving S-groups who had been in a position to end the session immediately by a break off. S-groups who had been second movers had always been offered an amount higher than their alternative, and it was economically more efficient for them to accept immediately rather than to break off immediately.

Table 7.6: Prevailing monetary motivations underlying break off discussions, I-sessions

Motivation	IS-groups												
	#	1.1	2.1	3.1	4.1	5.1	6.1	7.1	8.1	9.1	10.1	11.1	12.1
PREVAILING MONETARY own group													
Economic efficiency	12	•	•	•	•	•	•	•	•	•	•	•	•
PREVAILING MONETARY opponent group													
Economic efficiency	12	•	•	•	•	•	•	•	•	•	•	•	•
	IW-groups												
	#	1.2	2.2	3.2	4.2	5.2	6.2	7.2	8.2	9.2	10.2	11.2	12.2
PREVAILING MONETARY own group													
Economic efficiency	8			•		•	•		•	•	•	•	•
PREVAILING MONETARY opponent group													
Economic efficiency	11	•	•	•	•	•		•	•	•	•	•	•

(shaded) group initiating a break off
• motivation occuring in at least one round

But even for first movers the argument is only reasonable if groups assume the first offer made to them to be lower than their alternative. Groups made this argument after some rounds of bargaining knowing that their opponent's first offer was higher than their outside option. Since, in addition, they could have accepted the actual offer being not lower than the first offer, these break off discussions have to be called primarily non-payoff-oriented, even though they are motivated by economic efficiency.

Table 7.7: Prevailing nonmonetary motivational factors underlying break off discussions, I-sessions

Motivating factors	IS-groups #	1.1	2.1	3.1	4.1	5.1	6.1	7.1	8.1	9.1	10.1	11.1	12.1
PREVAILING NONMONETARY own group													
Economic efficiency	2									●			●
Power	11	●		●	●	●	●	●	●	●	●	●	●
Negative reciprocity	10 (11)	●		●	●	●	*)	●	●	●	●	●	●
PREVAILING NONMONETARY opponent group													
Economic efficiency													
Power													
Negative reciprocity	9				●	●	●	●	●	●	●	●	●
	IW-groups #	1.2	2.2	3.2	4.2	5.2	6.2	7.2	8.2	9.2	10.2	11.2	12.2
PREVAILING NONMONETARY own group													
Economic efficiency													
Power	9			●	●	●	●		●	●	●	●	●
Negative reciprocity	9 (11)		*)	●	●	●	●	*)	●	●	●	●	●
PREVAILING NONMONETARY opponent group													
Economic efficiency	2								●	●			
Power	(12)	**)	**)	**)	**)	**)	**)	**)	**)	**)	**)	**)	**)
Negative reciprocity	12	●	●	●	●	●	●	●	●	●	●	●	●

(shaded) group initiating a break off (12.1, 5.2, 6.2)

● motivating factor occuring in at least one round

*) Negative reciprocity was a motivation for making low offers and/or no concessions, yet it did not result in break off discussions for own group

**) W-groups interpret the higher alternative of S-groups as an „advantageous endowment“

7.3.2 Power

Analyzing bargaining behavior without taking into account power relations leaves out an important feature of social interactions. *Power* is understood as the *capability to influence others in order to make them behave in a way in which they otherwise would not chose to act.*[132] In order to analyze the power motivation which may lead subjects to a certain behavior we first explain the notion and the sources of power in our experiment.

In economics when bargaining experiments have been analyzed the concept of power or strength (in the sense of power) of the parties involved is usually expressed in terms of the characteristics of the game under consideration . For instance Rapoport et al. (1990) referring to Rubinstein's (1982) sequential bargaining model defines strength by calling the player with the lower bargaining cost for each period the stronger player. No opting out possibility exists in this model.

Klemisch-Ahlert (1996) defines strongness of the players in terms of their payoff functions which are different for both parties. Uhlich (1990) as well as Kuon and Uhlich (1993) define power in terms of alternatives, assigning higher power to the player receiving the higher guaranteed payoff when deciding to opt out. Choosing the outside option constitutes a source of power since it is thus possible to reduce the other's payoff, although at some cost to oneself.[133]

In psychology additional sources of power have been stated as being important in bargaining experiments (see Gruder, 1970). Bargainers may exercise power by refusing to negotiate in the sense defined in Section 5.4, they may abstain from making offers by shifting the initiative, or they may deny to acknowledge offers made by their opponents in persevering their own demand. This could (and did) motivate their counterpart to retaliate in kind, resulting in a stalemate mutually unprofitable in terms of fictitious payoff per hour. In order to induce the other side to make decisions more favorable to themselves, the party threatens, or actually sabotages the negotiation[134].

Another source of power is to affect the other group's payoff by the nature of their choices. The players are dependent on each other for final payoffs. The amount each group will receive is determined in part by their own and, in part, by their opponent's choice. By the nature of their proposals one party may alter the other group's outcome. This may result in a pattern

[132]C.f. Heckhausen (1989, p. 361), Rheinberg (1995, p. 93). See also the power concepts of Dahl (1957), Thibaut and Kelley (1959, pp. 100), Harsanyi (1976, pp. 163).

[133]Other authors defining power or strength in a similar sense are e.g. Shaked and Sutton (1984), Güth, Schmittberger, and Schwarze (1982), Selten (1981, 1987), Kahn and Murnighan (1993), Güth (1995).

[134]C.f. groups 4.1; 5.1; 6.1; 7.1; 10.1; 12.1, 17.1; 7.2; 10.2; 12.2.

of decisions over a series of rounds. In Section 5.5 we identified bargaining patterns displaying how groups try to implement their power by attempting to influence the other side to change their behavior.

Subjects sometimes complained that they were not allowed to engage in direct face-to-face bargaining since they perceived the indirect communication which takes place through proposals and the pattern of decisions as ambiguous. They thought that their exercise of power would be more efficient in direct communication. Other players opposed by arguing that in face-to-face bargaining the other party could attempt to exercise their power, and they themselves in turn could be influenced. We, however, did not allow direct bargaining in our experiment, since we were interested in the motivations of our participants which we doubted to be able to detect if they negotiated directly. We feared that they might argue strategically in order to influence the opponent group as much as possible and to directly employ their power to gain at the other's expense.

The analysis of power in social relationships has to distinguish between different types stressing the difference in the qualitative nature of power. In our experiment *coercive- or punishment power* (Heckhausen, 1989, Raven and Kruglanski, 1970) exists due to the rules of the game allowing *both S- and W-groups* to reduce the other's share, to persevere with one demand or even lower the offer and, most importantly, to break off the negotiation. Appendix B shows that many groups, S- as well as W-groups, readily utilize these response options. Therefore attributing power only to the player with the lower cost or the higher achievable payoff resp. alternative neglects an important aspect of the nature of power. The negotiation process has to be taken into account in an appropriate way inasmuch it may call forth reactions and retaliative decisions[135] the importance of which for potential and actual break offs will be analyzed in the next section.

Both parties in our experiment are capable of exerting power. Behaving accordingly and taking an apt decision makes their power effective. The *motivational* aspect of power has to be taken into consideration since the motivation of power comprises the *intention* to influence others. The existence of the power motivation may displace economic efficiency.

Note that an essential aspect of the power motivation is the *feeling* of power, strength, importance or prestige (Heckhausen, 1989, Rheinberg, 1995), the "inner experience" as McClelland (1975) termed it. This feeling of power is characteristic for S-groups[136]. It results in an aspiration level of nearly all

[135] Raven and Kruglanski (1970) stress that coercive power in order to be effective, may involve threats of punishments. In Section 5.4 we showed that groups readily used this possibility given by the rules of the game.

[136] Even if they do not employ their power and behave according to the notion of

S-groups being higher than the Equal Split.

In the remaining part of this section we will analyze the motivation of power in connection with non-payoff-oriented break off discussions which was explicitly stressed by 11 of the 12 S-groups and 9 of the 12 W-groups (c.f. Table 7.7).

In our experiment the capability to exert power is symmetric for both groups. The effect of such behavior, however, is asymmetric in that (i) the range of offers being acceptable for themselves is much larger for S-groups than for W-groups[137] and (ii) S-groups' alternatives are up to four times higher than those of W-groups. The asymmetry in guaranteed payoffs induces the above mentioned strong feeling of power in S-groups[138] even though they realize that discussing a break off could finally result in a loss given that all groups were offered an allocation larger than their alternative. Their behavioral goal is to enforce their position perceived as stronger by achieving a payoff *higher* than W-groups, which means higher than the Equal Split in sessions ending by agreement. In sessions ending by conflict they receive the larger alternative and thus get more than W-groups. A higher payoff they try to enforce if necessary at the cost of a break off.

W-groups have a feeling of power, too, since final agreement outcomes of S-groups are contingent on W-groups' consent and since they also are able to initiate a break off. They also try to enforce their demand if necessary at the cost of a break off. The power argument for S-groups loses its validity if W-groups *re-evaluate* the outcome of the game in case of a break off in that the pecuniary variable is not the decisive one any more, and the low alternative ceases to matter. This is what happened in sessions ending by a conflict induced by W-groups[139].

It is interesting to see that S-groups do not attribute any power motivation to W-groups (see Table 7.7). W-groups, on the other hand, admit only a slightly stronger position to S-groups, qualified as an "advantageous endowment". The asymmetry in alternatives does not result in an equivalent

---

bargaining making steady concessions to reach an agreement

[137]If in the worst case W-groups were not willing to offer more than the Equal Split then offers acceptable for themselves reach from $v(1)$ to 160, comprising a range of 33 resp. 65 points. But even if they consider 185 (the highest agreement outcome in I-sessions) an acceptable offer this range still amounts to only 58 resp. 90 points. If, however, S-groups demand $v(12)$ - $v(2)$ in the worst and 161 (at least 1 point more than ES) in the most advantageous case they face a range of demands acceptable for themselves of 128 resp. 96 points.

[138]Typical statements are: - We are going to enforce our more powerful position. - We will squeeze them. - We are in a power position. - We have the power. - We have bargaining power.

[139]We will analyze the process of re-evaluation in Section 7.6

asymmetry in the feeling of power resp. weakness.[140] This finding complies with our statement in Section 5.2.1 and 5.2.2 that most W-groups are not impressed by the difference between alternatives.

Simon (1957, 1961)[141] points out that anticipation of consequences[142] acts as a constant motivation without expressed threats being necessary. Thus the intensity of power is dependent on the opponent's anticipation on how likely it is that, in our case, the latent threat of a break off is exercised. From Table 7.7 we see that all W-groups admit a slightly stronger position to S-groups and that all but one S-group express a feeling of power. Table 7.5 shows that all W-groups argue on BOP in nonmonetarily motivated break off discussions, i.e. in a substantial part of the negotiation they realize the danger that S-groups might break off. Thus the power of S-groups is larger than of W-groups in terms of final payoffs.

An interesting structure of break off discussions being induced by prevailing nonmonetary motives also suggests that this power relation holds: there is a seemingly high number of sessions in which the willingness of S-groups to induce a conflict is discussed in a higher percentage of rounds by S- *as well as* by W-groups than all other possible combinations. The Binomial Test confirms that a significantly higher number of groups than randomly expected discuss non-payoff-oriented break offs by S-groups ($p = 0.03$, one-sided). The "sword of Damocles" (as termed by some participants) is likely to serve as a motivation for W-groups to be willing to concede higher payoffs than the Equal Split.

7.4 Reciprocity, a Social Norm with Two Faces

As was pointed out earlier another very important *noneconomic* motivational factor for behavior is reciprocity, the existence of which may also displace economic efficiency. We characterize *reciprocity* as the *phenomenon that subjects tend to reward others who treat them adequately (positive reciprocity) and to behave noncooperatively to those who do harm to them (negative reciprocity).*

We intentionally do not use the terms fair or unfair for defining positive or negative reciprocity, since in our experiment subjects used the term fair in order to indicate equitable allocations. As we saw, fairness does not have

[140] Typical statements are: - The difference in alternatives is not that much. - The difference in alternatives doesn't play a role. - Our opponents can't put pressure on us. - We have to agree on their final outcome. - Our opponents only think that we are weaker. Groups 1.2.1; 2.2.1; 3.2.1; 4.2.6, 4.2.11, 4.2.15; 7.2.2; 8.2.7; 10.2.2, 10.2.57; 11.2.2; 12.2.4, 12.2.6, 12.2.12.

[141] See also Heckhausen (1989).

[142] Being called by Simon (1961) the "rule of anticipated reactions" (p. 129, 234).

an unambiguous meaning. Neither is it obvious according to which fairness concept a treatment is perceived as adequate or harmful behavior.

As was previously mentioned psychologists studied the phenomenon of reciprocal behavior already in the Sixties stressing the normative aspects of reciprocal exchange in social relationships. Social norms as generally accepted standards of conduct influence the behavior of persons. People may be *motivated* to adhere to social norms which have to be regarded analogous to motives if they are internalized as behavioral standards of subjects. Their behavior then is motivated by the desire to comply with own normative standards[143].

7.4.1 Economic Literature on Reciprocity

It is only recently that reciprocity, sometimes under the heading of fairness or reciprocal fairness, re-attracted the research interest of economists[144]. In a growing number of papers reciprocity as a motivational variable explaining people's behavior has been investigated. Since this subject is so widely discussed we in this section will give a short and necessarily incomplete overview on important papers dealing with reciprocity by means of sometimes quite different methodological approaches to explain this phenomenon.

Rabin (1993) incorporates fairness into a formal model taking into consideration that peoples' well-being might be affected by the treatment of others. He does this by defining a kindness function which measures how kind one player is being to his opponent. His framework incorporates as stylized facts that people are driven by positive as well as by negative reciprocity, and that fairness influences behavior most when material stakes are small. He shows that assuming reciprocally motivated subjects may generate results that differ significantly from the outcomes of models that consider fully rational agents.

Fehr and his coauthors report results from investigating changing conditions in experimental labor markets. In these papers the gift exchange view of labor relations is studied by making either or both market sides capable of responding to the previous action of the trading partner. Workers had the possibility in reacting to employers' wage offers by making a costly effort decision. In some setups firms had the opportunity to punish or to reward workers after they had chosen high or low efforts. The data show that the existence of opportunities for reciprocation may significantly alter market outcomes: workers do not generally choose the money maximizing, i.e. minimal, effort levels. Instead, in response to low wages they choose low effort levels and in response to high wages they go for high effort levels (Fehr, Kirchler,

[143] C.f. Gouldner (1960), Berkowitz and Daniels (1964), Goranson and Berkowitz (1966), Greenberg and Frisch (1972), Heckhausen (1989)

[144] Exceptions, among others, are Axelrod (1984), Frank (1988), Sen (1990).

Weichbold, and Gächter, 1998a). Firms obviously anticipated that paying high wages will induce workers to reciprocate. Workers reported that in fact their effort decisions were dependent on the wages they were offered. This implicit exchange of "gifts" even prevails in competitive markets resulting in wages above the competitive level (Fehr, Kirchsteiger, and Riedl, 1993).

Also in other experimental setups, Fehr and his coauthors find that the opportunity of behaving reciprocally yield outcomes that differ considerably from predictions of economic theory assuming fully rational and selfish agents (Kirchler, Fehr, and Evans, 1995; Fehr and Tyran, 1997; Fehr, Gächter, and Kirchsteiger, 1996, 1997; Fehr and Gächter, 1998; Fehr, Kirchsteiger, and Riedl, 1998b).

In contrast to the 'stylized facts' Rabin quoted as evidence from the psychological literature, Cameron (1995), and Fehr and Tougareva (1996) show that reciprocity also prevails if stakes are two to three times higher than the monthly income of experimental subjects.

Charness (1996) adapted the experimental procedure of Fehr et al. He demonstrates that in a simulated labor market an employee's level of costly effort provision does not only highly depend on wage but that causal attribution matters in the sense that the method by which a wage is generated (chosen by the employer, drawn from a bingo cage, or chosen by a third party) has a substantial effect on effort. The perception of employer volition seems to be a factor influencing reciprocity.

Bolton and Zwick (1995) designed an experiment in which they test the anonymity hypothesis - which attributes subjects' behavior in ultimatum games deviating from the equilibrium prediction to the fact of being observed by the experimenter - against the punishment hypothesis - which independent of any experimenter influence assigns this behavior to the willingness of experimental subjects to punish unfair treatment. They stress that if it were true that experimenter observation distorts behavior of experimental subjects and hence data collected by experimental methods, serious methodological consequences would result. Bolton and Zwick, however, conclude that the punishment hypothesis can explain almost all of the observed deviation from perfect equilibrium whereas the anonymity hypothesis can explain only a small fraction.

Berg, Dickhaut, and McCabe (1995) developed the following investment game: an anonymous investor can pass any portion of his initial monetary endowment to an anonymous receiver which is tripled in being transferred. The receiver can now choose to give back to the investor any part of the tripled sum of money. It is common knowledge that both investor and receiver cannot make a binding contract and that they will never get to know who their opponent was. The results of Berg, Dickhaut, and McCabe show that reciprocity exists as a basic element of human behavior and that trust can be and is used for mutual gain. People respond reciprocally when given the opportunity, they risk some amount of money in the belief that there would be reciprocity even in a double-blind setting.

Jacobsen and Sadrieh (1996) replicated the experiment by Berg et al. (1995) in a video experiment. By this methodological device they were able to make use, as we did, of the direct observation of experimental subjects. The results of their experiment can be seen as supportive and analogous to those of the analyses previously cited: A majority of investors exhibits trust in reciprocity and a majority of receivers reciprocate. Moreover, by analyzing the transcripts they found that altruistic motives of charity, money maximization motives and reciprocity as gratitude for in-game kindness were the most important ones that induced investors and/or receivers to pass parts or all of the initial endowment or of the return.

Hoffmann, McCabe, and Smith (1995, 1997) and McCabe, Rassenti, and Smith (1996) combine evidence from repeated game theory and experimental economics with an approach of evolutionary psychology assuming that humans have special and highly developed cognitive mechanisms for dealing with social exchange problems, referred to as a reciprocity algorithm.

McCabe, Rassenti, and Smith (1996) examined decision making in two-person extensive form game trees allowing subjects to choose between a subgame where backward induction is self-evident and a subgame where reciprocity can be used as a means of achieving a cooperative outcome. They observe substantial cooperation in plays where subjects play a randomly chosen counterpart only once as well as in plays where subjects play each counterpart in the population exactly once with alternating roles. The authors stress that this finding is consistent with reciprocity being an innate characteristic of many people. However, they qualify their results in posing the question whether their findings would carry over if subjects were matched with persons whom they perceive as opponents "ready to exploit any opportunity for gain" (p. 13428).

Hoffmann, McCabe, and Smith (1997) go a step further in assuming that negative and positive reciprocity have emerged as solutions to important socio-economic activities, and emergence of some social institutions can be explained as attempts to encourage reciprocity.

Most of the above mentioned authors incorporate or at least favor to incorporate reciprocity into utility functions. Güth, however, whom this research sometimes reminds of a "neoclassical repairshop", as he maliciously states (Güth, 1995), proposes a behavioral theory based on a dynamic reasoning process. He discusses how choices of boundedly rational decision makers could emerge assuming a behavioral repertoire based on former experiences, which could include reciprocity aspects, and their recommendations for similar situations. This is done in a general perspective (Güth, 1995, 1997a) as well as in the particular choice problem of ultimatum bargaining (Güth, 1997b).

That reciprocity is guiding people's behavior in the "real world" is reported by Bewley (1997) in a study employing a completely different approach. In a field study he interviewed persons who are actively involved in the labor market (business people in companies of different types of businesses and temporary labor services, headhunters, counsellors of the unemployed, labor leaders, labor lawyers and management consultants, but no unemployed). He found that reciprocity works as described above: In order to promote cooperation, a prerequisite for high productivity is morale which is more important than for instance financial incentives. Since lasting reductions of wages are likely to effect morale and productivity by making employees believe that the company is unfair, firms refrain from lowering wages in a recession for their existing personnel.

7.4.2 Reciprocity in Break Off Discussions

After having shown that reciprocity became a major issue in economic research by being incorporated into economic models and/or being tested by experiments we analyze the prevalence of this phenomenon in our experiment.

Arguing on BOW and/or BOP even if the amount offered or assumed to be offered is higher than the outside option is a reaction to previous actual or to anticipated bargaining behavior that is perceived as noncooperative, inadequate, inacceptable, i.e. as hostile[145] treatment. Therefore in the following, we will attend to *negative reciprocity* only. Table 7.7 shows that in *nearly all* groups negative reciprocity is a motivational basis for non-payoff-oriented BOW and BOP.

We identified several behavioral features from the transcripts which groups in our experiment perceive as hostile and which are accompanied by non-payoff-oriented break off discussions (see Table 7.8).

Again the Equal Split proves to be an important issue. In Section 7.3.2 we pointed out the following asymmetry: S-groups (except for group 2.1) claim *more* than the Equal Split since due to their higher alternative they want to achieve a higher payoff than W-groups. Therefore, most S-groups perceive an offer not higher than the Equal Split already as hostile behavior. To the contrary, many W-groups, at least for a substantial part of the negotiation, believe the Equal Split to be an adequate division of the coalition value.

[145] The importance of hostility is stressed by Raven and Kruglanski (1970) and Heckhausen (1989), the latter focusing on an attribution theoretic point of view.

Table 7.8: Behavior perceived as hostile by own group and/or assumed being perceived as hostile by opponent group

Hostile behavior	IS-groups #	1.1	2.1	3.1	4.1	5.1	6.1	7.1	8.1	9.1	10.1	11.1	12.1
***perceived by* own group**													
Offer W-group =< *Equal Split*	8 (9)	•			•	•	*)	•	•	•	•		I
Demand S-groups > *Equal Split*													
Opponent's *concessions* not adequate[a,b,c,d]	8 (10)			•	•	*)	*)	•	•	•	•	•	•
Own *bonus* not adequate	5				•			•	•	•			•
Opponent's *surplus* too high	1									•			
Opponent's *payoff* too high													
***perceived by* opponent group**													
Offer W-group =< *Equal Split*													
Own *concessions* not adequate[c,f,g]	9				•	•	•	•	•	•	•	•	•
Bonus to opponent not *adequate*	7				•	•	•	•	•	•	•		
Own *surplus* too high	2				•						•		
Own *payoff* too high													

Hostile behavior	IW-groups #	1.2	2.2	3.2	4.2	5.2	6.2	7.2	8.2	9.2	10.2	11.2	12.2
***perceived by* own group**													
Offer W-group =< *Equal Split*													
Demand S-groups > *Equal Split*	6 (7)				•			*)	•	•	•	•	•
Opponent's *concessions* not adequate[a,b,c,d]	9 (10)			•	•	•	•	*)	•	•	•	•	•
Own *bonus* not adequate	6				•		•			•	•	•	•
Opponent's *surplus* too high	1						•						
Opponent's *payoff* too high	7				•	•	•			•	•	•	•
***perceived by* opponent group**													
Offer W-group =< *Equal Split*	8	•		•	•		•		•	•	•		•
Own *concessions* not adequate[c,f,g]	12	•	•	•	•	•	•	•	•	•	•	•	•
Bonus to opponent not *adequate*	11	•	•	•	•	•	•	•	•	•	•		•
Own *surplus* too high	3				•				•	•			
Own *payoff* too high	4	•	•					•					•

[shaded] group initiating a break off

• hostile behavior occurring in at least one round

a) opponent's (first) offer too low
b) no opponent's concessions at all
c) opponent's threat (offer is lower than previous one(s))
d) in relation to own concession(s)
e) own (first) offer too low
f) no own concessions at all
g) own threat (offer is lower than previous one(s))
*) Negative reciprocity was a motivation for making low offers and/or no concessions, yet it did not result in break off discussions for own group

They perceive an offer *lower* than the Equal Split as hostile treatment inducing BOD.

Related to this finding is that groups expect a *bonus* in addition to their alternative for not breaking off. For S-groups this bonus has to be more than the difference between Equal Split and $v(1)$. For W-groups the additional amount is not as explicitly stated as with S-groups. But whenever this topic is discussed it is clear that this bonus has to be substantially higher than an ε, thus contradicting clearly game theoretic equilibrium assumptions in ultimatum bargaining. It is interesting to note that Binmore, Shaked, and Sutton (1989) clearly see that "... in real life, epsilon would need to be chosen sufficiently large not to be dismissed as negligible" though theory idealizes it to be zero (p. 756). According to this statement subjects in our experiment obviously perceived the experimental setting as a real life situation. And in fact, observing on the tapes their deep engagement in the task shows that at least when discussing break offs they take the experiment as serious as real world events.

Another important feature influencing subjects' tendencies to negative reciprocity is concession behavior. Going against the notion of bargaining by persevering demands or refusing to make adequate concessions arouses hostility that is answered by break off discussions. Obviously not only the final outcomes but also the negotiation process have to be taken into account when personal attitudes in bargaining experiments are to be evaluated.

The perception of being treated badly and/or the anticipation of malevolent behavior causes spiteful statements indicating that behavior induced by prevailing nonmonetary motives is taken into consideration ruling out economic efficiency. Typical statements being just the opposite to those in Section 7.3.1 are:

- Punishing/hurting the opponent outweighs the own loss.[146]
  (Den anderen bestrafen, ihm wehtun entschädigt für den eigenen Verlust.)

- People do not always behave rational.
  (Leute verhalten sich nicht immer rational.)

- It is funny to annoy the opponent group.
  (Es ist lustig, die anderen zu ärgern.)

- Bad luck for the opponent.
  (Pech für die anderen.)

[146]See Heckhausen (1989) who reports on this effect when discussing the norm of negative reciprocity

- Pay back in the opponent's own coin.
  (In gleicher Münze heimzahlen.)

- Teach a lesson to the opponent group.
  (Den anderen eine Lehre erteilen.)

- Pure spitefulness may cause the opponent's break off.
  (Reine Boshaftigkeit kann sie zum Abbruch bewegen.)

- They will get their own back on us.
  (Sie wollen uns eins auswischen, uns in die Pfanne hauen.)

- They will take us for a ride.
  (Sie wollen uns übers Ohr hauen.)

From the above analysis we conclude that negative reciprocity plays an important role in bargaining. Subjects take into consideration and/or actually punish those who do not treat them adequately, and they assume correctly that their opponents may behave in the same way. However, there is an asymmetry between S- and W-groups in anticipating the opponent's acceptance behavior. Moreover, our findings support the punishment hypothesis stated by Bolton and Zwick (1995). This is the more important since in our experimental setup there was no anonymity for subjects. To the contrary, they have been observed directly and have been videotaped.

The nonmonetary, yet not irrational element that is inherent in a person's intention to make use of its retaliative power may also act as a stabilizing factor in social interactions. Greenberg (1978) and Frank (1988) point out that being correctly anticipated to act in a negative reciprocal way even if retaliation is considerably costly may protect against exploitation.[147] This mechanism is assumed to hold when explaining first movers' high offers in ultimatum bargaining.

7.5 Emotions

In the last sections we established that power and negative reciprocity are motivating factors being crucial for potential and actual break offs indicated by non-payoff-oriented break off discussions. In addition we found that emotions guide the behavior of participants in our experiment. Therefore in this section we will concentrate on the influence of emotions, especially anger.

[147] Frank (1988, pp. 254, 255) states that non-payoff-oriented behavior is often an advantage : "There are many problems that purely self-interested persons simply cannot solve. [...] They cannot threaten credibly to walk away from unfair transactions that will increase their wealth. Nor can they deter aggressors when retaliation would be prohibitively costly".

In psychology the importance of emotions is an acknowledged fact[148]. Weiner (1987) states that actions depend to a great extend on a specific instigating emotion, and that emotion is likely to be elicited by a particular interpretation of a situation.

7.5.1 Emotions as Determinants for Primarily Non-Payoff-Oriented Break Off Discussions

Frank (1988) devotes his book "Passions within Reason" to the analysis of the strategic role of the emotions. He states that contrary to the reasoned pursuit of self-interest, passions and other 'non-rational' sources of motivation do serve subjects' interests well when facing problems which cannot be solved by rational action. Solving these problems would require to commit oneself to behave in a way that may later prove to be contrary to one's interest. Acting according to certain emotions and being known for that enables people to make commitments that otherwise would not be credible even though these commitments involve avoidable losses.

We in our experiment found that already the perceived (and obviously in real world situations experienced) possibility of emotion-guided behavior made the above mechanism hold. Despite the fact that there was no later relationship[149] being thought of as reacting to emotions by a possible break off prevented most groups from making persevering demands to exploit their opponents.

In order to show that and how frequently participants articulate emotions and attitudes which motivate themselves or could have motivated their opponents we quote when and how often the exact words mentioned below have been used. These factors also have been at work even if subjects did not mention them explicitly.

- *Anger (Ärger)*
  groups 1.1.7; 3.1.8; 4.1.32, 4.1.25, 4.1.26, 4.1.46; 5.1.5, 5.1.9; 5.1.26; 6.1.2, 6.1.18, 6.1.22, 6.1.24; 7.1.3, 7.1.29; 10.1.2, 10.1.6, 10.1.53, 10.1.88; 12.1.1; 13.1.5, 13.1.8; 16.1.1; 17.1.9, 17.1.12; 19.1.24; 20.1.10; 1.2.1; 3.2.5, 3.2.14; 5.2.9, 5.2.12; 7.2.4, 7.2.25, 7.2.29, 7.2.29, 7.2.35; 8.2.17, 8.2.19; 9.2.4, 9.2.9; 10.2.51; 11.2.6; 13.2.1, 13.2.4, 13.2.6; 16.2.21; 18.2.15; 19.2.13, 19.2.14, 19.2.19, 19.2.22, 19.2.37
- *Defiance (Trotz)*
  groups 9.1.32; 10.1.52; 19.2.33

[148] See e.g. McClelland (1985), Gergen and Gergen (1986), Heckhausen (1989), Rheinberg (1995).

[149] Inexperienced subjects were told that they played the game only once. It was only after the session had finished that they were asked whether they would be willing to participate in another experienced session.

- *Dictatorship in the sense of coercion (Diktat)*
  groups 2.1.3; 9.1.4; 5.2.9, 5.2.12; 12.2.17
- *Envy/Begrudging (Neid/Mißgunst)*
  groups 7.1.1, 7.1.3; 10.1.2, 10.1.9, 10.1.36; 17.1.14; 3.2.3; 4.2.6, 4.2.11; 5.2.5, 5.2.9, 5.2.22; 6.2.14, 6.2.17, 6.2.22, 6.2.23; 7.2.2, 7.2.7, 7.2.25, 7.2.29; 8.2.1, 8.2.3, 8.2.5, 8.2.17; 12.2.7
- *Fear (Angst)*
  groups 3.1.2, 3.1.4; 4.1.9; 5.1.4; 9.1.12; 10.1.6, 10.1.11, 10.1.19; 11.1.19; 18.1.7; 4.2.33, 4.2.40; 5.2.7, 5.2.13, 5.2.15; 9.2.4, 9.2.5, 9.2.31; 10.2.10, 10.2.71; 19.2.5, 19.2.19; 20.2.4, 20.2.8
- *Greed (Gier)*
  groups 15.1.19; 10.2.85
- *Pride/Self-esteem (Stolz)*
  groups 9.1.16; 11.1.10; 5.2.7, 5.2.9
- *Revenge (Rache)*
  groups 4.1.142, 4.1.24; 6.2.10, 6.2.14, 6.2.15, 6.2.16
- *Self-respect (Ehre)*
  groups 10.1.10; 13.1.8; 5.2.25; 11.2.7; 12.2.18; 19.2.17, 19.2.27
- *Spiteful/-ness (Bösartig/-keit)*
  groups 4.1.14; 5.1.16; 15.1.19; 5.2.1; 7.2.23, 7.2.33; 8.2.10, 8.2.18; 9.2.10, 9.2.26

Note that W-groups articulate these emotions and attitudes in much more rounds than S-groups.

In our experiment *anger* is the emotion that proved to be most important in connection with break off discussions induced by prevailing nonmonetary motives. This basic sentiment is one of the very prevalent emotions (anger, pity, guilt, gratitude and shame) the importance of which is agreed upon in psychology[150]. As Weiner (1987) points out, anger is determined by perceptions of causality and seems to be assigned to an antecedent negative, self-related outcome or event which is attributed to factors controllable by others. Anger tends to evoke retaliation or moving psychologically against others. Weiner reports on data showing that emotions (in his study anger and pity) appear to be the immediate and direct motivators of behavior.

These results are supported by the findings in our experiment. Given the mechanism of negative reciprocity, the perception of hostile treatment

[150] See McClelland (1985), Gergen and Gergen (1986), Heckhausen (1989), Rheinberg (1995), Homans (1961).

causes anger. Subjects in our experiment get annoyed and angry about their opponents' proposals resulting in tension, tough counterproposals, sarcasm, and a very aggressive terminology calling forth break off discussions resulting in some final break offs. Participants characterize their opponents as "idiots, stupid, loony, impertinent, stubborn, ridiculous, absurd", they are "fed up!", they call for "revenge, electroshock, thrashing". They use terms like "shit, declaration of war. Let they have it! Smash their face in! Fight until the last drop of blood!"

7.5.2 Economic Literature Taking Account of Emotions

The subject of emotions is finding growing interest among researchers in economics. As described earlier, models have been developed that encorporate emotions into utility functions (Rabin, 1993). Huang and Wu (1992) focus on anger and pride being decisive emotional factors in the adversarial process of litigation, the issue they are concentrating on. They show that responses induced by these emotions can increase the number of cases brought to trial and make the threat of going to trial a credible one. The introduction of these emotional responses into game theoretic models can result in behavior that could not be explained otherwise.

Camerer and Thaler (1995) favor an approach in line with the work of Rabin (1993) and acknowledge existence of emotions. They state that responders in ultimatum bargaining may be upset by getting obviously unfair proposals and proposers gradually react to that anger.

Dufwenberg and Gneezy (1996) explicitly encorporate emotional considerations into their model, by allowing for the emotion of guilt. They report on an experiment designing the situation of a person who finds a wallet in the street and is unobserved. Game theory predicts that the finder will not return the wallet because he anticipates that the owner will not reimburse him for his honesty even though both persons are interested in the more efficient outcome of returning the wallet and reimbursing the finder properly. Dufwenberg and Gneezy among other issues tested for guilt and found that the owners' behavior was consistent with a theory of guilt based on psychological game theory[151].

The original title of Mitzkewitz and Nagel (1993) "Envy, Greed and Anticipation in Ultimatum Games with Incomplete Information: An Experimental Study"[152] indicates that the authors believe emotions to be an explanatory factor in social interaction. In different experimental setups termed "offer and demand games" they study the behavior of proposers and the reaction of responders in order to present a theory of boundedly rational behavior. The

---

[151] C.f. Geanakoplos, Pearce, and Stacchetti (1989)

[152] C.f. Mitzkewitz and Nagel (1991)

most frequently used fairness criterion in demand games guiding responders actions is resistance to visible unfairness by rejecting proposals that display obviously greedy proposers. On the other hand proposers tend to change the directions of their individual strategies after having made wrong anticipations and become more envious.

Klemisch-Ahlert (1996) reports that envy plays a role when money is allocated in her audiotaped bargaining experiment. Subjects in one group could agree on an allocation of payoffs that gave both participating groups the same amount of money, or they could agree to an allocation that gave one group the same amount as before but the other group a 50% higher share. One group did not agree on the latter strongly Pareto optimal outcome because they "did not want to give money away". Klemisch-Ahlert conclude envy to be the reason for this decision.

7.6 Motivational Explanation of Potential and Actual Break Offs

In the last sections we established that power, negative reciprocity and emotions are crucial for potential and actual break offs. In this section we want to describe the process from the perception of opponent's behavior to potential and/or actual break offs. Figure 7.2 gives a diagrammatic description of the dynamics which we will explain in the rest of this section.

Given the capability in our experiment to retaliate which results in negative reciprocity, subjects' power motivation is a decisive factor for justifying the level of their aspirations. Their feeling of power results in certain actions by their opponents being seen as hostile treatments, and thus influences their bargaining behavior. From the perception of being treated inappropriately anger arouses.

The most important point to stress is that anger causes subjects to *re-evaluate* the outcome of the game. Monetary issues become totally minor matters, and emotional factors, e.g. self-esteem, self-respect, envy, greed, defiance, spite (Stolz, Ehre, Neid, Habgier, Trotz, Bösartigkeit) dominate economic efficiency. Negative reciprocity together with *re-evaluation* mentioned above induces the intention to punish, provokes spiteful behavior and thus non-payoff-oriented break off discussions. Finally break offs result in some groups.[153]

This process corresponds to the description by Raven and Kruglanski (1970) who state that hostility and a desire to punish another may manifest

[153]Had subjects been playing on their own at least five more had been likely to break off.

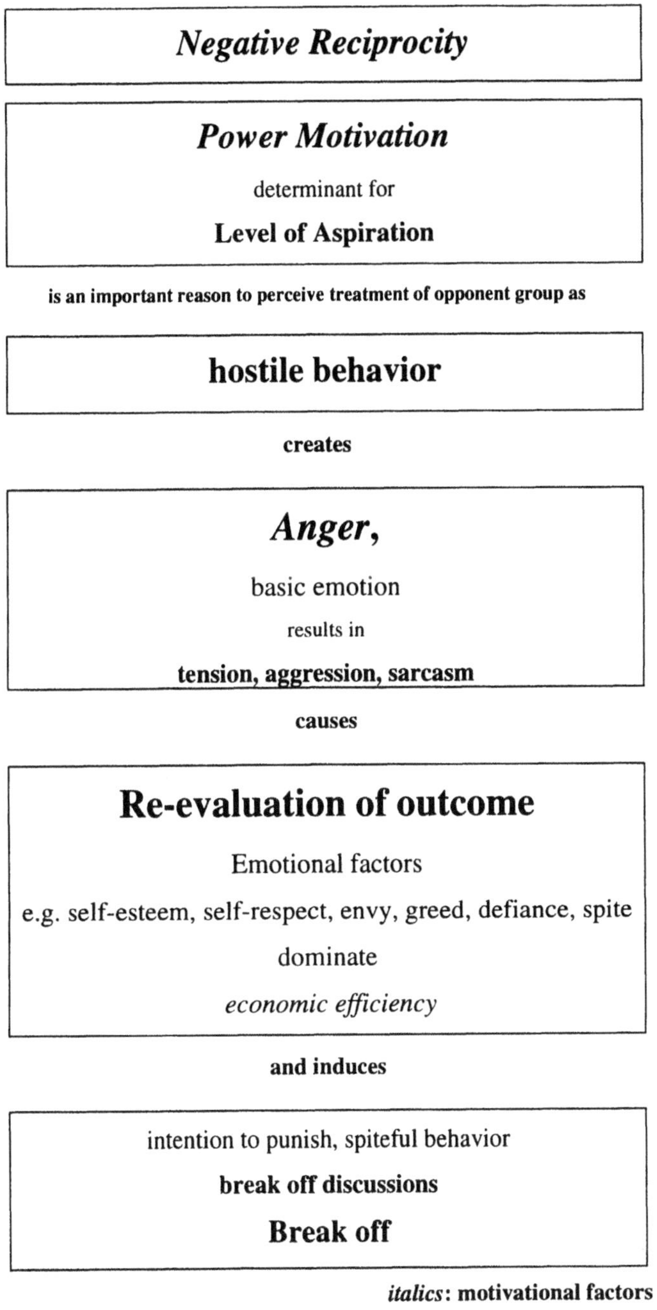

Figure 7.2: Motivations and emotional factors causing potential and actual break offs

itself in the use of coercive power in order to increase self-esteem and to show superiority over the other. It will likely lead to the influencee's abandoning the social relationship entirely.

Groups who were willing to break off showed release of the tension that had been visible as long as they felt themselves obligated to economic efficiency and the "dictatorship" of their opponents. Money had ceased to be of importance. Yet, what proved to be important was a feeling of surrender which would have resulted had they agreed to an outcome "dictated" or imposed by their counterparts and which they did not want to bear.

Members of a W-group rejecting a Split-the-Difference-proposal argued: "Pride and money fight against each other. I don't allow the high payoff to the others," and just before ending the session by conflict "Let's break off as a matter of self-respect! The money I don't care!" These remarks correspond to what Frank (1988) wrote on persons who are guided by emotions and reject one-sided offers: "Most know perfectly well that to accept would increase their wealth, yet they reject with not the slightest trace of regret" (p. 255).

Can we distinguish any differences between groups who only discussed break offs, and those who actually broke off? From Table 7.5 we saw that in 20 out of 24 I-groups subjects had non-payoff-oriented break off discussions in sometimes quite high percentages of rounds, but only 3 groups ended the session by conflict. The same is true for E-sessions, and only one break off occurred. Certainly, there are personal and situational factors determining when an offer or a sequence of offers is perceived as so inadequate that a break off is initiated. These effects we did not analyze. But there are two features of the bargaining process that may hint at an impending conflict: (i) those groups are likely to be punished who violate the notion of bargaining, i.e. that both partners have to make concessions, and (ii) an agreement is expected around mid-payoffs.

Firstly, the diagrams of the bargaining process show that in five groups (5.1, 6.1, 12.1, 12.2, 17.1) a negotiation behavior is predominant that does not show any cooperation (c.f. Appendix B and our analysis of strategic ideas in Section 5.5). The main feature of these bargaining patterns is that proposals are in a close relation or correspond to the initial very high aspiration level, and considerable concessions are not made. All those sessions ended by a break-off in which at least one group showed this behavior.[154]

Secondly we pointed out in Section 6.4 that one appearance of the equity principle complies with the common principle in bargaining to expect an agreement in or near the middle between two demands. Opponents of

[154]The same is true for the one session ending by a break off and belonging to those sessions of the Kuon-Uhlich-experiment which we analyzed in this study. C.f. Appendix C, Session 45.

conflict initiating groups obviously violate this principle in persistingly demanding amounts that are considerably (in our experiment around 20%) higher than the middle between their initial proposals. Obviously W-groups tend to punish those counterparts who are too greedy: with one exception, agreement outcomes in I- and E-sessions do only deviate around 5% from the mid-payoff to the benefit of S-groups.

7.7 Conclusion

What did we learn from the analysis of break off discussions? The evaluation of the transcripts of our experiment reveal that potential and actual break offs are an important feature of bargaining. We found significant correlates of break off discussions. Subjects' behavior is motivated not only by economic, but also by noneconomic factors, motivations, emotions and social norms. The inclination to behave in a way termed as non- or irrational in traditional microeconomic and game theory stems from negative reciprocity, motivating subjects to retaliate treatment perceived as inacceptable, and a feeling of power induced by the capability given by the rules of the game to punish hostile behavior. Anger, one of the basic emotions, is provoked causing a re-evaluation of the outcome of the game. As a result of this re-evaluation, emotional factors dominate the economic motivation, and break offs are taken into consideration or are actually initiated.

The process of re-evaluation described above possibly illustrates what Roth (1995a) had in mind when he wrote: "... bargainers may be concerned with more than their own payoffs in evaluating the outcome of bargaining" (p. 328).

Chapter 8

Conclusive Remarks: How Do Business People Decide?

Selten (1997) made a remark that reality is still full of undiscovered regularities and that we have to discover them. We showed in this study that by observing subjects and videotaping their discussions important behavioral regularities could be made visible. The most important ones are that behavior is guided by aspirations and prominence, that decisions are influenced by equity and fairness aspects, and that actions are affected by motivations, emotions and social norms.

One could argue that the subjects in our experiment are students and that their decisions are different from what people would do who in firms are responsible for everyday business decisions. We therefore conducted a small sample of questionnaire interviews in order to get insight into how business people would resolve our bargaining problem. The English translation of this questionnaire is to be found in Appendix G.

To make the problem interesting for business people we framed it into a joint venture decision. We were afraid that confronting people with an abstract problem who are not trained in thinking in this way[155] would induce them to refrain from answering our questions. And even in this framing people had difficulties since the problem was simplified and reduced to bargaining only about the profit of a joint venture (JVP). Business people are used to make much more complicated decisions. If they think about a cooperation project they take into account aspects of employment, turnover, market entry, gaining know-how, problems of plant capacity and other problems as was stated in comments on the questionnaire.

Since we asked people from various businesses we as an example gave profits on different levels to have persons identify with the task. Too low a profit with respect to firm size would have presented the joint venture as an

[155]None of them had a high school degree, three of them are owners of a workshop.

unattractive problem. Thus, the environment of the questionnaire interview is different from our experiment with respect to framing and several amounts of the coalition value.

Table 8.1: Characteristics of business people answering the questionnaire

Person Number	Types of Businesses	Position of Person Answering the Questionnaire	Number of Employees
1	Manufacturing	Manager of the sales department of a machine manufacturing company	18
2	Services	Owner of a dry cleaning firm	25
3	Services	Owner of a dry cleaning firm	5
4	Services	Owner of a dry cleaning firm	15
5	Health services	Owner of a physiotherapist office	15
6	Professional service company	Certified public accountant, executive in an audit and consulting firm	3,500

Table 8.1, 8.2, 8.3 show the types of businesses, the position of the persons answering the questionnaire, the number of employees and the answers to our questions. The most important finding of this small sample is that from the answers we can conclude that allocation decisions of five of the six persons are guided by *equity* considerations. As in our experiment different appearances of the equity principle influence decision makers[156]: the Equal Split, Split the Difference, Proportional Split and, as an iterated equity principle, the middle between Proportional Split and outside option. Two persons apply different equity norms when deciding as an S- or W-person.

When giving the reasons why the proposed bargaining result was aimed at persons 3 and 6 explicitly mention aspects of fairness. Person 2 states that "fair play" requires a Proportional Split if a fruitful cooperation is to be expected. Person 6, in contrast, would strive for an Equal Split of the Surplus since this allocation fits to his understanding of fairness. He argues that the appropriate negotiable amount, in our notation the proper standard of distribution, has to be the surplus and not the total JVP since the distribution of half of the JVP is already fixed by the outside options. The Proportional Split he declines because the difference in absolute terms between profits is too high.

Also person 5 cares for the difference between profits but from a controversial perspective: demanding 70% of JVP ensures a profit to the stronger partner which is more than twice as high as the profit of the weaker partner. According to the power relation of profits, a payoff which corresponds to only double the amount of the W-person is seen as inadequate.

[156]Persons no. 1, 2, 3, 5, 6.

Table 8.2: Answers of business people to our bargaining problem: Allocation of joint-venture profit

Person Number	**Allocation of joint-venture-profit (JVP) *)**					
	Partner with *higher* realizable profit (g1)			Partner with *lower* realizable profit (g2)		
	DM 1,000,000	DM 500,000	DM 100,000	DM 1,000,000	DM 500,000	DM 100,000
1	Preferred: *Proportional Split (P)* DM 800,000 Minimally: larger than *Equal Split* > DM 500,000			Preferred: *Proportional Split* DM 800,000 Minimally: lower than *Middle between P and Alternative g2* < DM 850,000		
2	*Proportional Split* DM 800,000	75 % of JVP DM 375,000	70 % of JVP DM 70,000	60 % of JVP DM 600,000	60 % of JVP DM 300,000	60 % of JVP DM 60,000
3	*Proportional Split* DM 800,000	*Proportional Split* DM 400,000	*Proportional Split* DM 80,000	*Proportional Split* DM 800,000	*Proportional Split* DM 400,000	*Proportional Split* DM 80,000
4	(i) 70 % of JVP[a)] DM 700,000 (ii) 60 % of JVP[b)] DM 600,000	dto. DM 350,000 dto. DM 300,000	dto. DM 70,000 dto. DM 60,000	(i) 70 % of JVP[a)] DM 700,000 (ii) 60 % of JVP[b)] DM 600,000	dto. DM 350,000 dto. DM 300,000	dto. DM 70,000 dto. DM 60,000
5	Preferred: *Proportional Split* DM 800,000 yet larger than *Equal Split* > DM 500,000	Preferred: 70 % of JVP DM 350,000 dto. > DM 250,000	Preferred: 70 % of JVP DM 70,000 dto. > DM 50,000	*Equal Split* DM 500,000	*Equal Split* DM 250,000	*Equal Split* DM 50,000
6	Preferred: *Split the Difference* DM 650,000 Minimally: additional profit DM 200,000 JVP for g1 DM 600,000			Preferred: *Split the Difference* DM 650,000 Minimally: additional profit up to DM 300,000 JVP for g1 up to DM 700,000		

*) Amounts are in terms of payoffs for g1, i.e. demands of g1 resp. offers of g2

italics: Allocation guided by Equity Principle

b) If g2 has *no* essential influence in the joint venture

c) If g2 *has* influence in the joint venture, e.g. on sales prices

Table 8.3: Answers of business people to our bargaining problem: Break off taken into consideration

Person Number	**Break off taken into consideration** Partner with *higher* realizable profit (g1) DM 1,000,000	DM 500,000	DM 100,000	Partner with *lower* realizable profit (g2) DM 1,000,000	DM 500,000	DM 100,000
1	*Equal Split* or less DM 500,000			*Middle between P and Alternative g2* DM 850,000		
2				If JVP for g2 is not larger than 115% of profit in non-cooperation > DM 460,000	> DM 230,000	> DM 46,000
3	If JVP for g1 << *P* [a]	dto.	dto.	If JVP for g1 >> *P* [a]	dto.	dto.
4	(i) If JVP for g1 is smaller than 70% of total JVP[b] < DM 700,000 (ii) If JVP for g1 is smaller than 60% of total JVP[c] < DM 600,000	< DM 350,000 < DM 300,000	< DM 70,000 < DM 60,000	(i) If JVP for g2 is smaller than 30% of total JVP[b] > DM 700,000 (ii) If JVP for g2 is smaller than 40% of total JVP[c] > DM 600,000	> DM 350,000 > DM 300,000	> DM 70,000 > DM 60,000
5	*Equal Split* DM 500,000	*Equal Split* DM 250,000	*Equal Split* DM 50,000	> *Equal Split* > DM 500,000	> *Equal Split* > DM 250,000	> *Equal Split* > DM 50,000
6	< (*Split the Difference* - 50,000) < DM 600,000			> (*Split the Difference* + 50,000) > DM 700,000		

*) Amounts are in terms of payoffs for g1, i.e. demands of g1 resp. offers of g2

italics: Allocation guided by Equity Principle

a) Amount not specified

b) If g2 has *no* essential influence in the joint venture

c) If g2 *has* influence in the joint venture, e.g. on sales prices

As in our experiment, there are persons (2, 5) who would not have come to an agreement had they to play against themselves.

Another factor influencing the proportion demanded seems to be the level of profit: persons 2 and 5 offer a higher percentage to the weaker partner if the profit level decreases.

Even though interviewees point out that a break off should be avoided as far as possible they stress that cooperation should not be enforced at any cost. Nearly all persons state the conditions when a break off should be taken into consideration. It is argued that negotiations should be broken off if the potential partner would try to enforce his conditions[157]. Person 2 specifies the "ε" which would induce him not to break off to be higher than 15% of his outside option.

Two persons comment that their decisions are influenced by experience resp. emotions. Person 2 states that he, as the owner of a workshop being a skilled manual worker, is unable "to put business decisions into formulae". He acts according to experience and his professional sense. Person 5 states that the potential break off is a purely emotional decision. Monetary aspects would demand different behavior.

We see that among other factors notions of equity and fairness influence decisions. This has been shown not only by videotaping subjects in our experiment and asking them by questionnaires. The studies by Bewley (1997) and Königstein (1997) yield similar results. Contrary to the critique quoted in Section 3.1.1 the influence of equity norms and fairness aspects seems to be a robust phenomenon in different experimental settings and different techniques of getting to learn what influences people's decisions. We hope that these findings will contribute to videotaping becoming an accepted scientific method.

The statements on break offs show clearly that also in business life break offs are a usual decision alternative even if offers are higher than outside options and that behavior guided by prevailing nonmonetary motives has to be taken into account.

In game theory behavior of economic agents not guided by full rationality is assumed not to be present, and therefore in many situations actual behavior of experimental subjects cannot be explained. It is characterized as an anomaly. According to Thaler (1988, p.195) "... an empirical result qualifies as an anomaly if it is difficult to 'rationalize' or if implausible assumptions

[157] If the other person "attempts to take the partner to the cleaners" (wenn der andere versucht, mich über den Tisch zu ziehen) (persons 3, 6), if cooperation comes down to "dictation" (Kooperation würde zu einem Diktat führen) (person 2), if cooperation costs too much (person 5).

are necessary to explain it within the paradigm".[158] This interpretation of an anomalous empirical result refers to one of the meanings of anomaly, namely the deviation from a general rule or method (c.f. Webster, 1966). And if this notion is applied, subjects' behavior as observed in our experiment, especially break off behavior, has to be characterized as an anomaly.

However, anomaly can also be defined as a deviation from what is usual or normal, something that is irregular (c.f. Webster, 1966). We saw that, for instance in ultimatum games, behavior qualified as anomalous proved to be a very robust phenomenon. And actual and potential break offs which according to game theory should not occur we did observe very frequently. The empirical results referred to by Thaler are by no means irregular and unusual. Consequently, they are not to be qualified as anomalies according to the second interpretation. Do these findings not suggest that it is not the behavior that has to be explained by implausible hypotheses but rather that it is the paradigm that rests on implausible assumptions?

[158] See also the paper by Camerer and Thaler (1995).

Appendix A

Introduction of Experimental Subjects

You participate in a bargaining experiment where two groups negotiate with each other. To evaluate the communication process within the groups the experiment is recorded on video.

The goal of the game is to maximize your own profit while bargaining on a coalition value.

The game ends if one group accepts the proposed division of the other group, or if one group breaks off the negotiation. If there is an agreement, **each** member of the group receives the payoff the group agreed upon. If there is a break off of negotiations, **each** member of the group receives the guaranteed payoff for his/her group (the alternative).

I will now explain the negotiation process from the bargaining protocol. The other group received an identical bargaining protocol.

You have been randomly chosen to make the first (second) proposal. A money payoff, called the coalition value, amounts to 320 points. If there is a breakoff of the negotiation, the guaranteed payoff for group 1 is 96 (128) points and the guaranteed payoff for group 2 is 64 (32) points.

Please discuss which of the following four decision alternatives the group is to be choosing, and please discuss also the reasons why the group chooses just this decision:

1. You make a proposal on the division of the coalition value to your opponent group. The proposal has to be nonnegative and integer-valued.

2. You shift, i.e. the initiative to make a proposal passes to the other group without your making a proposal.

3. You accept the proposal of your opponent group.

4. You break off the negotiation.

Agree upon one of the four possibilities. Write down the result of your discussion into the column of the protocol that is provided for your group. Each member of the group has to confirm this entry by his/her signature.Your proposed allocation of the coalition value will then be transmitted to your opponent group.

Following each bargaining round please fill in one copy of the questionnaire. It will be collected afterwards.

After having finished the experiment each member of the group will be paid either the accepted share of the coalition value or the guaranteed payoff for his/her group. Each point is worth 0,10 DM.

Try to maximize your own profit!

There is no time constraint.

Are there any questions?

Bargaining Protocol		Date Starting time End			Session No. Group No. Page 1		
Current Proposal					Payoffs		
Proposal		Group 1 receives	Group 2 receives	Signatures	Coalition	Alternative	
No.	of group no.					Group 1	group 2
1	1				320	128	32
2	2						
3	1						
4	2						
5	1						
6	2						
7	1						
8	2						
9	1						
10	2						
11	1						
12	2						
13	1						
14	2						
15	1						
16	2						

Appendix B

Negotiation Processes

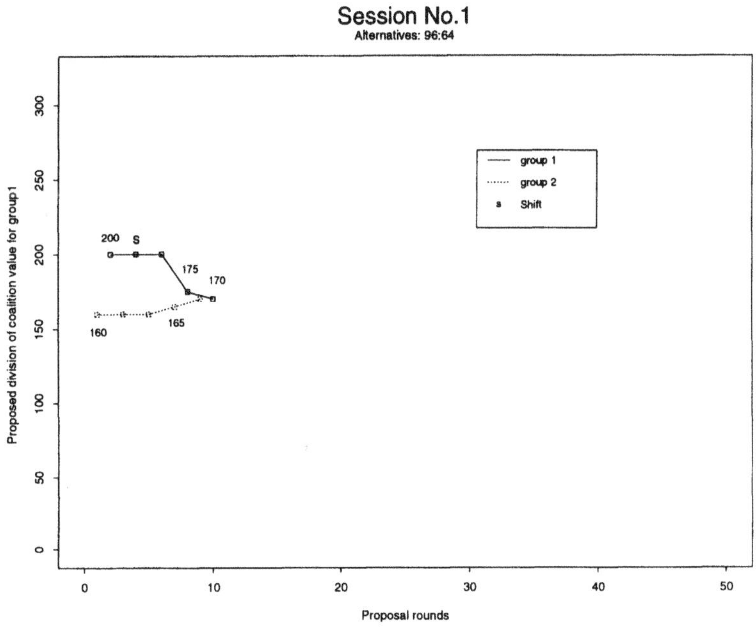

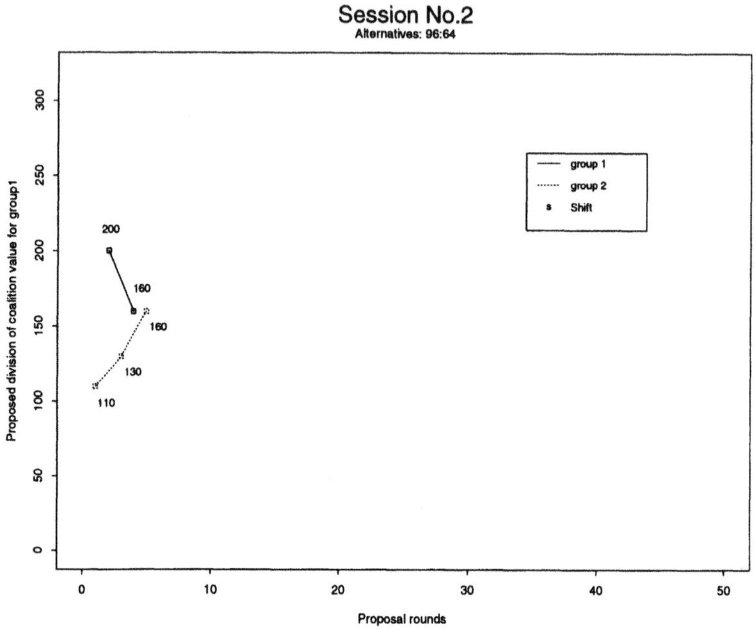
Session No.2
Alternatives: 96:64
group 1
group 2
s Shift
200
160
160
130
110
Proposed division of coalition value for group1
0
50
100
150
200
250
300
0
10
20
30
40
50
Proposal rounds

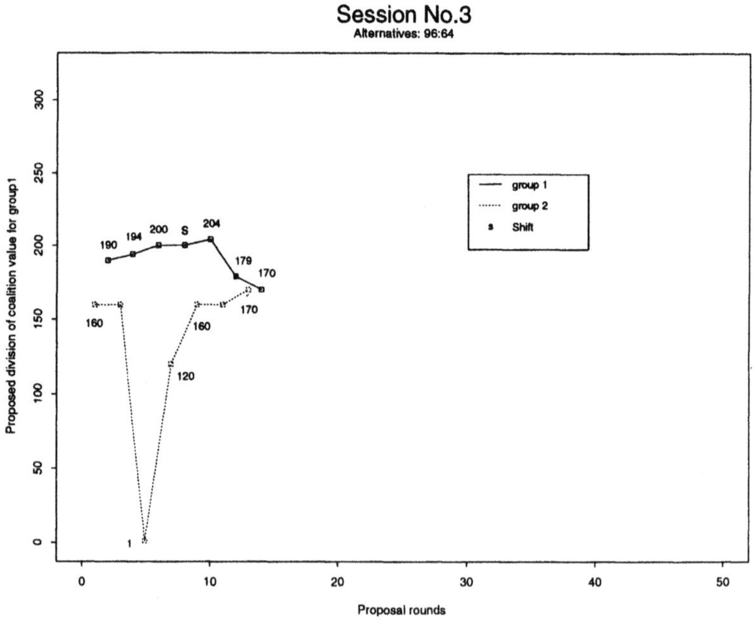
Session No.3
Alternatives: 96:64
group 1
group 2
s Shift
190
194
200
S
204
179
170
160
160
170
120
1
Proposed division of coalition value for group1
0
50
100
150
200
250
300
0
10
20
30
40
50
Proposal rounds

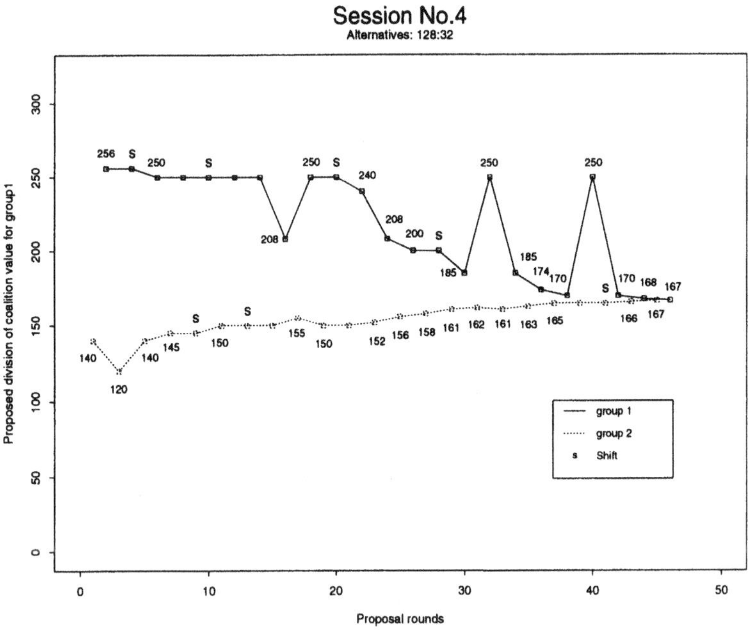
Session No.4
Alternatives: 128:32
Proposed division of coalition value for group1
Proposal rounds
0
50
100
150
200
250
300
0
10
20
30
40
50
256 S 250 S 250 S 240 250 250
208 208 200 S 185 185 174 170 S 170 168 167
S S
140 120 140 145 150 155 150 152 156 158 161 162 161 163 165 166 167
group 1
group 2
s Shift

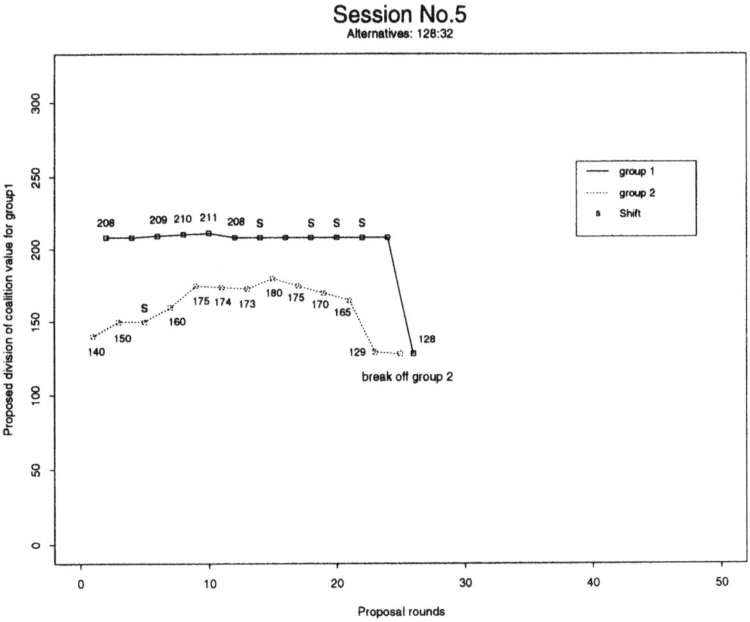
Session No.5
Alternatives: 128:32
Proposed division of coalition value for group1
Proposal rounds
0
50
100
150
200
250
300
0
10
20
30
40
50
208 209 210 211 208 S S S S
S
175 174 173 180 175 170 165
140 150 160
129 128
break off group 2
group 1
group 2
s Shift

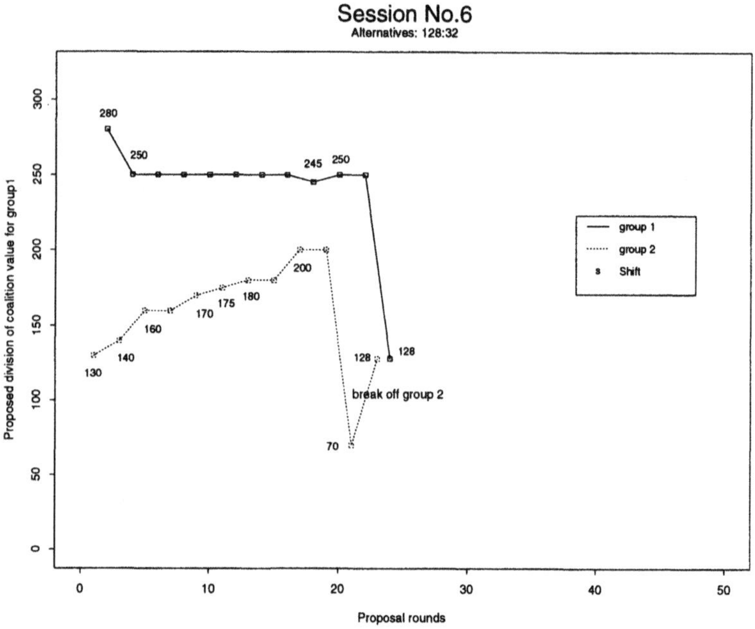
Session No.6
Alternatives: 128:32
Proposed division of coalition value for group1
Proposal rounds
280
250
245
250
200
180
175
170
160
140
130
128
128
break off group 2
70
group 1
group 2
Shift

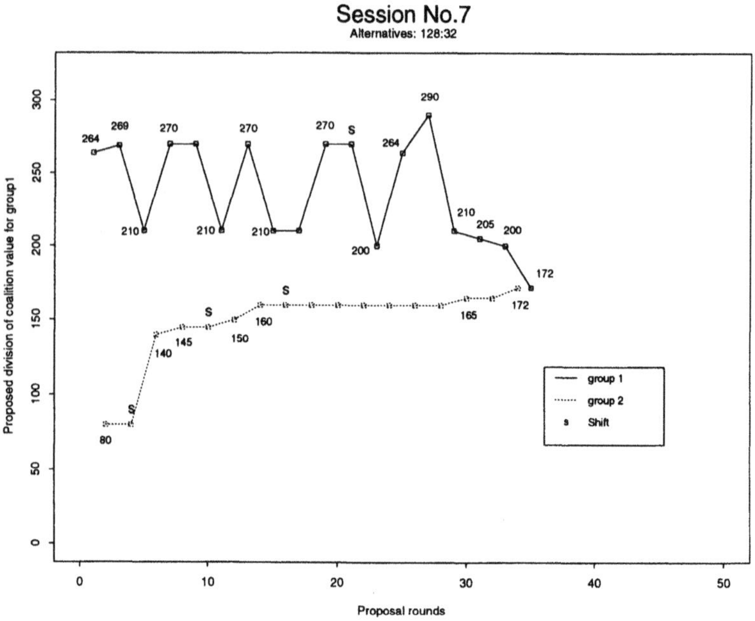
Session No.7
Alternatives: 128:32
Proposed division of coalition value for group1
Proposal rounds
264
269
270
270
270
290
264
210
210
210
200
210
205
200
172
165
172
160
150
145
140
80
group 1
group 2
Shift

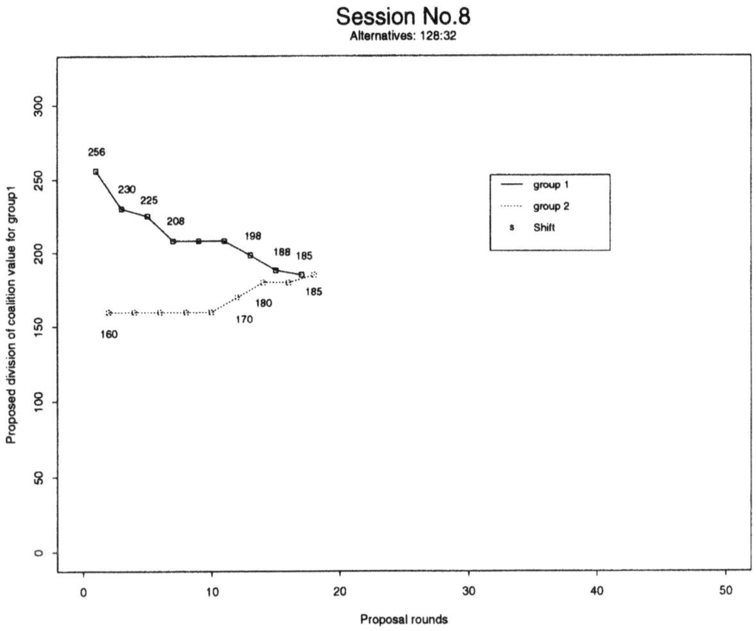
Session No.8
Alternatives: 128:32
Proposed division of coalition value for group1
Proposal rounds
group 1
group 2
s Shift
256
230
225
208
198
188
185
185
180
170
160
0
50
100
150
200
250
300
0
10
20
30
40
50

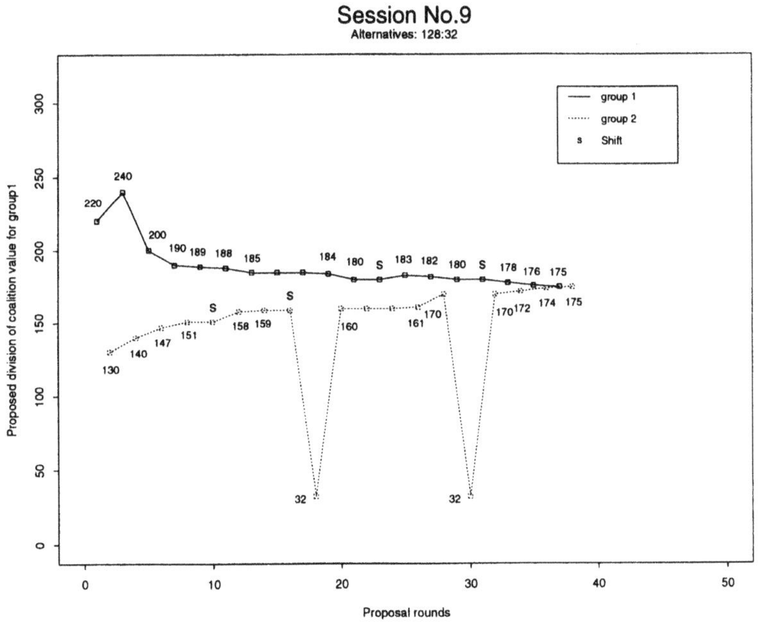
Session No.9
Alternatives: 128:32
Proposed division of coalition value for group1
Proposal rounds
group 1
group 2
s Shift
240
220
200
190
189
188
185
184
180
S
183
182
180
S
178
176
175
S
S
158
159
151
147
140
130
160
161
170
170
172
174
175
32
32
0
50
100
150
200
250
300
0
10
20
30
40
50

Session No.10

Alternatives: 96:64

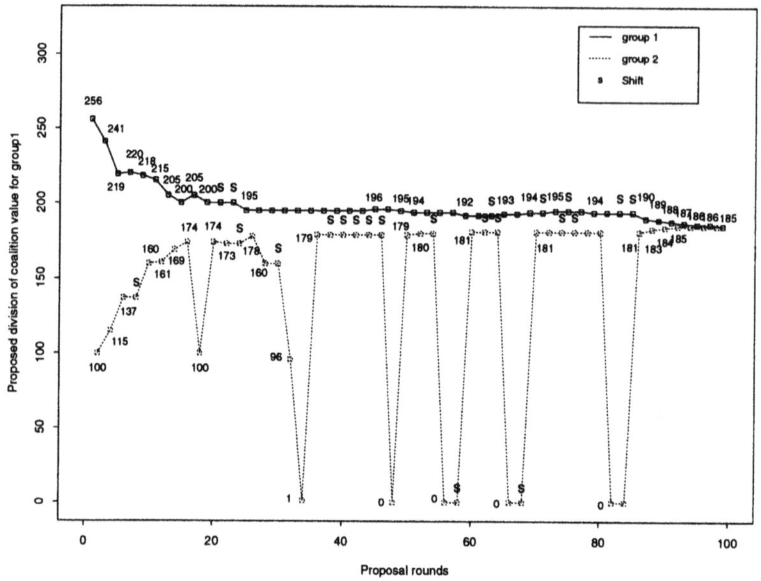

Session No.11

Alternatives: 96:64

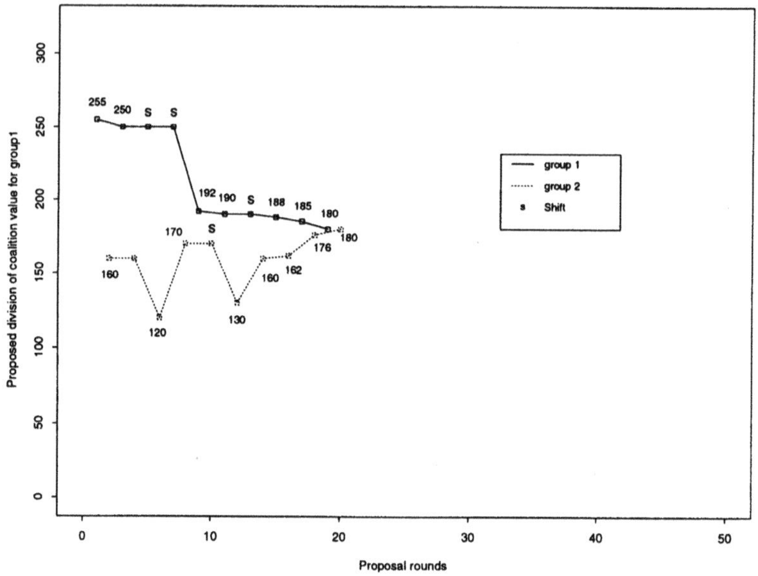

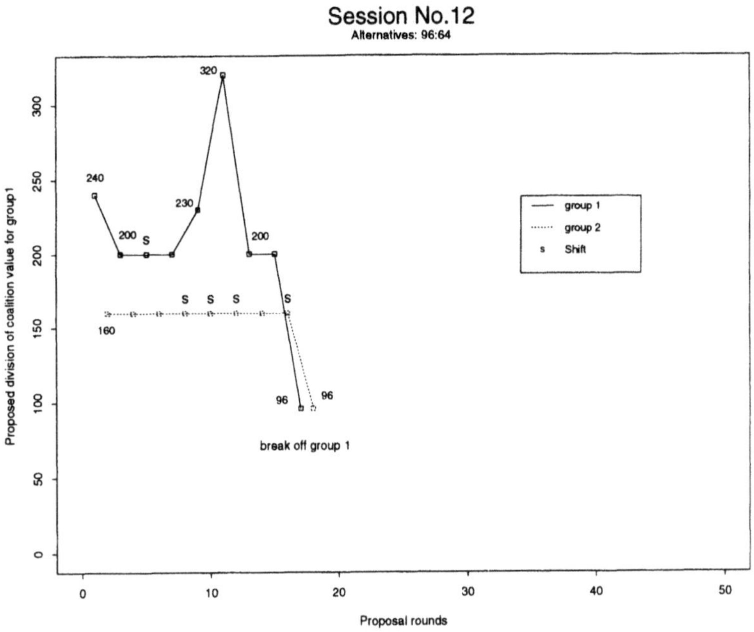

Session No.12
Alternatives: 96:64
Proposed division of coalition value for group1
Proposal rounds
320
240
230
200
S
200
S S S S
160
96
96
break off group 1
group 1
group 2
s Shift

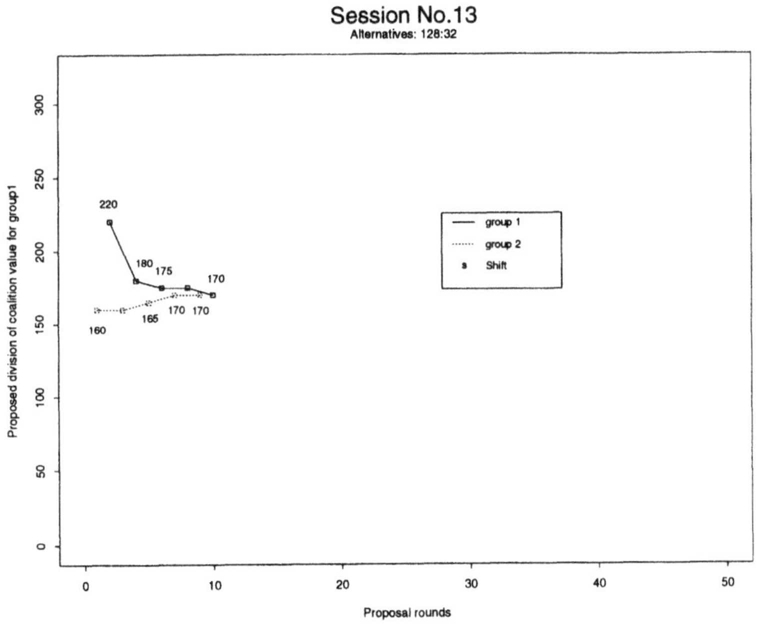

Session No.13
Alternatives: 128:32
Proposed division of coalition value for group1
Proposal rounds
220
180
175
170
165
170 170
160
group 1
group 2
s Shift

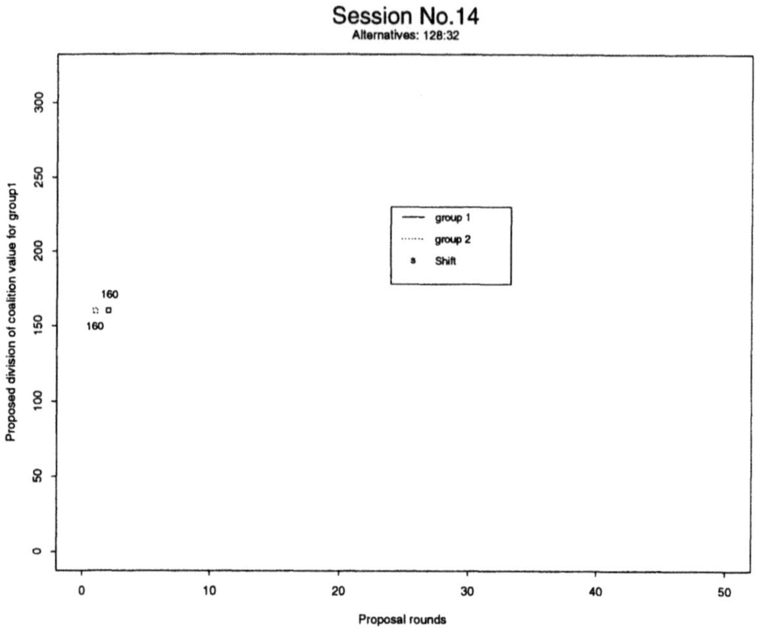
Session No.14
Alternatives: 128:32
group 1
group 2
Shift
160
160
Proposed division of coalition value for group1
Proposal rounds

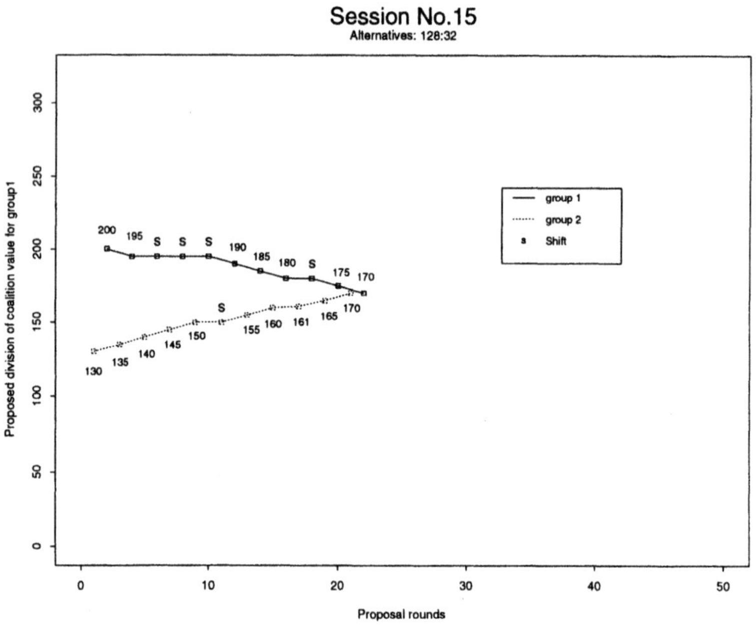
Session No.15
Alternatives: 128:32
group 1
group 2
Shift
200
195
190
185
180
175
170
130
135
140
145
150
155
160
161
165
170
Proposed division of coalition value for group1
Proposal rounds

Session No.16
Alternatives: 128:32

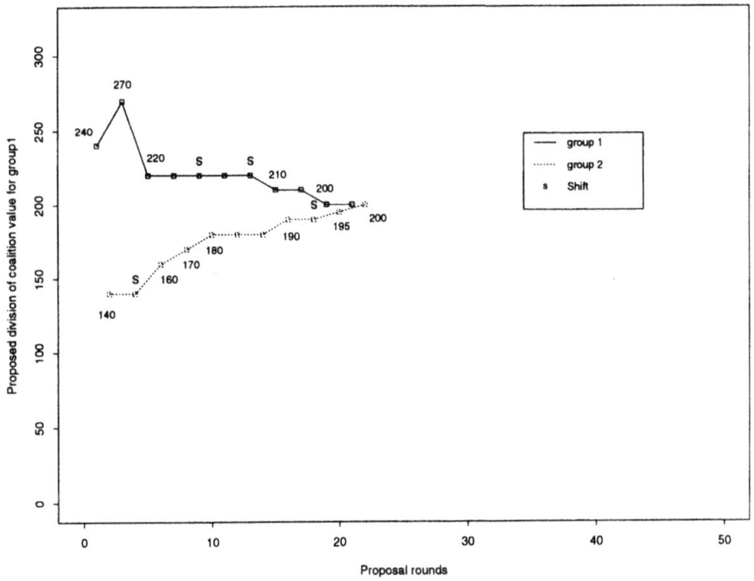

Session No.17
Alternatives: 128:32

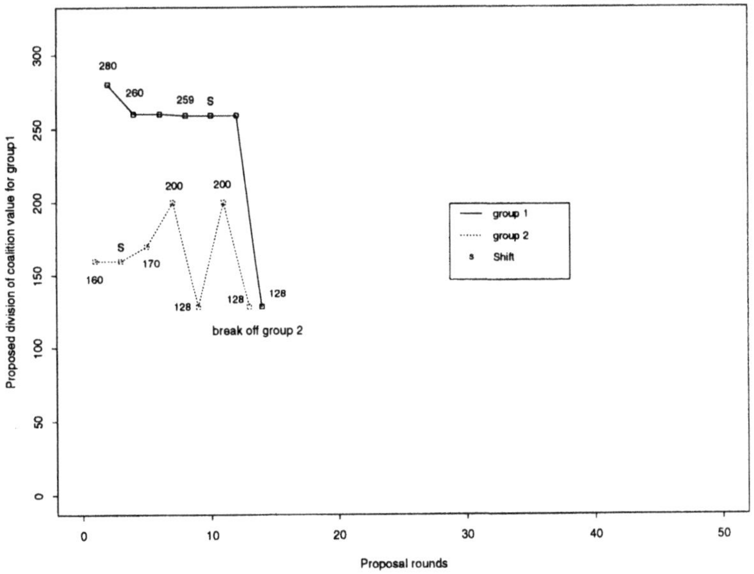

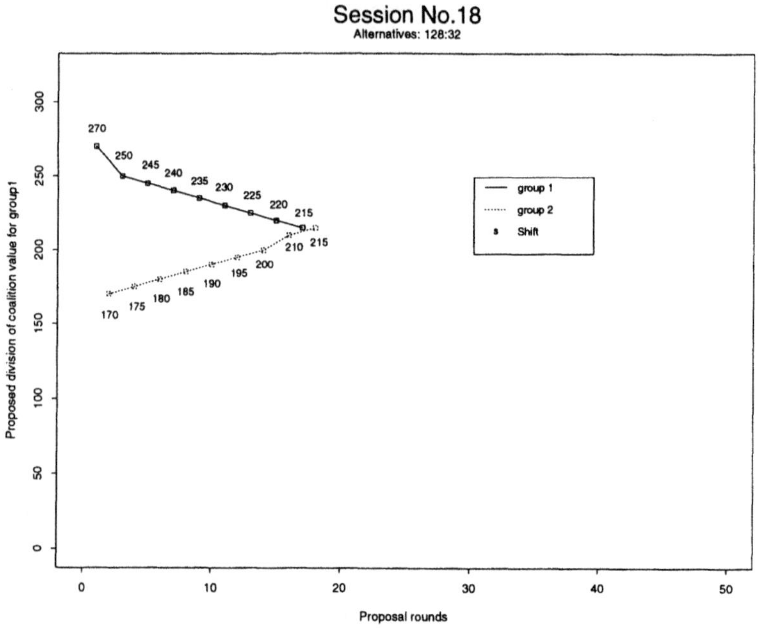
Session No.18
Alternatives: 128:32
Proposed division of coalition value for group1
Proposal rounds
group 1
group 2
Shift
270
250
245
240
235
230
225
220
215
210
215
200
195
190
185
180
175
170

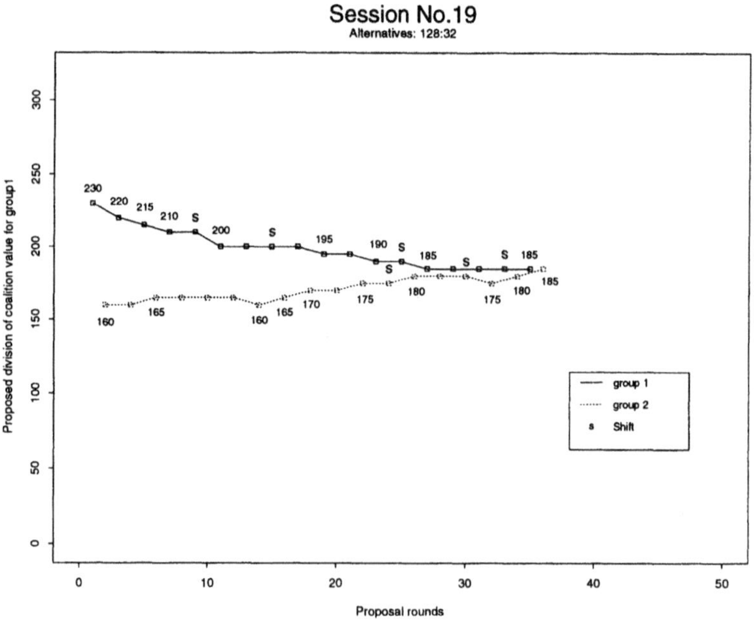
Session No.19
Alternatives: 128:32
Proposed division of coalition value for group1
Proposal rounds
group 1
group 2
Shift
230
220
215
210
200
195
190
185
185
160
165
160
165
170
175
180
175
180
185

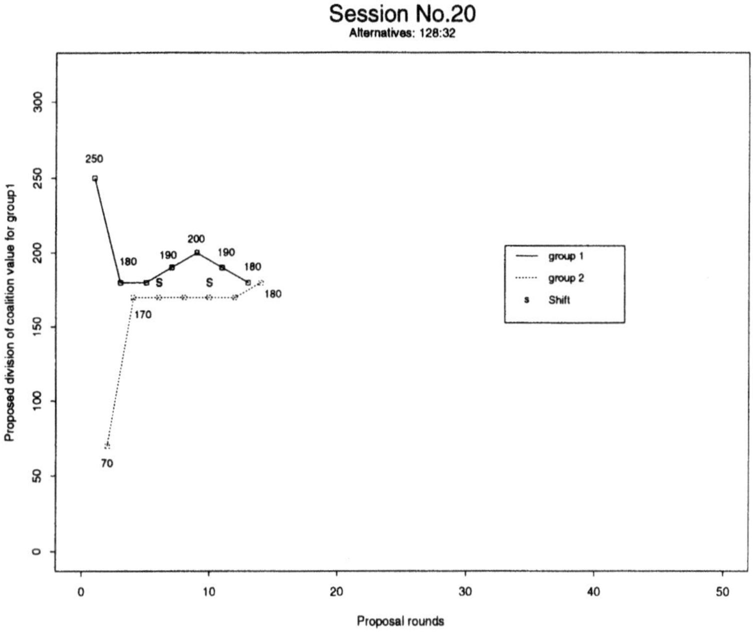

Session No.20
Alternatives: 128:32
Proposed division of coalition value for group1
Proposal rounds
250
180
190
200
190
180
180
170
70
S
S
group 1
group 2
s Shift
0
50
100
150
200
250
300
0
10
20
30
40
50

Appendix C

Negotiation Processes of the Kuon-Uhlich-Experiment

Coalition value: 320

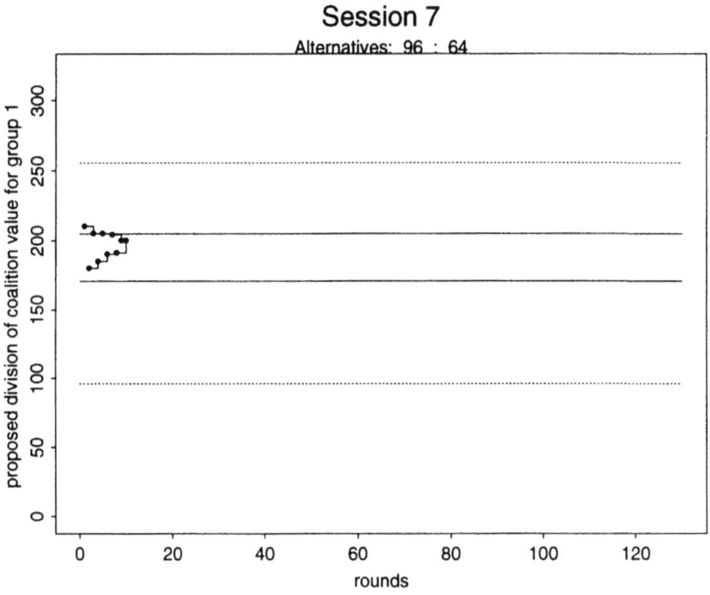

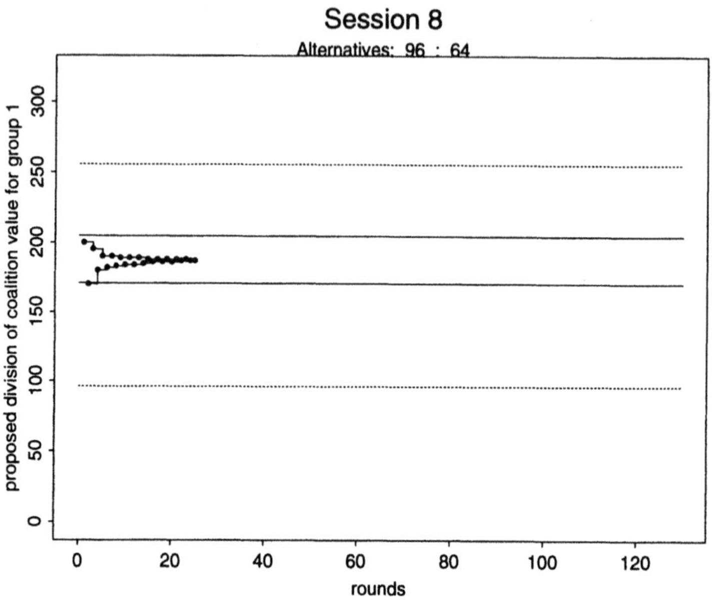
Session 8
Alternatives: 96 : 64
proposed division of coalition value for group 1
0
50
100
150
200
250
300
0
20
40
60
80
100
120
rounds

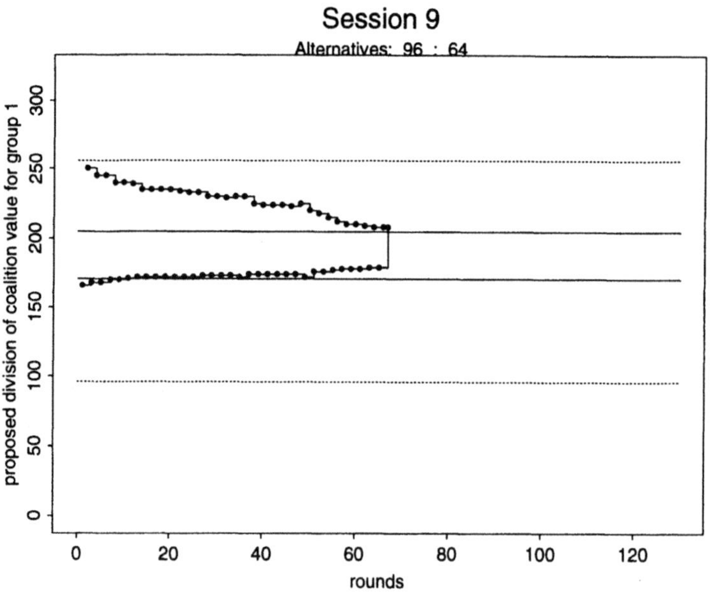
Session 9
Alternatives: 96 : 64
proposed division of coalition value for group 1
0
50
100
150
200
250
300
0
20
40
60
80
100
120
rounds

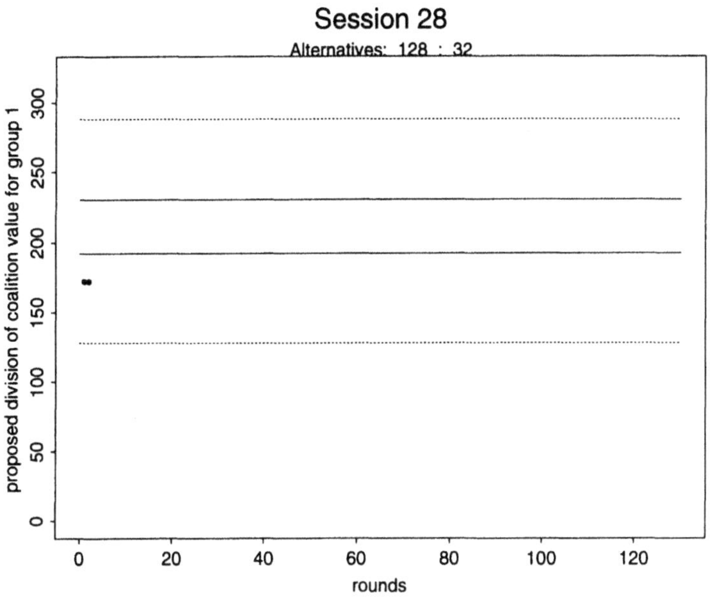
Session 28
Alternatives: 128 : 32
proposed division of coalition value for group 1
0
50
100
150
200
250
300
0
20
40
60
80
100
120
rounds

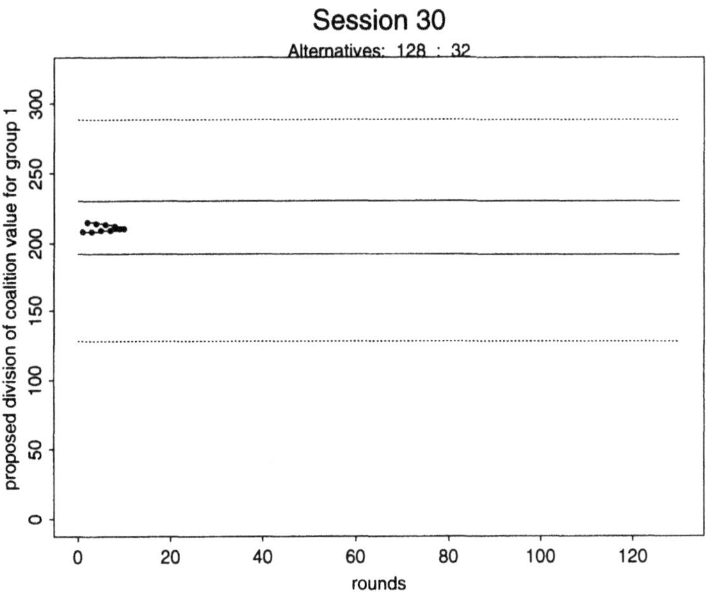
Session 30
Alternatives: 128 : 32
proposed division of coalition value for group 1
0
50
100
150
200
250
300
0
20
40
60
80
100
120
rounds

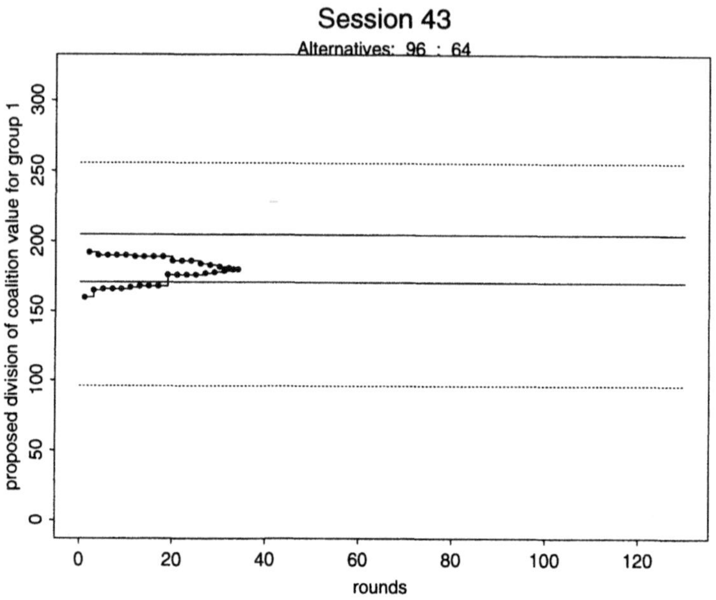
Session 43
Alternatives: 96 : 64
proposed division of coalition value for group 1
0
50
100
150
200
250
300
0
20
40
60
80
100
120
rounds

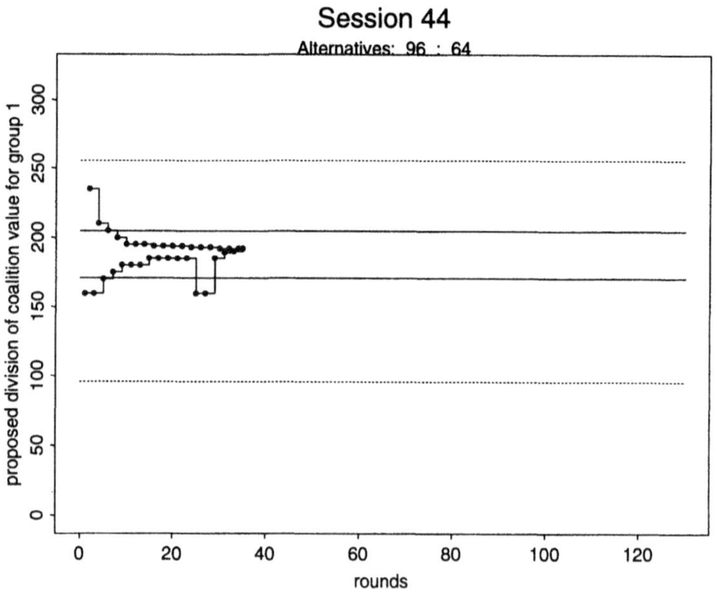
Session 44
Alternatives: 96 : 64
proposed division of coalition value for group 1
0
50
100
150
200
250
300
0
20
40
60
80
100
120
rounds

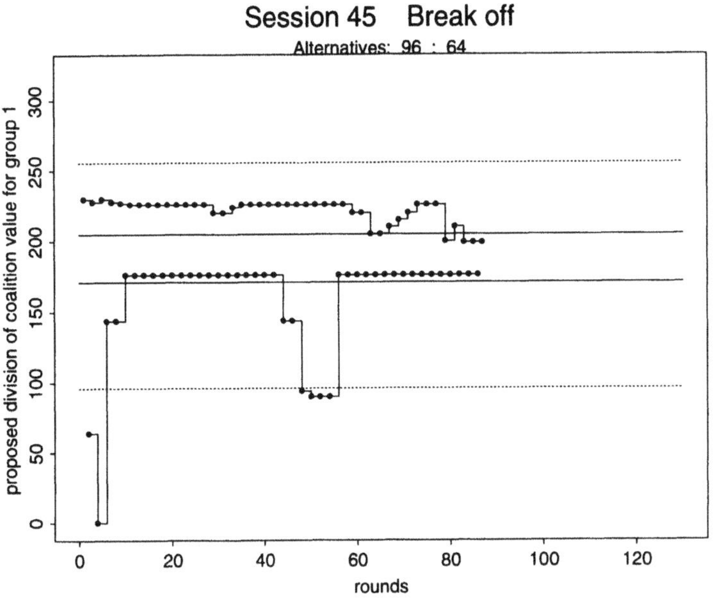
Session 45 Break off
Alternatives: 96 : 64
proposed division of coalition value for group 1
0
50
100
150
200
250
300
0
20
40
60
80
100
120
rounds

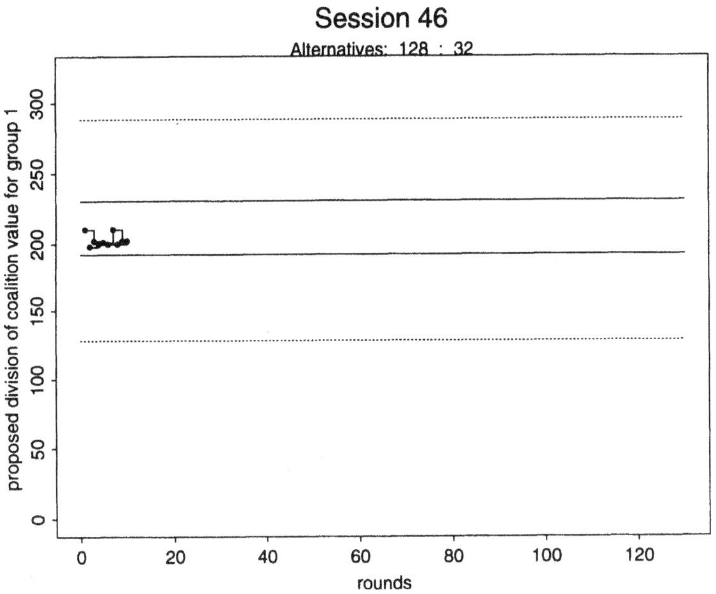
Session 46
Alternatives: 128 : 32
proposed division of coalition value for group 1
0
50
100
150
200
250
300
0
20
40
60
80
100
120
rounds

Session 47

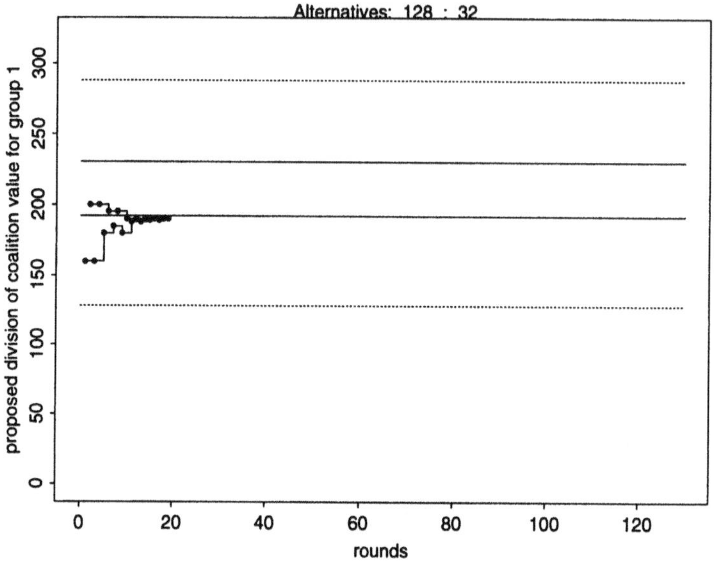

Session 48

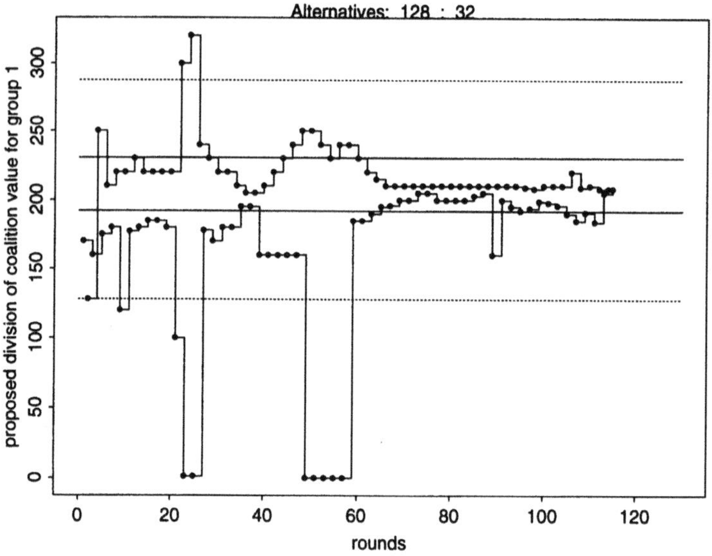

Appendix D

Allocations

In the first diagram we show the values of the allocations discussed during the negotiation. Bold face numbers are allocations discussed by group 4.1, numbers printed in a normal font are those of group 4.2. A column of numbers represents the allocations discussed by one group in one round.

In the following two diagrams we distinguish all allocations according to the members of groups 4.1 or 4.2 who proposed this allocation. Members of groups are represented by different characters: + for group member l (on the left side of the screen), • for group member m (in the middle of the screen), o for group member r (on the right side of the screen). If a value is to be exceeded or if an amount is not to be accepted, either $>$ or $<$ is found below or above the corresponding value, i.e. at least one of the group members is striving for a higher or lower payoff.

The alternately proposed divisions of the coalition value for both groups are also depicted. The thin solid line is valid for group 1, the dotted line is valid for group 2.

Payoffs are quoted in terms of payoffs for group 1, even if proposed allocations of group 2 are shown.

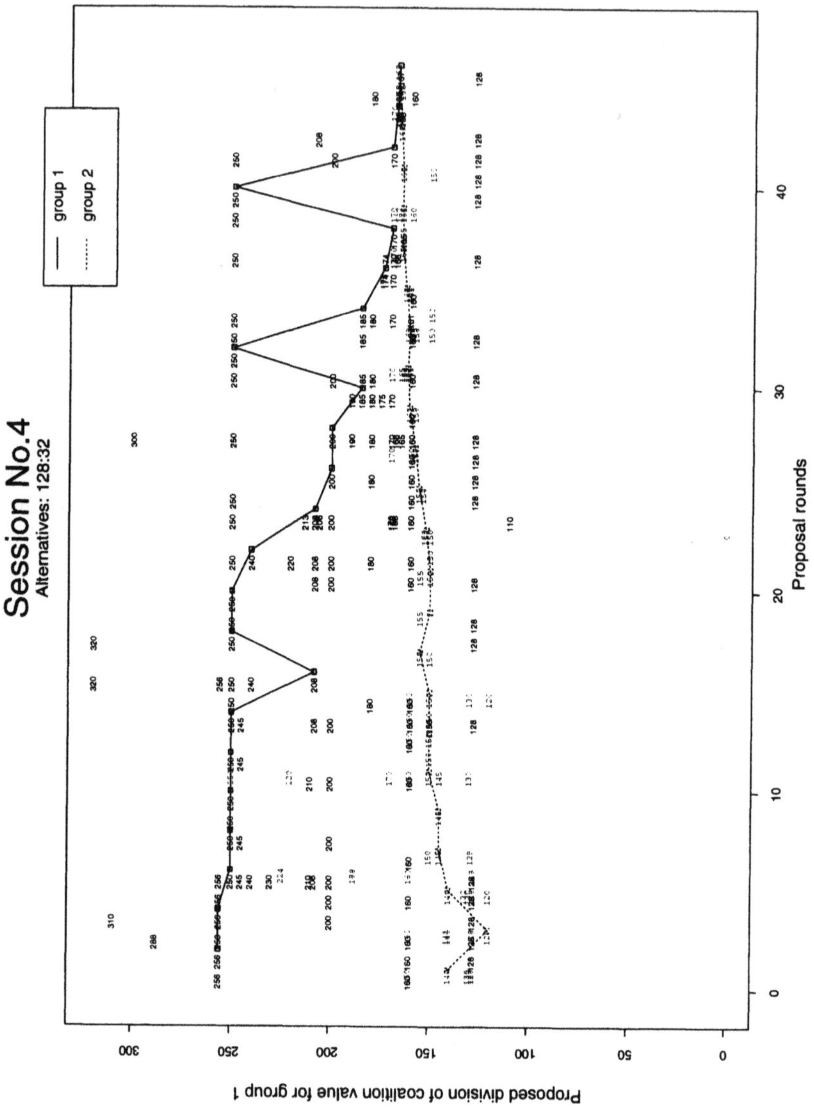
Session No.4
Alternatives: 128:32
group 1
group 2
Proposal rounds
Proposed division of coalition value for group 1

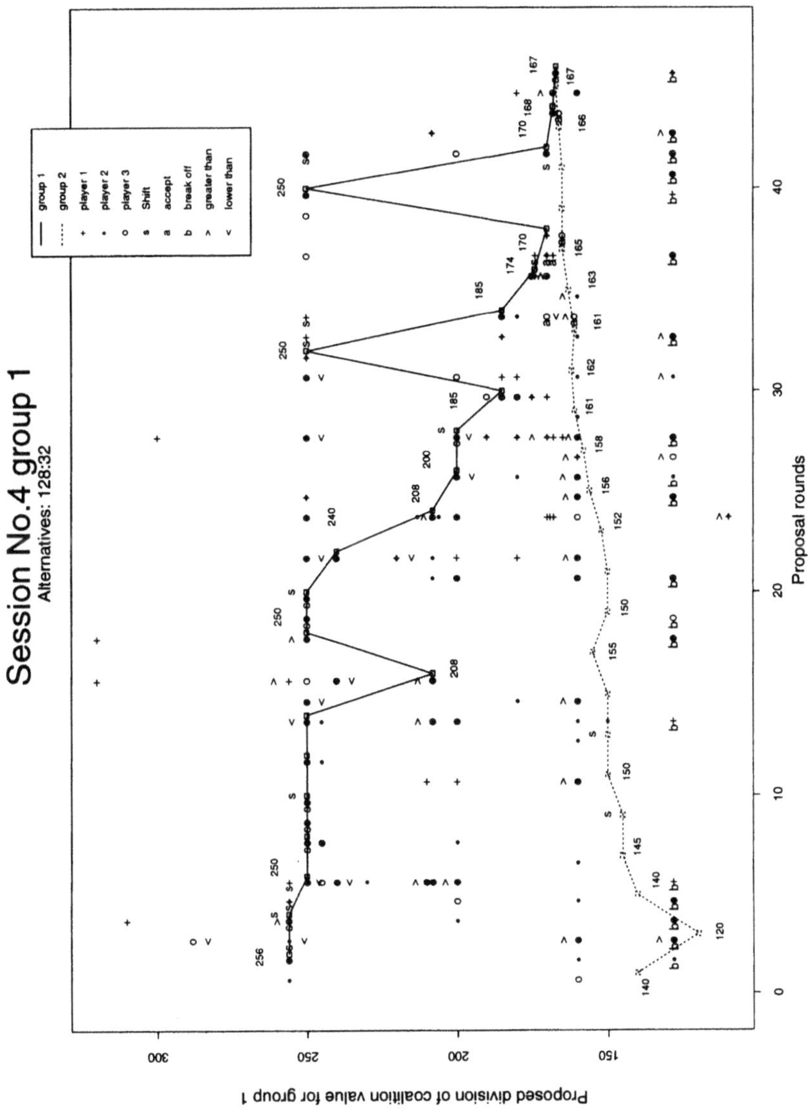
Session No.4 group 1
Alternatives: 128:32
group 1
group 2
player 1
player 2
player 3
Shift
accept
break off
greater than
lower than
Proposal rounds
Proposed division of coalition value for group 1

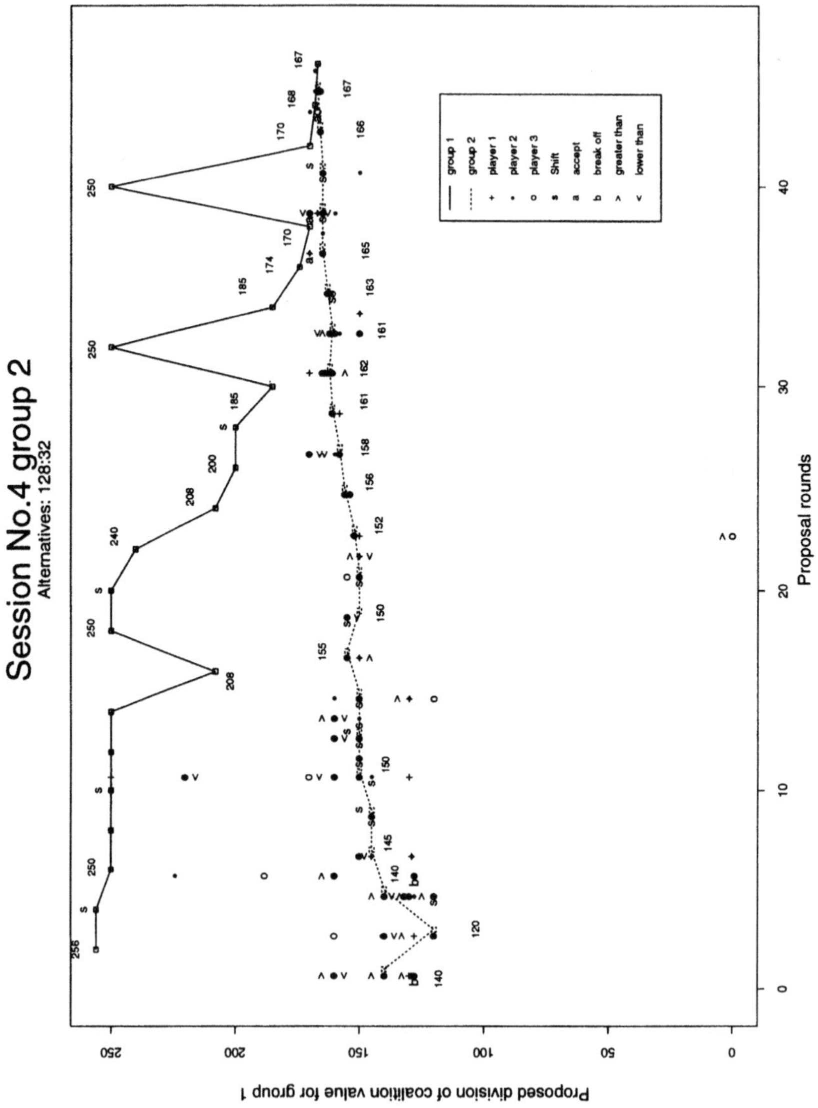
Session No.4 group 2
Alternatives: 128:32
Proposed division of coalition value for group 1
Proposal rounds
group 1
group 2
player 1
player 2
player 3
Shift
accept
break off
greater than
lower than

Appendix E

Formation and Adaptation of Aspiration Levels

The following figures show the adaptation of aspiration levels in terms of payoffs for group 1. The bold solid line shows the variation of aspiration levels. As before members of the groups are represented by different characters: + for group member l (on the left side of the screen), • for group member m (in the middle of the screen), ∘ for group member r (on the right side of the screen). If a lower bound is to be exceeded or if an upper bound is not to be accepted, either $>$ or $<$ is found below or above the corresponding value, i.e. at least one of the group members is striving for a higher or lower aspiration level. If this is valid for the whole group the line representing the aspiration levels becomes a bold broken line.

To relate aspiration levels to proposed divisions of the coalition value also the alternating proposals for both groups are depicted. The thin solid line is valid for group 1, the dotted line is valid for group 2.

Payoffs and aspiration levels are always quoted in terms of payoffs for group 1, even if aspiration levels for group 2 are shown.

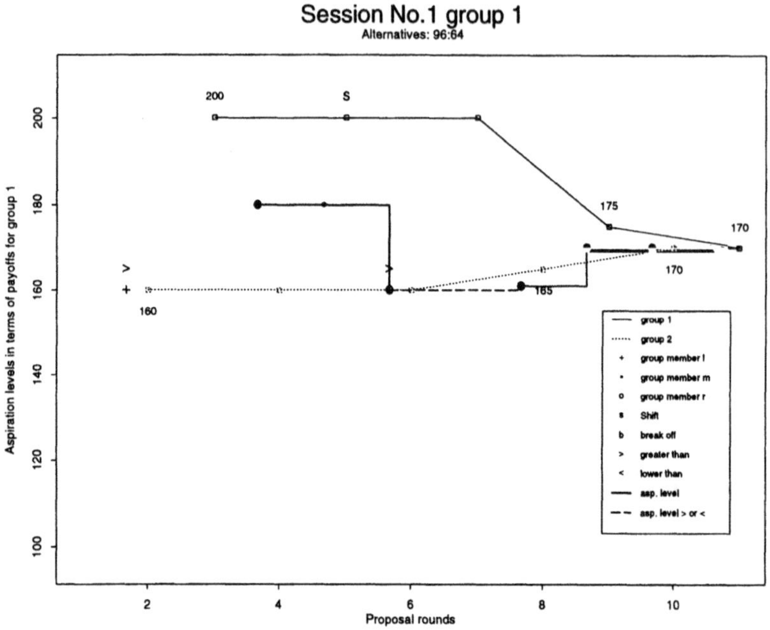
Session No.1 group 1
Alternatives: 96:64
Aspiration levels in terms of payoffs for group 1
Proposal rounds
200
S
175
170
170
165
160
group 1
group 2
group member l
group member m
group member r
Shift
break off
greater than
lower than
asp. level
asp. level > or <

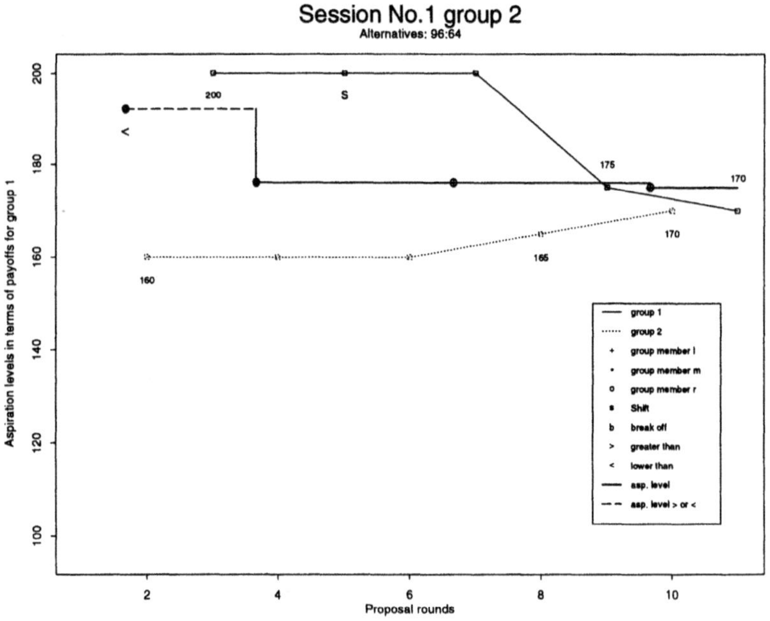
Session No.1 group 2
Alternatives: 96:64
Aspiration levels in terms of payoffs for group 1
Proposal rounds
200
S
175
170
170
165
160
group 1
group 2
group member l
group member m
group member r
Shift
break off
greater than
lower than
asp. level
asp. level > or <

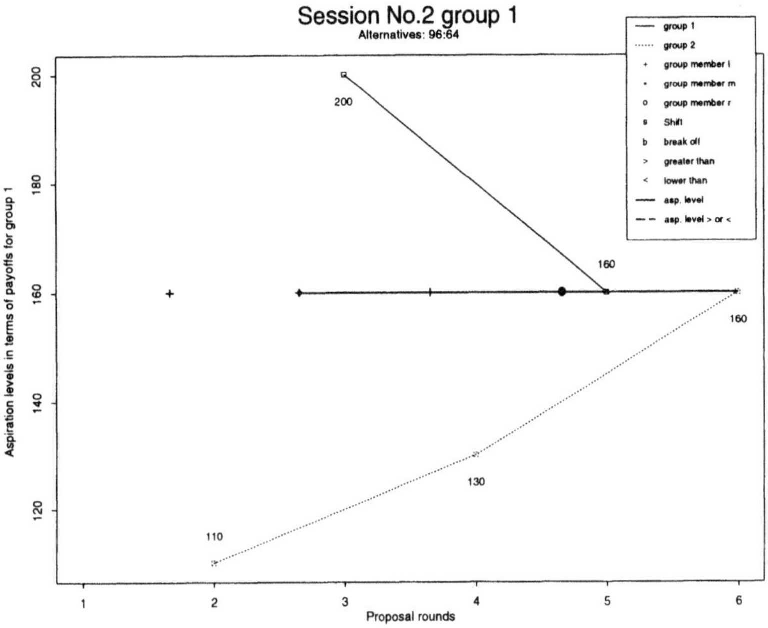
Session No.2 group 1
Alternatives: 96:64
group 1
group 2
group member l
group member m
group member r
Shift
break off
greater than
lower than
asp. level
asp. level > or <
200
160
160
130
110
Aspiration levels in terms of payoffs for group 1
120
140
160
180
200
1
2
3
4
5
6
Proposal rounds

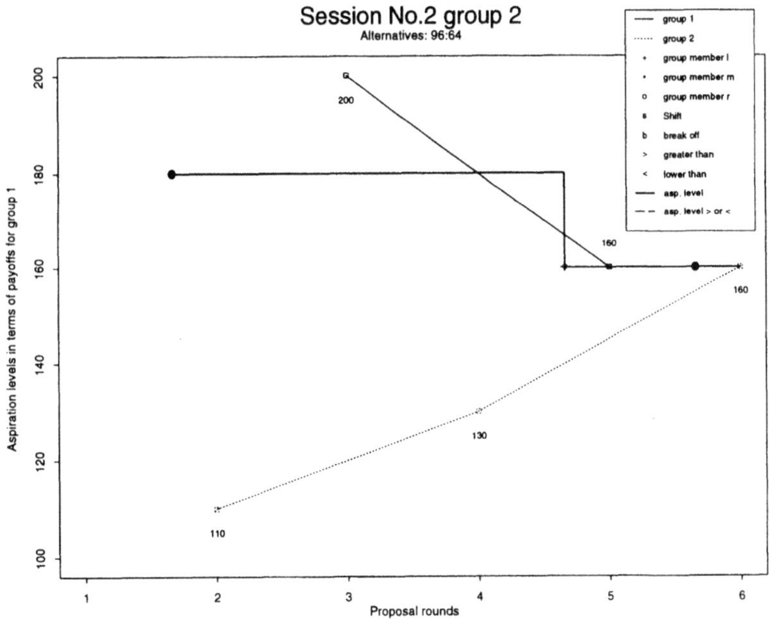
Session No.2 group 2
Alternatives: 96:64
group 1
group 2
group member l
group member m
group member r
Shift
break off
greater than
lower than
asp. level
asp. level > or <
200
160
160
130
110
Aspiration levels in terms of payoffs for group 1
100
120
140
160
180
200
1
2
3
4
5
6
Proposal rounds

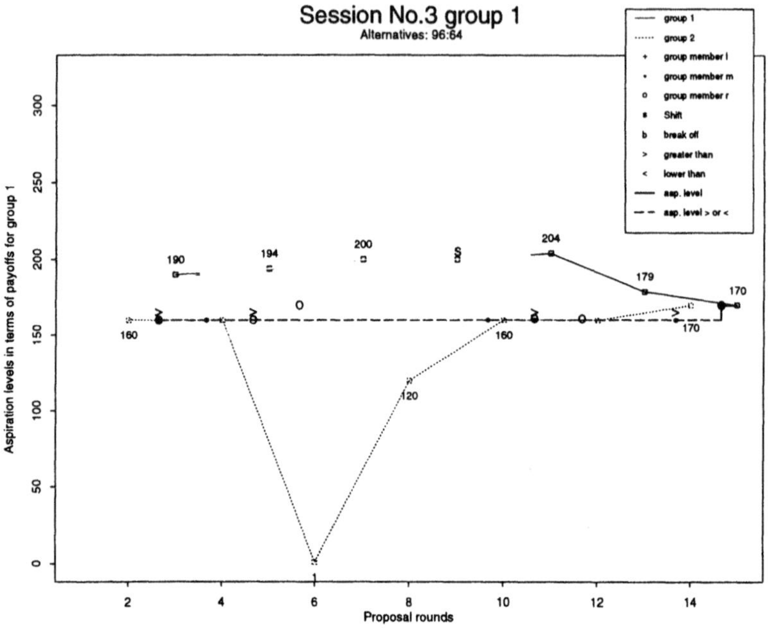
Session No.3 group 1
Alternatives: 96:64
group 1
group 2
group member l
group member m
group member r
Shift
break off
greater than
lower than
asp. level
asp. level > or <
Aspiration levels in terms of payoffs for group 1
Proposal rounds
190
194
200
204
179
170
160
120
1
S

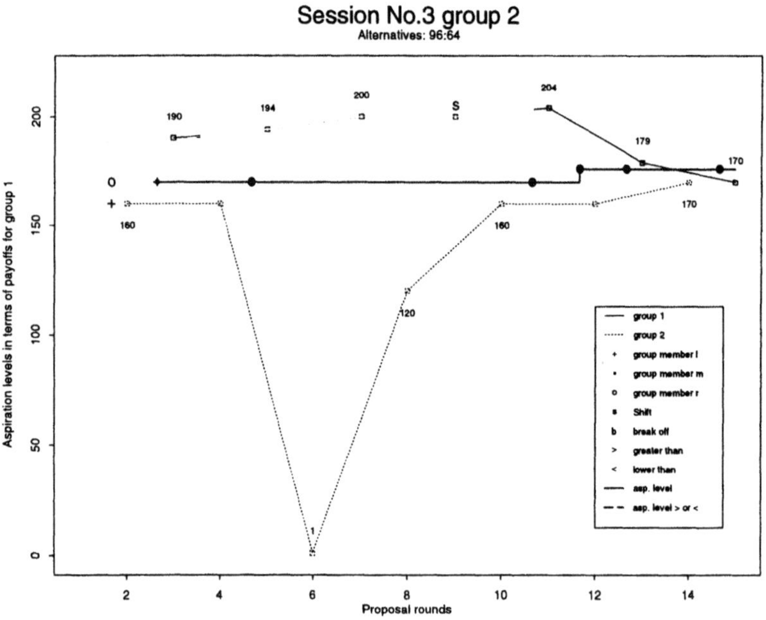
Session No.3 group 2
Alternatives: 96:64
group 1
group 2
group member l
group member m
group member r
Shift
break off
greater than
lower than
asp. level
asp. level > or <
Aspiration levels in terms of payoffs for group 1
Proposal rounds
190
194
200
204
179
170
160
120
1
S

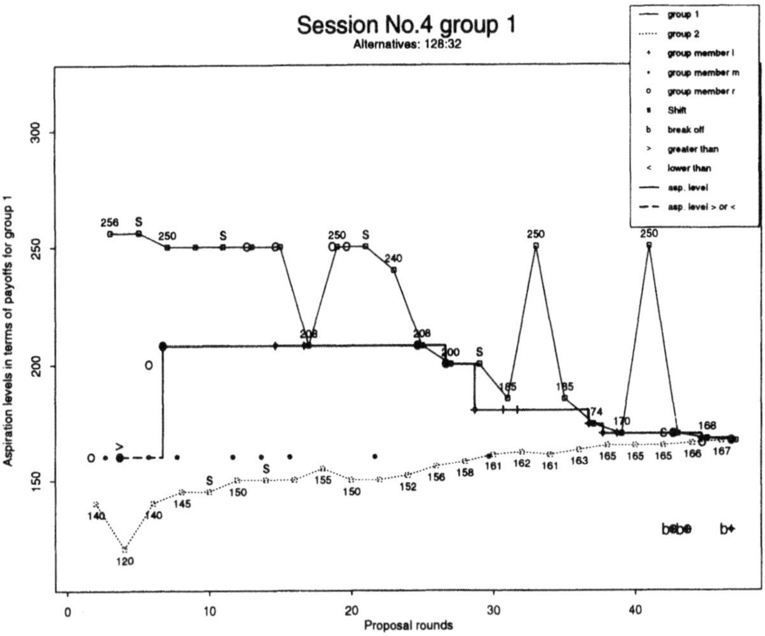
Session No.4 group 1
Alternatives: 128:32
group 1
group 2
group member l
group member m
group member r
Shift
break off
greater than
lower than
asp. level
asp. level > or <
Aspiration levels in terms of payoffs for group 1
Proposal rounds

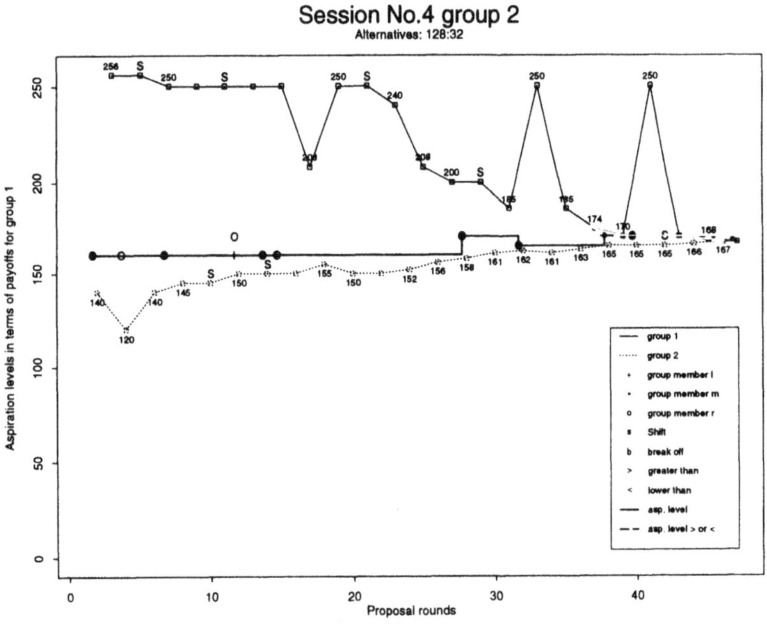
Session No.4 group 2
Alternatives: 128:32
group 1
group 2
group member l
group member m
group member r
Shift
break off
greater than
lower than
asp. level
asp. level > or <
Aspiration levels in terms of payoffs for group 1
Proposal rounds

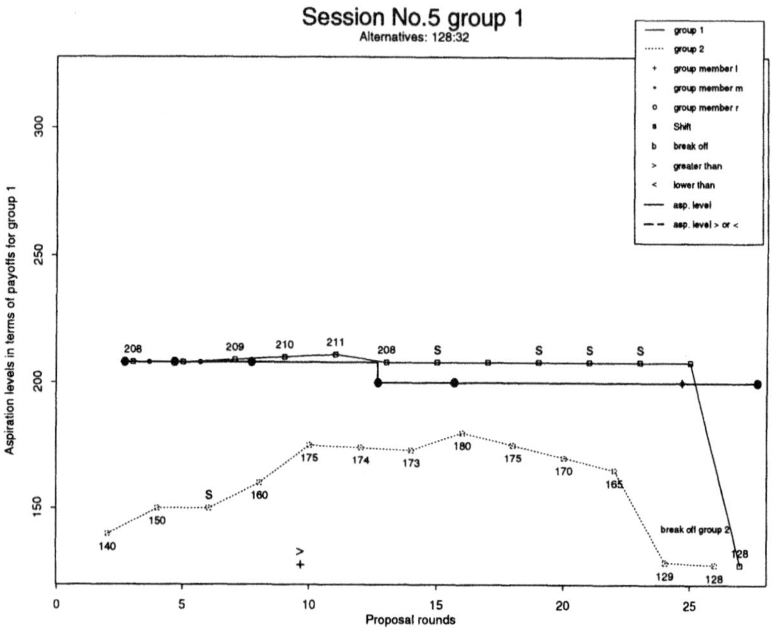
Session No.5 group 1
Alternatives: 128:32
group 1
group 2
group member l
group member m
group member r
Shift
break off
greater than
lower than
asp. level
asp. level > or <
Aspiration levels in terms of payoffs for group 1
Proposal rounds
break off group 2

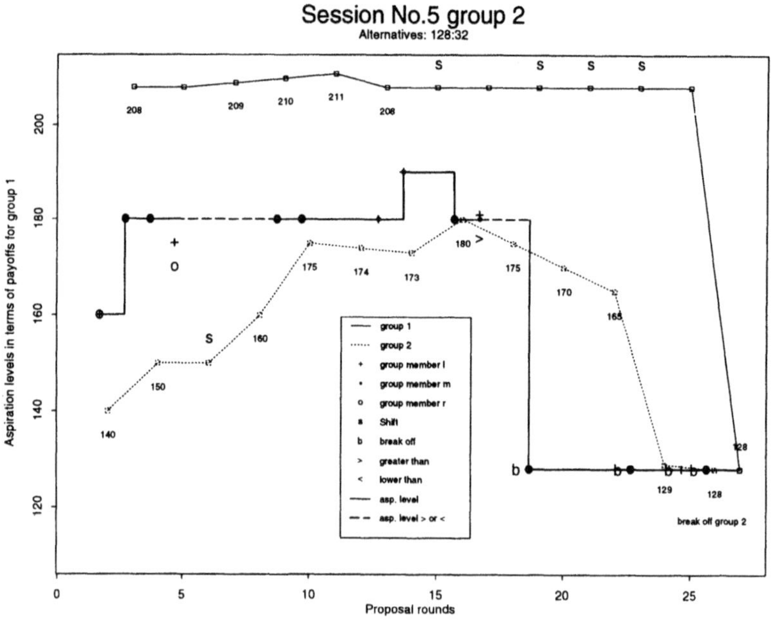
Session No.5 group 2
Alternatives: 128:32
group 1
group 2
group member l
group member m
group member r
Shift
break off
greater than
lower than
asp. level
asp. level > or <
Aspiration levels in terms of payoffs for group 1
Proposal rounds
break off group 2

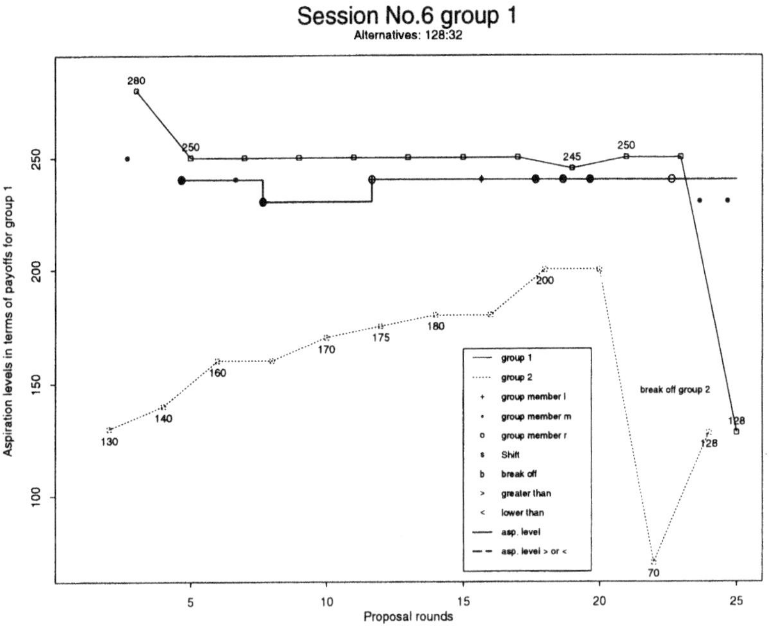
Session No.6 group 1
Alternatives: 128:32
Aspiration levels in terms of payoffs for group 1
Proposal rounds
280
250
245
250
200
180
175
170
160
140
130
128
70
break off group 2
group 1
group 2
group member l
group member m
group member r
Shift
break off
greater than
lower than
asp. level
asp. level > or <

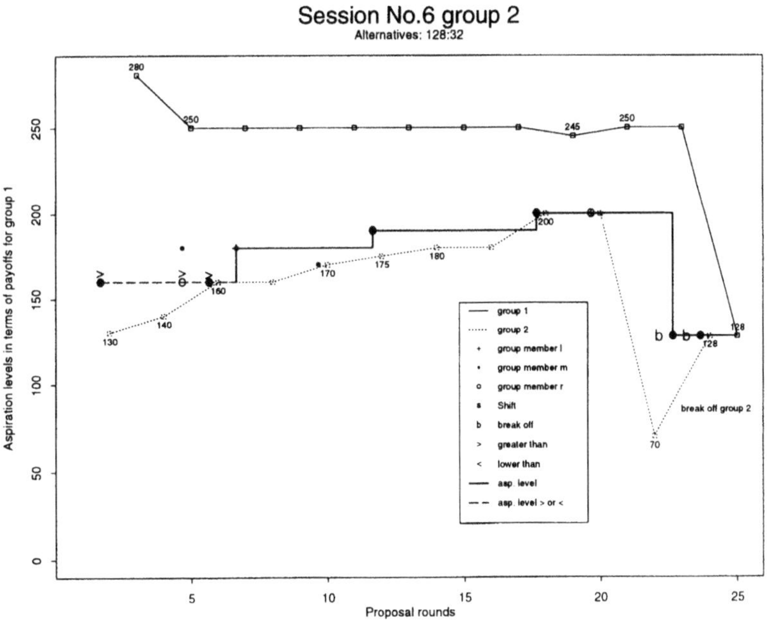
Session No.6 group 2
Alternatives: 128:32
Aspiration levels in terms of payoffs for group 1
Proposal rounds
280
250
245
250
200
180
175
170
160
140
130
128
70
break off group 2
group 1
group 2
group member l
group member m
group member r
Shift
break off
greater than
lower than
asp. level
asp. level > or <

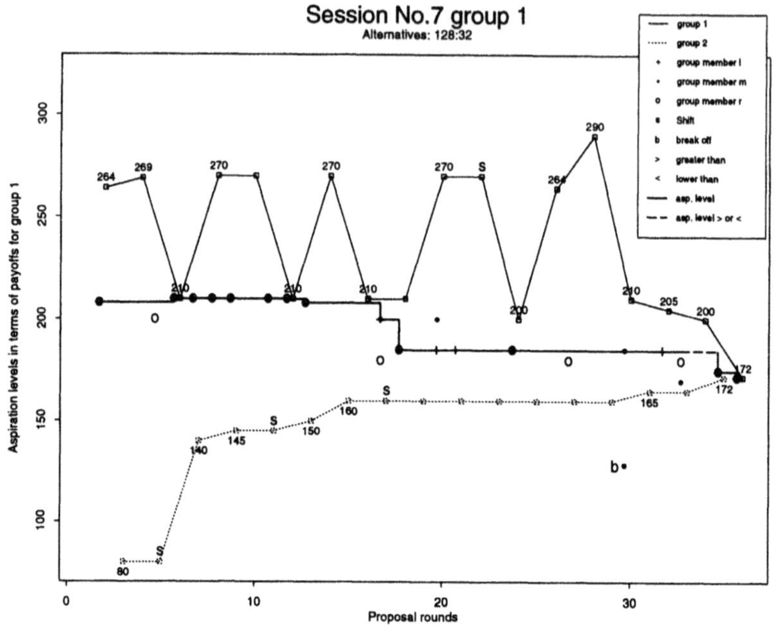
Session No.7 group 1
Alternatives: 128:32
group 1
group 2
group member l
group member m
group member r
Shift
break off
greater than
lower than
asp. level
asp. level > or <
Aspiration levels in terms of payoffs for group 1
Proposal rounds
264
269
270
270
270
290
210
210
210
200
210
205
200
172
172
165
160
150
145
140
80
S
b

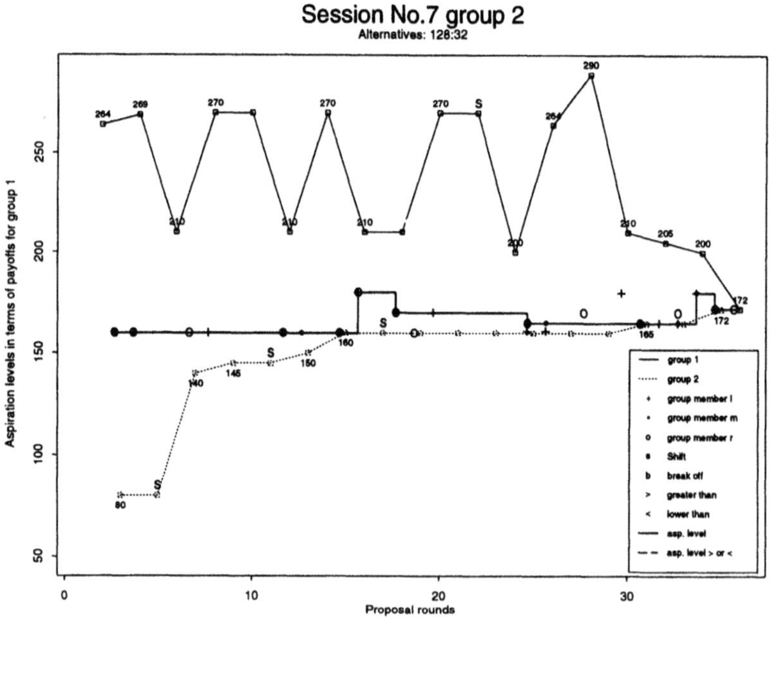
Session No.7 group 2
Alternatives: 128:32
group 1
group 2
group member l
group member m
group member r
Shift
break off
greater than
lower than
asp. level
asp. level > or <
Aspiration levels in terms of payoffs for group 1
Proposal rounds
264
269
270
270
270
290
210
210
210
200
210
205
200
172
172
165
160
150
145
140
80
S

Session No.8 group 1

Alternatives: 128:32

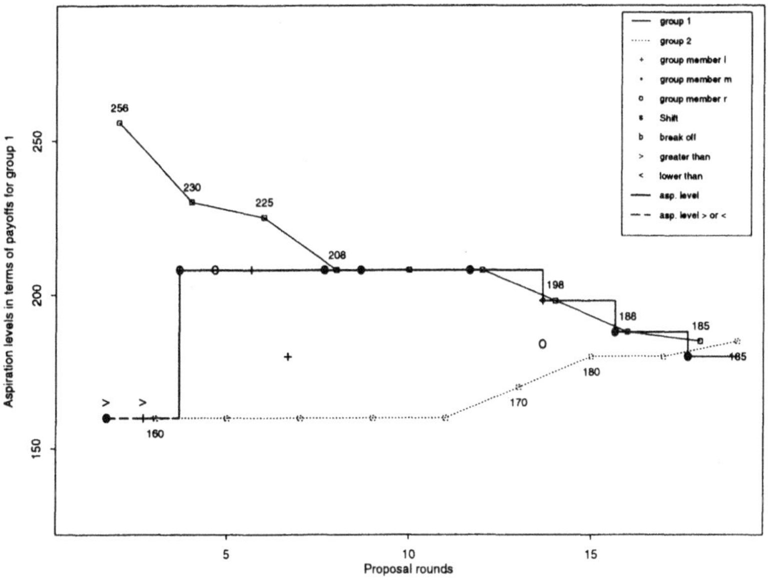

Session No.8 group 2

Alternatives: 128:32

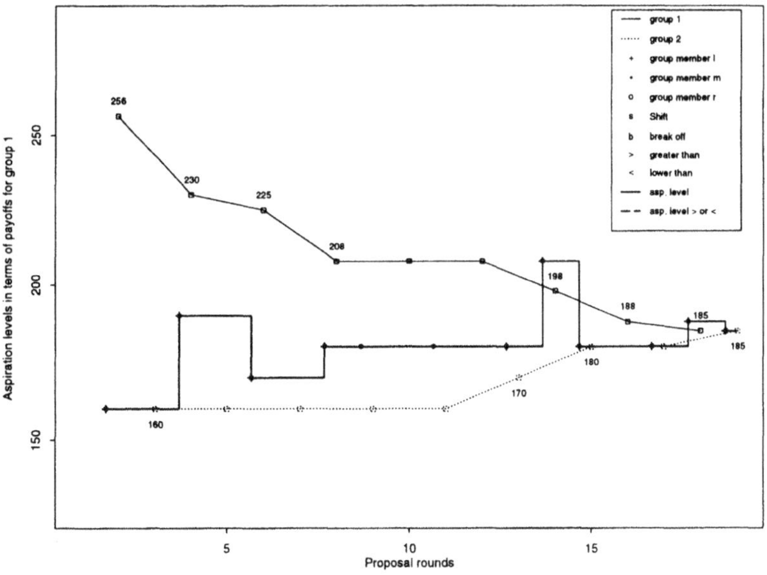

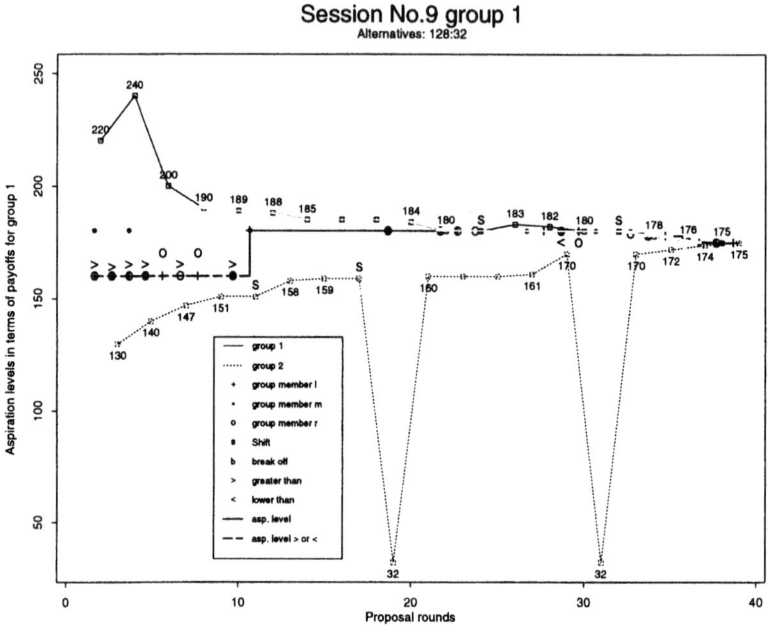
Session No.9 group 1
Alternatives: 128:32
Aspiration levels in terms of payoffs for group 1
Proposal rounds
group 1
group 2
group member l
group member m
group member r
Shift
break off
greater than
lower than
asp. level
asp. level > or <

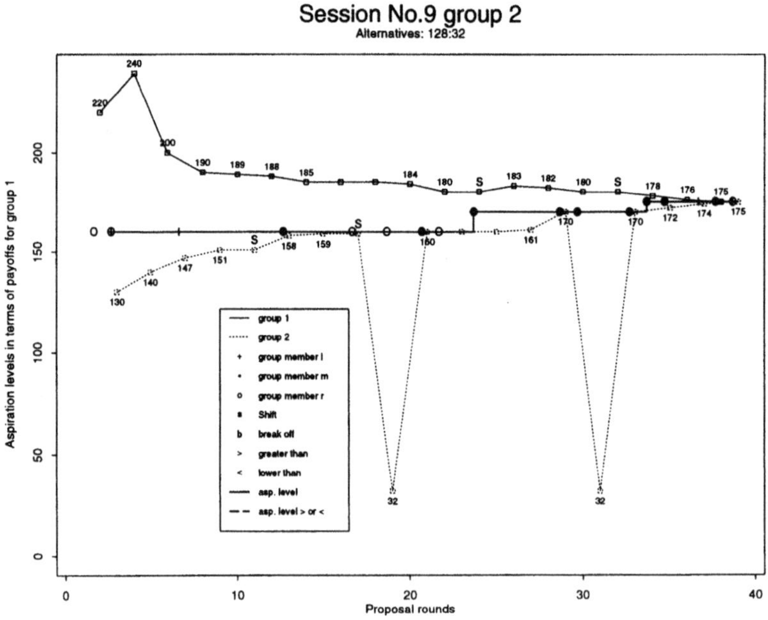
Session No.9 group 2
Alternatives: 128:32
Aspiration levels in terms of payoffs for group 1
Proposal rounds
group 1
group 2
group member l
group member m
group member r
Shift
break off
greater than
lower than
asp. level
asp. level > or <

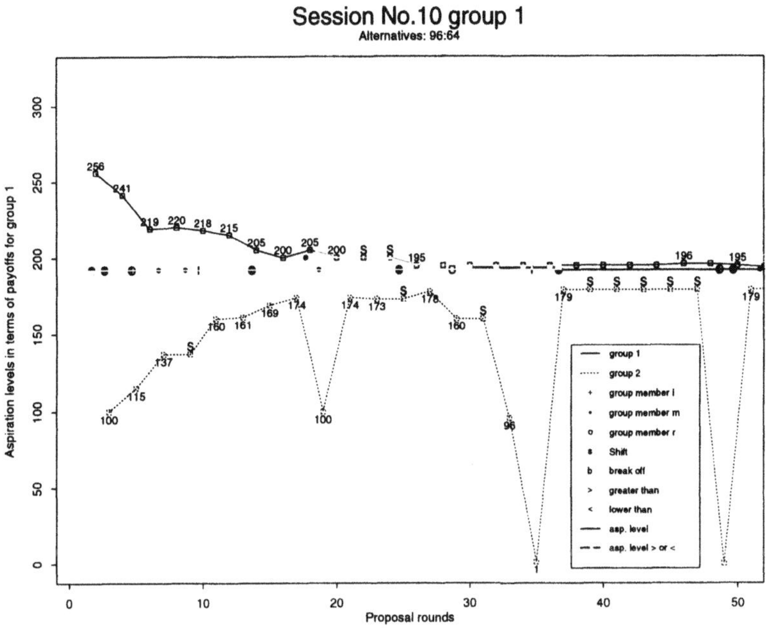
Session No.10 group 1
Alternatives: 96:64
Aspiration levels in terms of payoffs for group 1
Proposal rounds
group 1
group 2
group member l
group member m
group member r
Shift
break off
greater than
lower than
asp. level
asp. level > or <

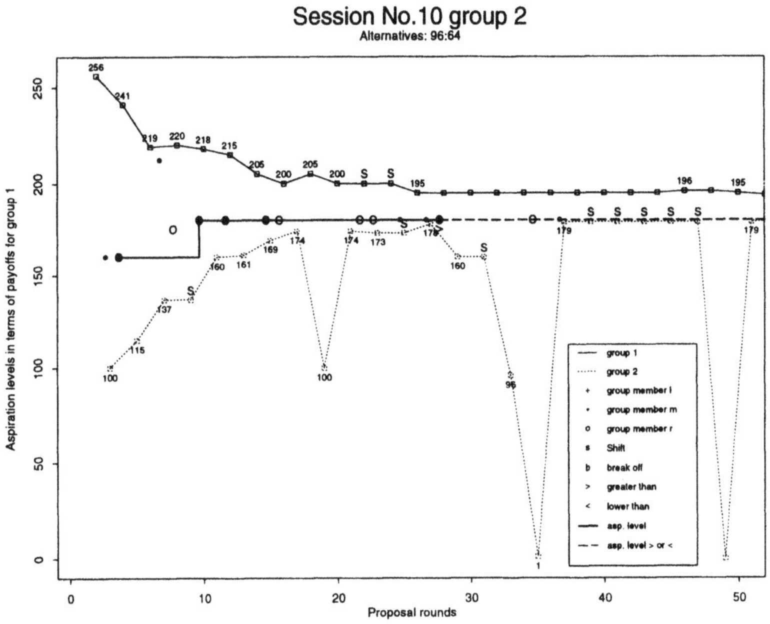
Session No.10 group 2
Alternatives: 96:64
Aspiration levels in terms of payoffs for group 1
Proposal rounds
group 1
group 2
group member l
group member m
group member r
Shift
break off
greater than
lower than
asp. level
asp. level > or <

Session No.10 group 1
Alternatives: 96:64

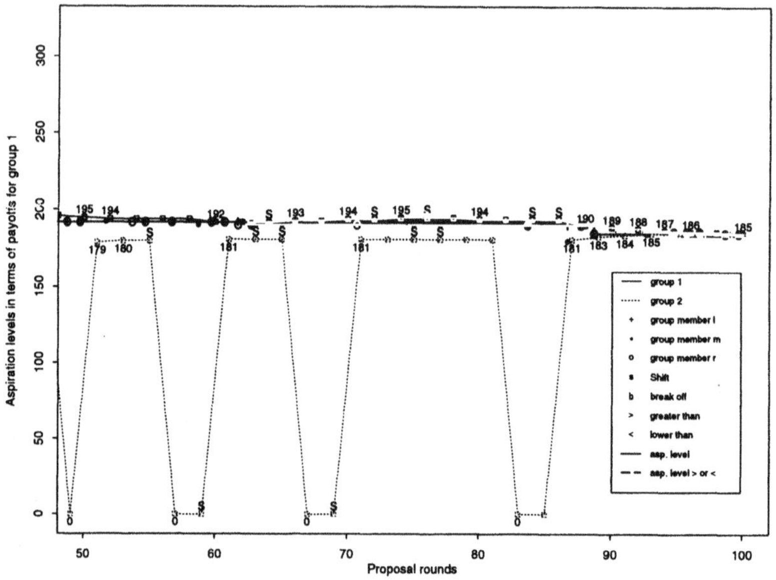

Session No.10 group 2
Alternatives: 96:64

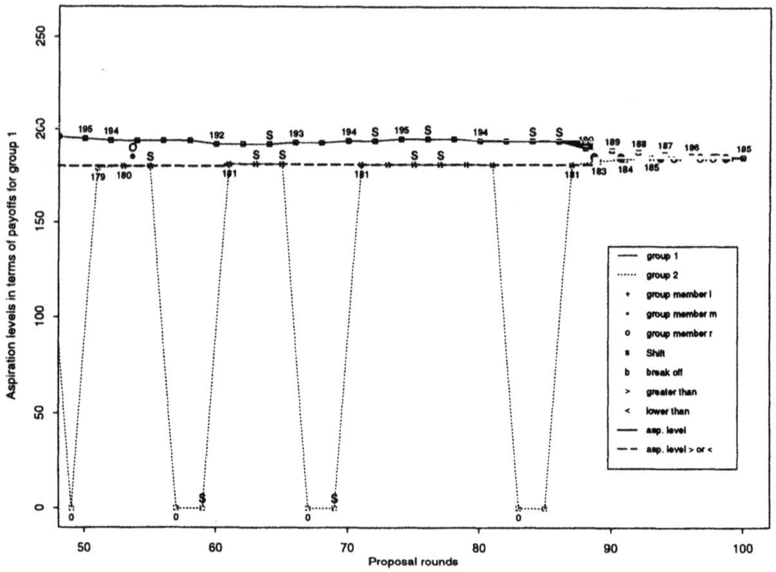

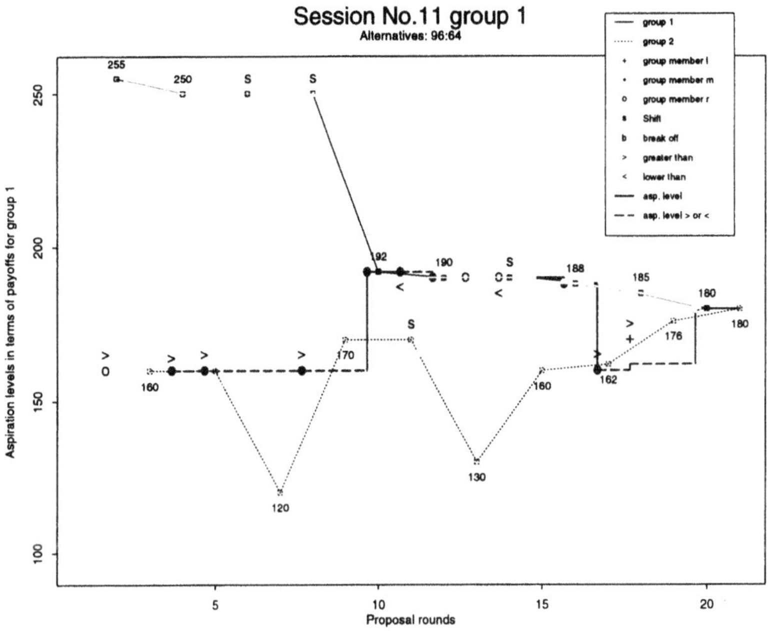
Session No.11 group 1
Alternatives: 96:64
group 1
group 2
group member l
group member m
group member r
Shift
break off
greater than
lower than
asp. level
asp. level > or <
Aspiration levels in terms of payoffs for group 1
Proposal rounds

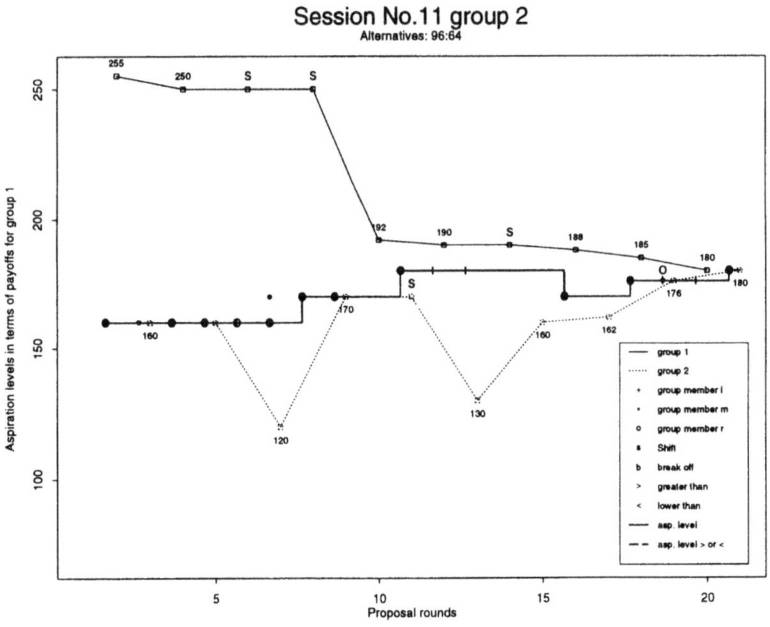
Session No.11 group 2
Alternatives: 96:64
group 1
group 2
group member l
group member m
group member r
Shift
break off
greater than
lower than
asp. level
asp. level > or <
Aspiration levels in terms of payoffs for group 1
Proposal rounds

Session No.12 group 1
Alternatives: 96:64

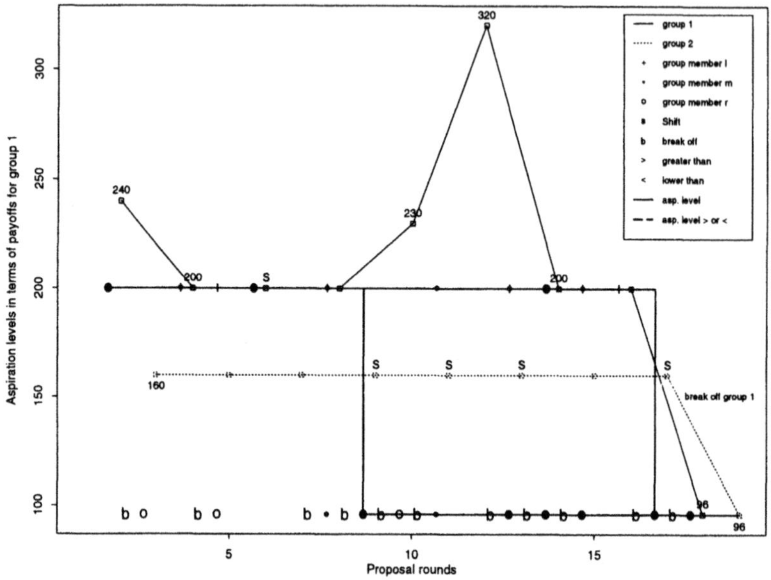

Session No.12 group 2
Alternatives: 96:64

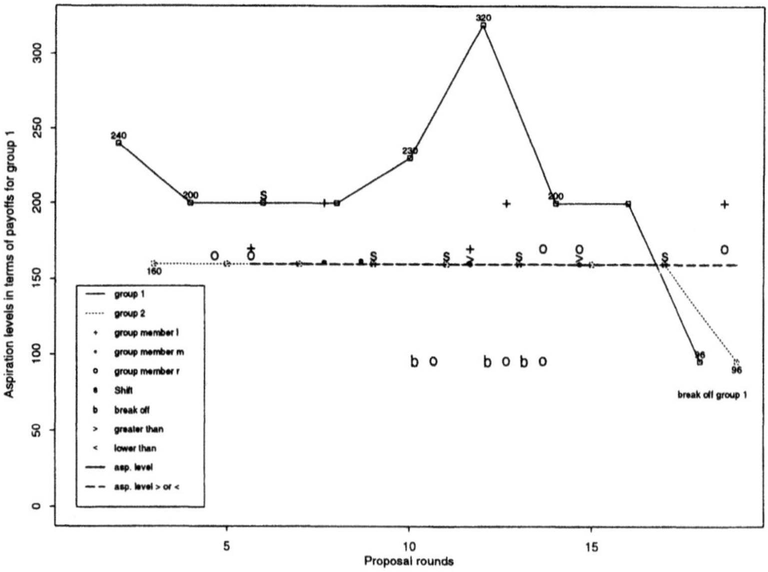

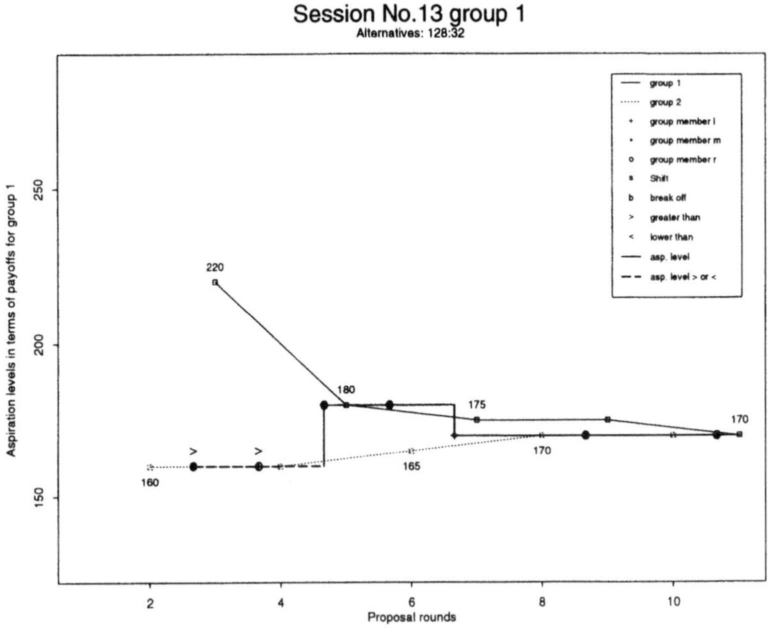
Session No.13 group 1
Alternatives: 128:32
group 1
group 2
group member l
group member m
group member r
Shift
break off
greater than
lower than
asp. level
asp. level > or <
Aspiration levels in terms of payoffs for group 1
Proposal rounds
220
180
175
170
165
160

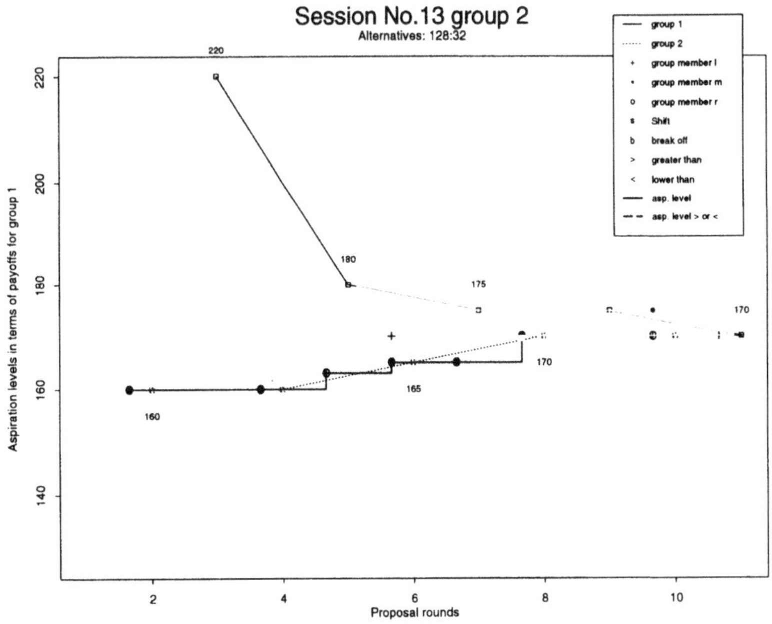
Session No.13 group 2
Alternatives: 128:32
group 1
group 2
group member l
group member m
group member r
Shift
break off
greater than
lower than
asp. level
asp. level > or <
Aspiration levels in terms of payoffs for group 1
Proposal rounds
220
180
175
170
165
160

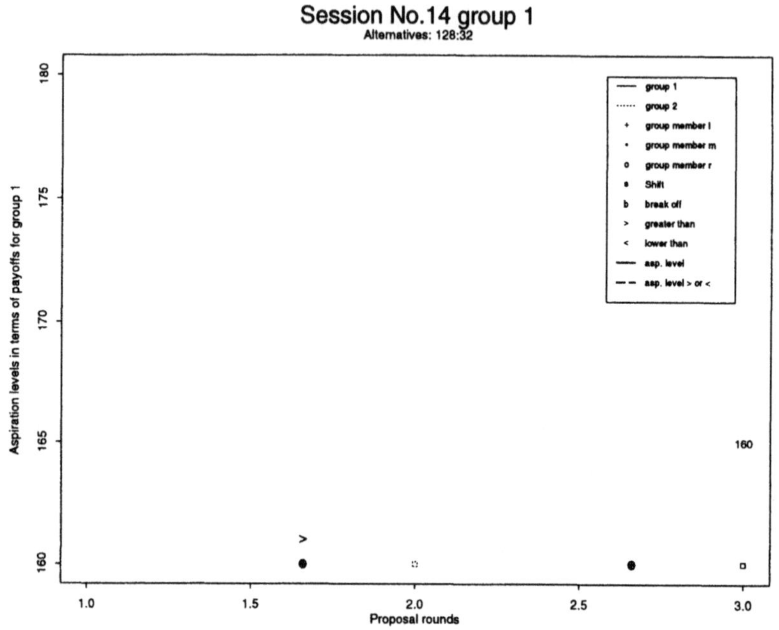
Session No.14 group 1
Alternatives: 128:32
Aspiration levels in terms of payoffs for group 1
Proposal rounds
group 1
group 2
group member l
group member m
group member r
Shift
break off
greater than
lower than
asp. level
asp. level > or <
160

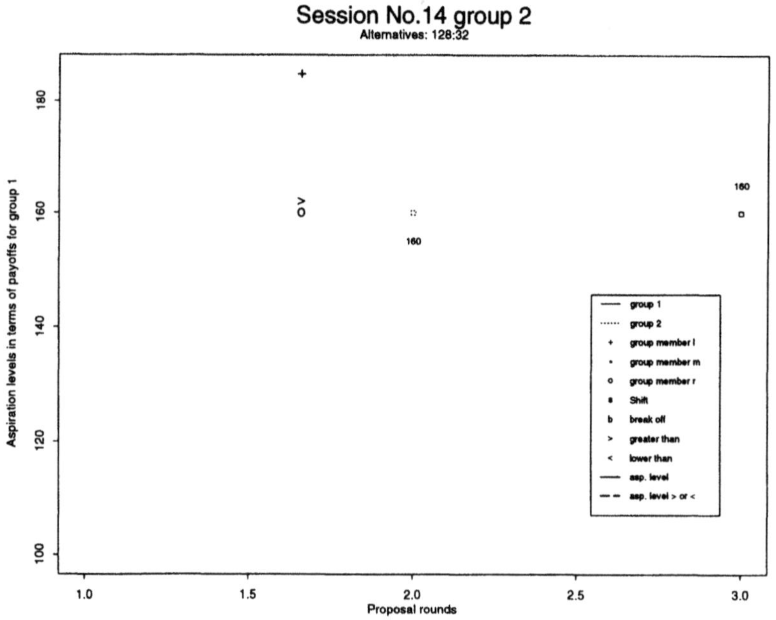
Session No.14 group 2
Alternatives: 128:32
Aspiration levels in terms of payoffs for group 1
Proposal rounds
group 1
group 2
group member l
group member m
group member r
Shift
break off
greater than
lower than
asp. level
asp. level > or <
160
160

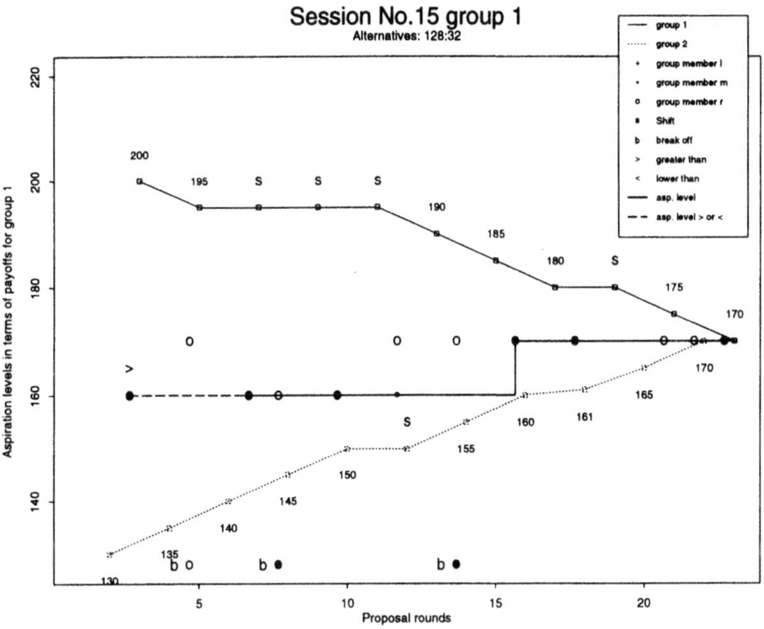
Session No.15 group 1
Alternatives: 128:32
Aspiration levels in terms of payoffs for group 1
Proposal rounds
5
10
15
20
140
160
180
200
220
group 1
group 2
group member l
group member m
group member r
Shift
break off
greater than
lower than
asp. level
asp. level > or <

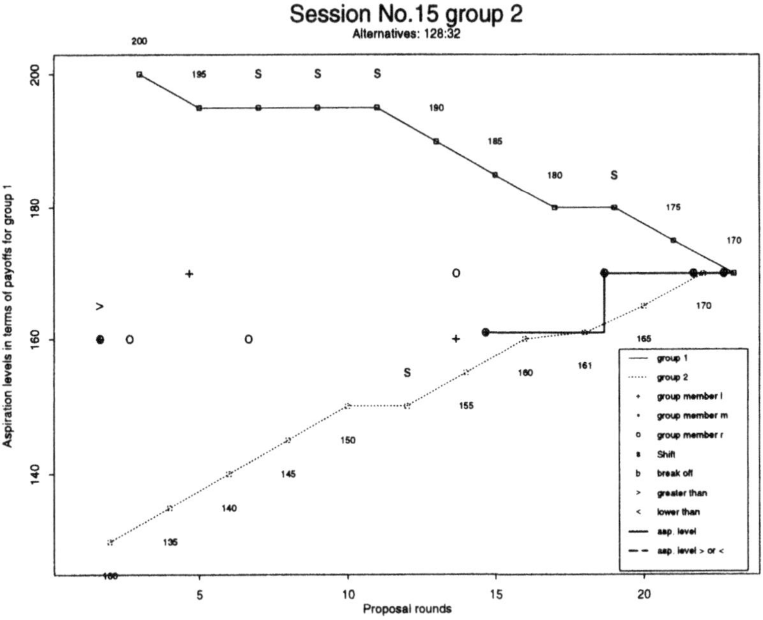
Session No.15 group 2
Alternatives: 128:32
Aspiration levels in terms of payoffs for group 1
Proposal rounds
5
10
15
20
140
160
180
200
group 1
group 2
group member l
group member m
group member r
Shift
break off
greater than
lower than
asp. level
asp. level > or <

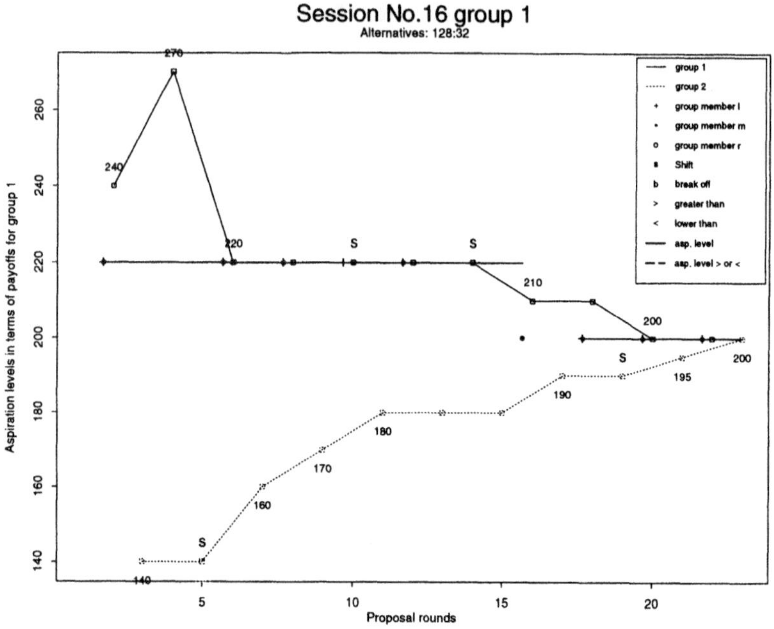
Session No.16 group 1
Alternatives: 128:32
Aspiration levels in terms of payoffs for group 1
Proposal rounds
group 1
group 2
group member l
group member m
group member r
Shift
break off
greater than
lower than
asp. level
asp. level > or <
270
240
220
210
200
195
190
180
170
160
140
S

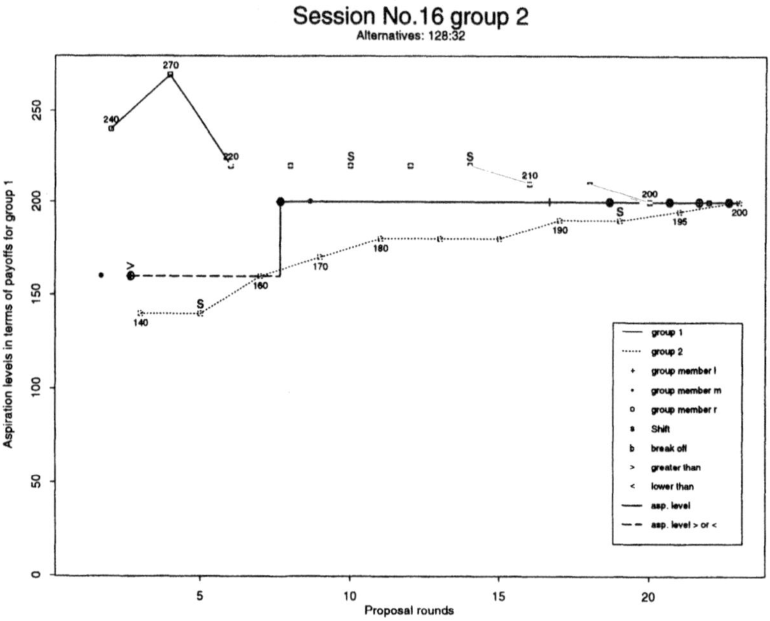
Session No.16 group 2
Alternatives: 128:32
Aspiration levels in terms of payoffs for group 1
Proposal rounds
group 1
group 2
group member l
group member m
group member r
Shift
break off
greater than
lower than
asp. level
asp. level > or <
270
240
220
210
200
195
190
180
170
160
140
S

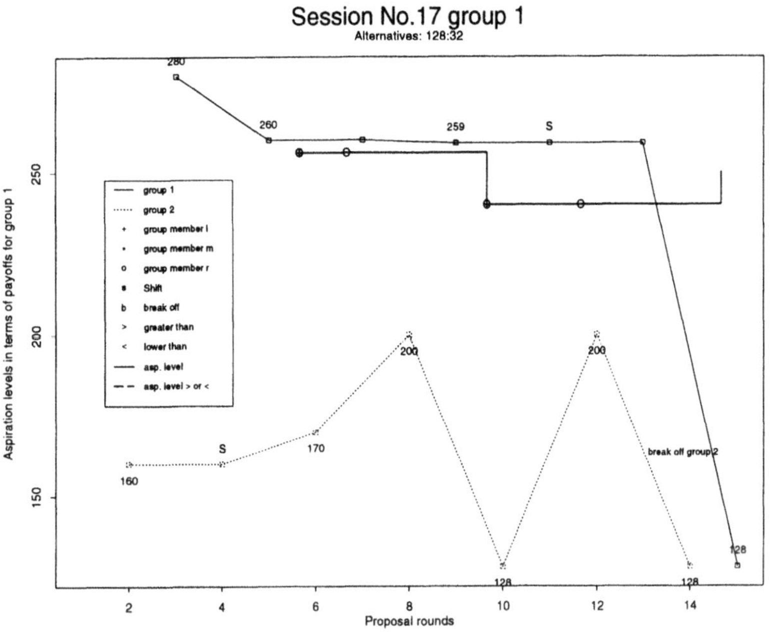
Session No.17 group 1
Alternatives: 128:32
Aspiration levels in terms of payoffs for group 1
Proposal rounds
group 1
group 2
group member l
group member m
group member r
Shift
break off
greater than
lower than
asp. level
asp. level > or <
280
260
259
S
S
170
160
200
200
128
128
128
break off group 2

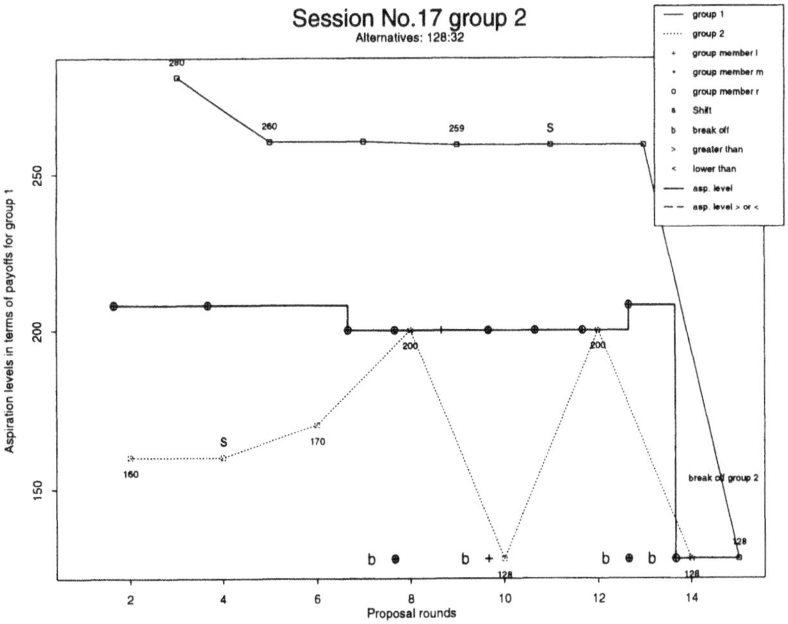
Session No.17 group 2
Alternatives: 128:32
Aspiration levels in terms of payoffs for group 1
Proposal rounds
group 1
group 2
group member l
group member m
group member r
Shift
break off
greater than
lower than
asp. level
asp. level > or <
280
260
259
S
S
170
160
200
200
128
128
128
break off group 2
b
b
b
b

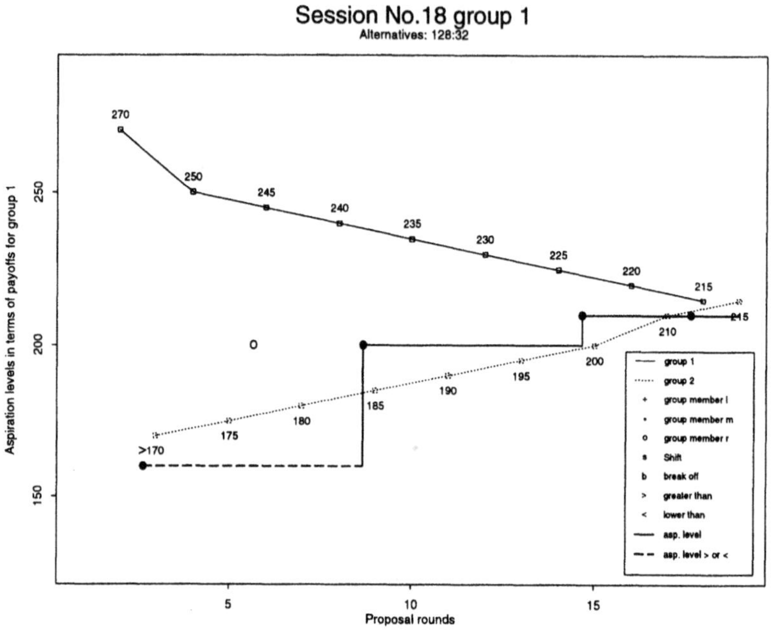
Session No.18 group 1
Alternatives: 128:32
Aspiration levels in terms of payoffs for group 1
Proposal rounds
group 1
group 2
group member l
group member m
group member r
Shift
break off
greater than
lower than
asp. level
asp. level > or <

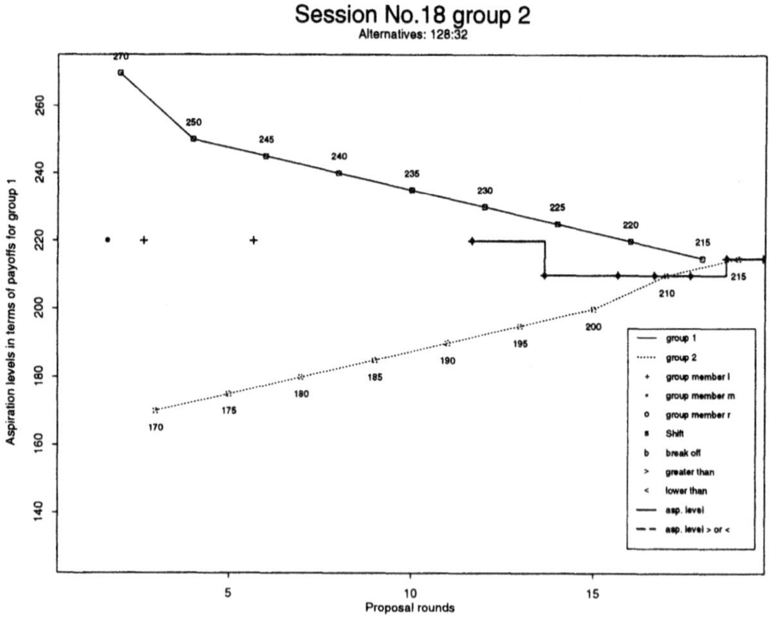
Session No.18 group 2
Alternatives: 128:32
Aspiration levels in terms of payoffs for group 1
Proposal rounds
group 1
group 2
group member l
group member m
group member r
Shift
break off
greater than
lower than
asp. level
asp. level > or <

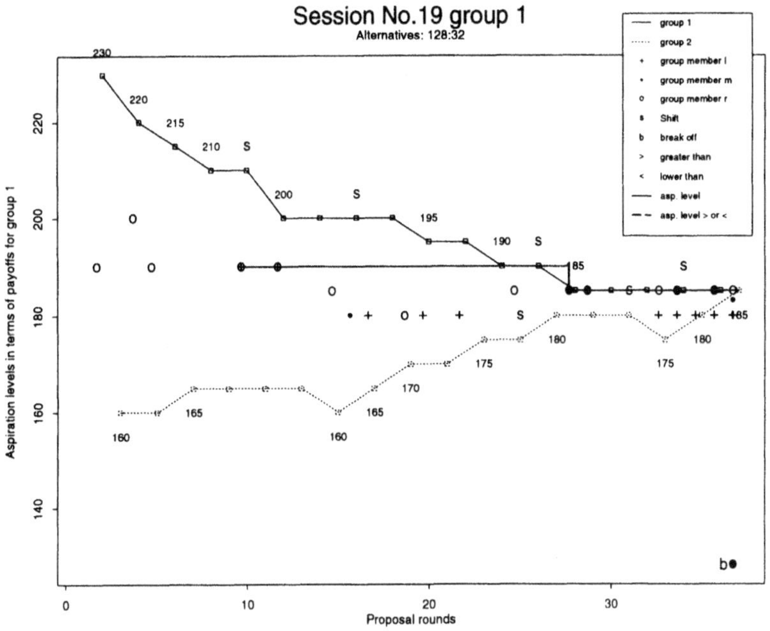
Session No.19 group 1
Alternatives: 128:32
group 1
group 2
group member l
group member m
group member r
Shift
break off
greater than
lower than
asp. level
asp. level > or <
Aspiration levels in terms of payoffs for group 1
Proposal rounds

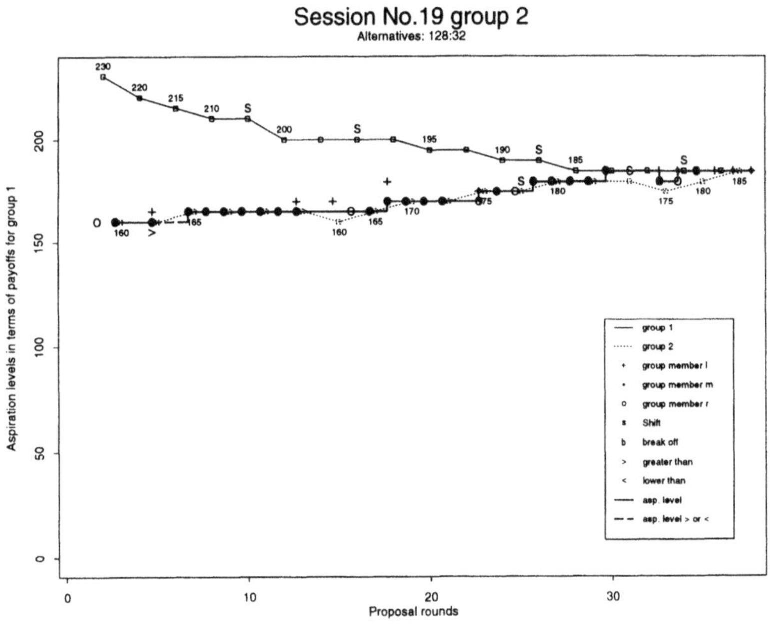
Session No.19 group 2
Alternatives: 128:32
group 1
group 2
group member l
group member m
group member r
Shift
break off
greater than
lower than
asp. level
asp. level > or <
Aspiration levels in terms of payoffs for group 1
Proposal rounds

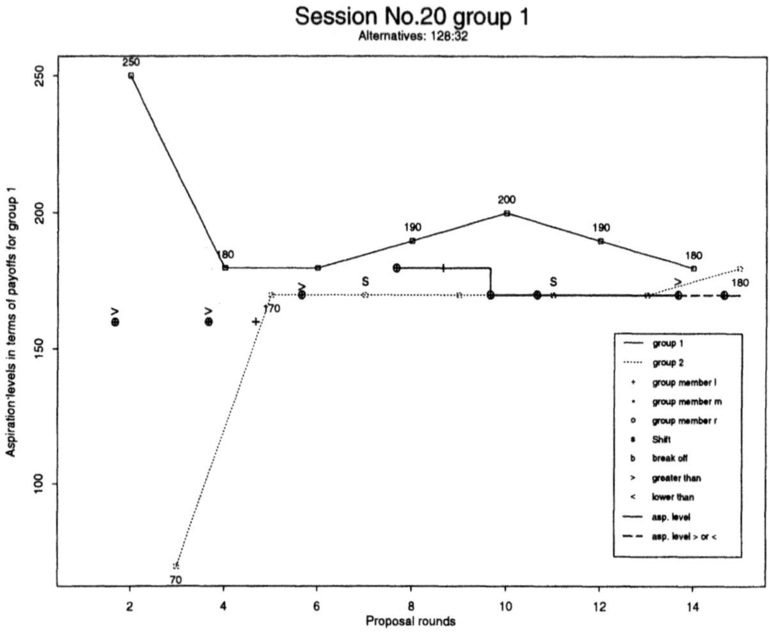
Session No.20 group 1
Alternatives: 128:32
Aspiration levels in terms of payoffs for group 1
Proposal rounds
250
180
190
200
190
180
180
170
70
group 1
group 2
group member l
group member m
group member r
Shift
break off
greater than
lower than
asp. level
asp. level > or <

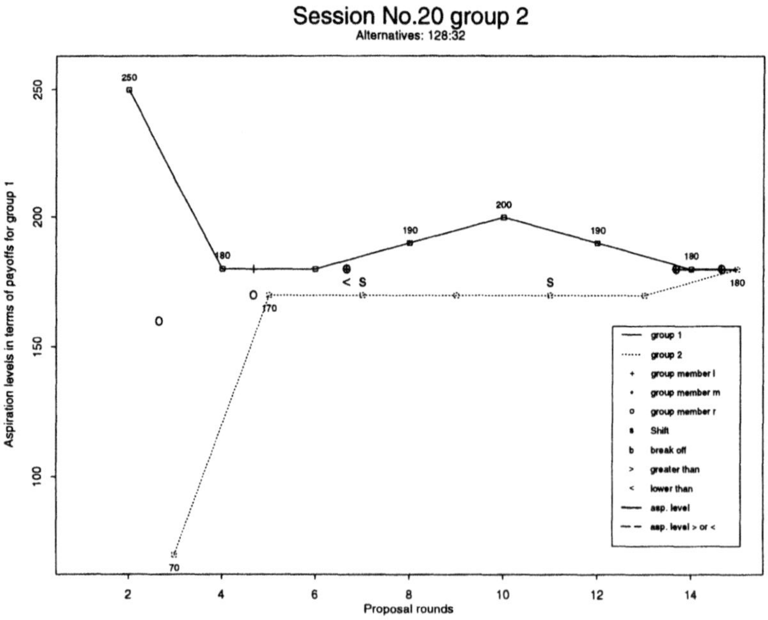
Session No.20 group 2
Alternatives: 128:32
Aspiration levels in terms of payoffs for group 1
Proposal rounds
250
180
190
200
190
180
180
170
70
group 1
group 2
group member l
group member m
group member r
Shift
break off
greater than
lower than
asp. level
asp. level > or <

Appendix F

Break Off Discussions

The following figures show break off discussions. Vertical broken lines mark the rounds in which break offs have been discussed. As before the horizontal bold line indicates aspiration levels, and members of the groups are represented by the different characters: + for group member l (on the left side of the screen), • for group member m (in the middle of the screen), ∘ for group member r (on the right side of the screen). The thin solid line represents demands of group 1, the dotted line represents offers of group 2.

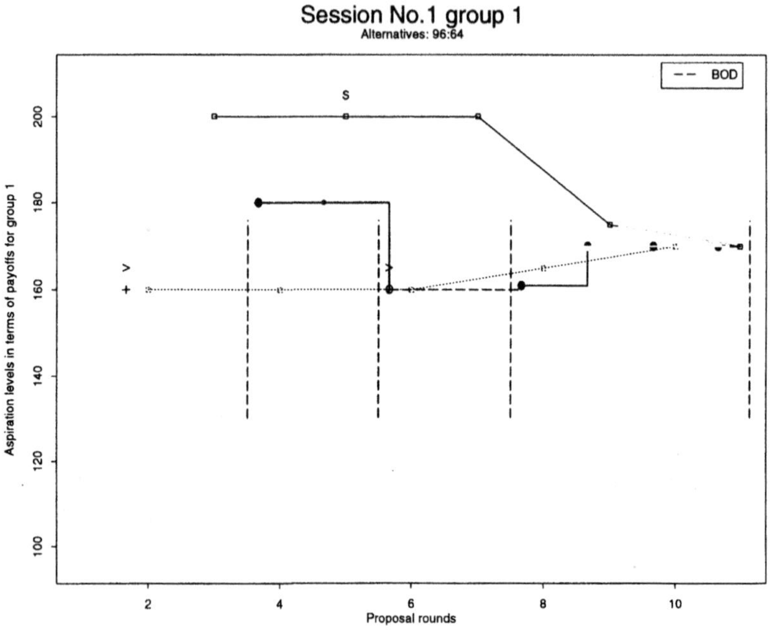
Session No.1 group 1
Alternatives: 96:64
BOD
S
Aspiration levels in terms of payoffs for group 1
100
120
140
160
180
200
2
4
6
8
10
Proposal rounds

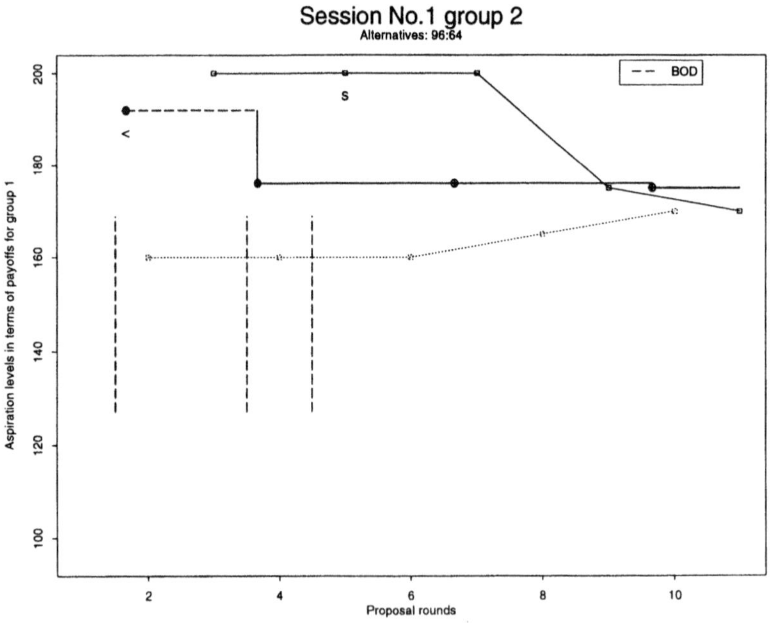
Session No.1 group 2
Alternatives: 96:64
BOD
S
Aspiration levels in terms of payoffs for group 1
100
120
140
160
180
200
2
4
6
8
10
Proposal rounds

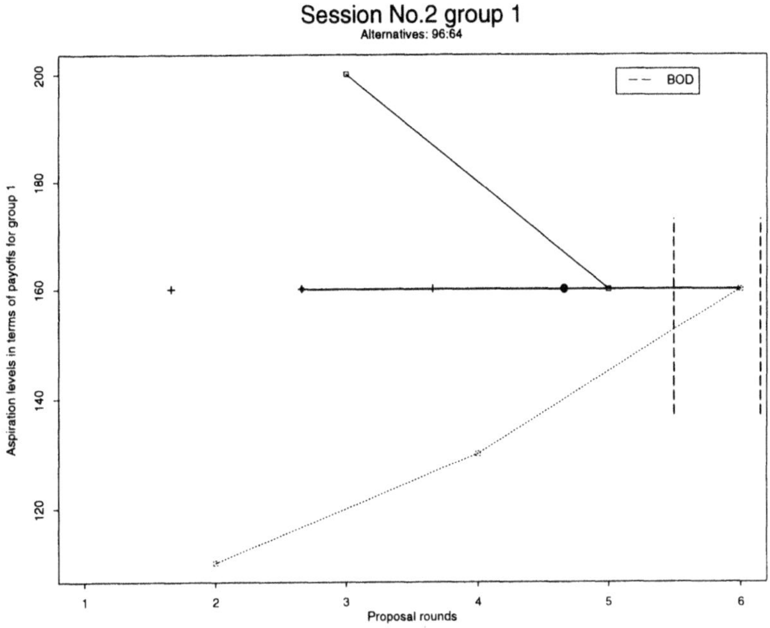
Session No.2 group 1
Alternatives: 96:64
BOD
Aspiration levels in terms of payoffs for group 1
Proposal rounds
200
180
160
140
120
1
2
3
4
5
6

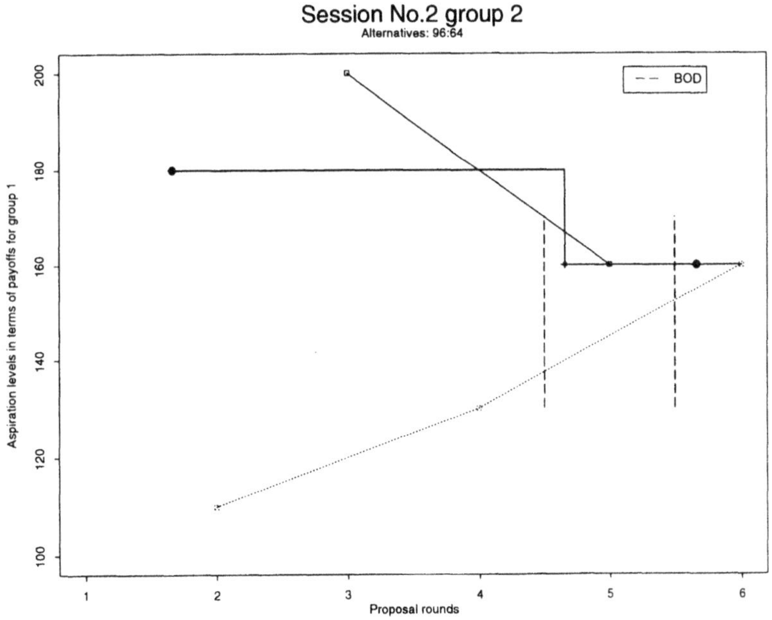
Session No.2 group 2
Alternatives: 96:64
BOD
Aspiration levels in terms of payoffs for group 1
Proposal rounds
200
180
160
140
120
100
1
2
3
4
5
6

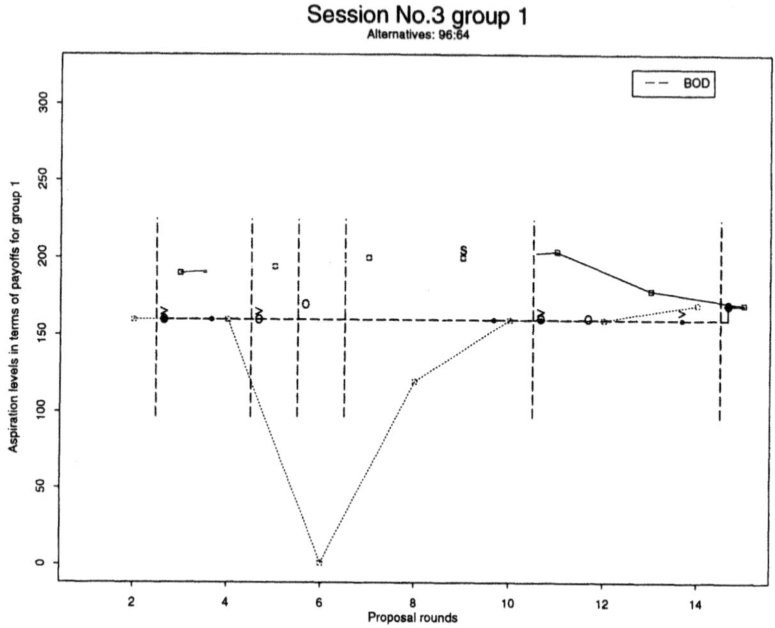
Session No.3 group 1
Alternatives: 96:64
BOD
Aspiration levels in terms of payoffs for group 1
Proposal rounds
0
50
100
150
200
250
300
2
4
6
8
10
12
14

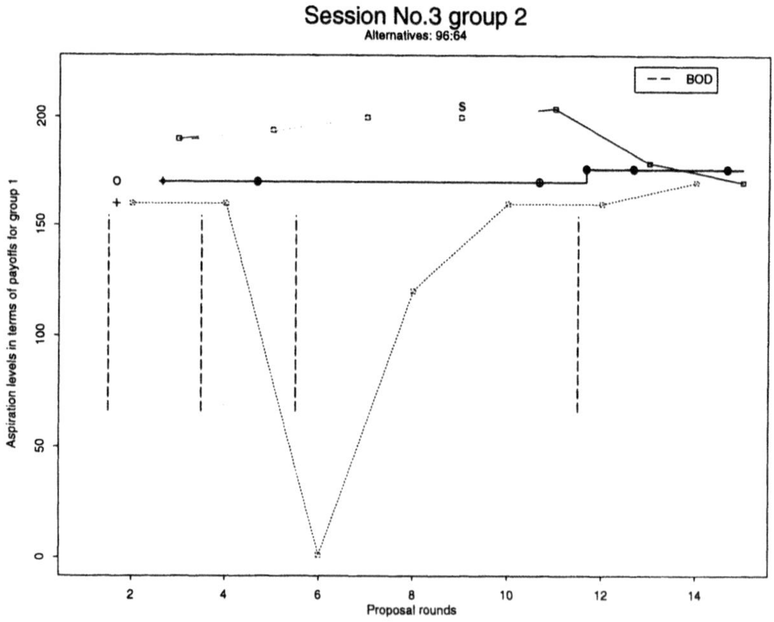
Session No.3 group 2
Alternatives: 96:64
BOD
Aspiration levels in terms of payoffs for group 1
Proposal rounds
0
50
100
150
200
2
4
6
8
10
12
14

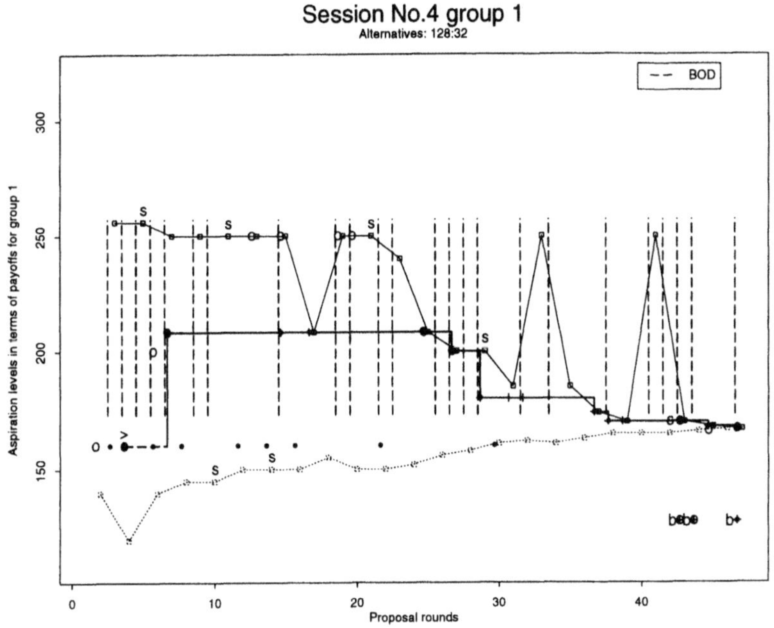
Session No.4 group 1
Alternatives: 128:32
BOD
Aspiration levels in terms of payoffs for group 1
Proposal rounds

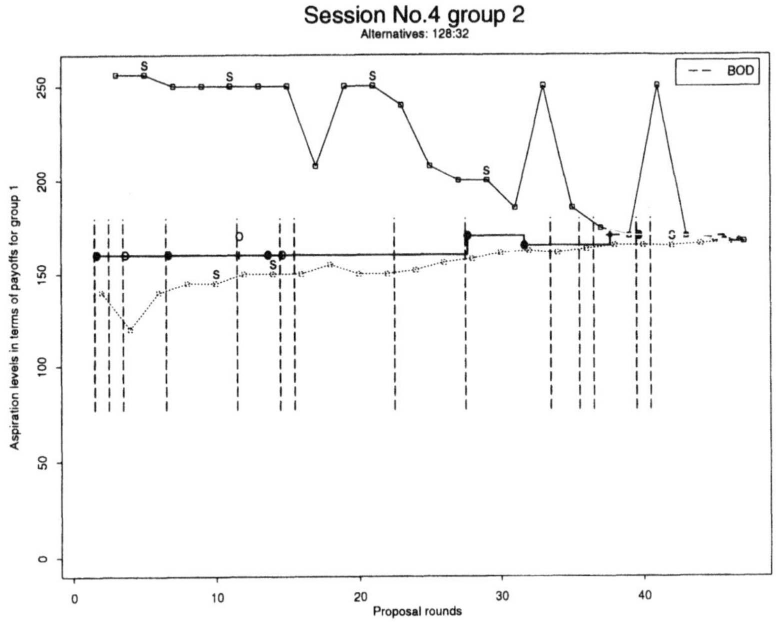
Session No.4 group 2
Alternatives: 128:32
BOD
Aspiration levels in terms of payoffs for group 1
Proposal rounds

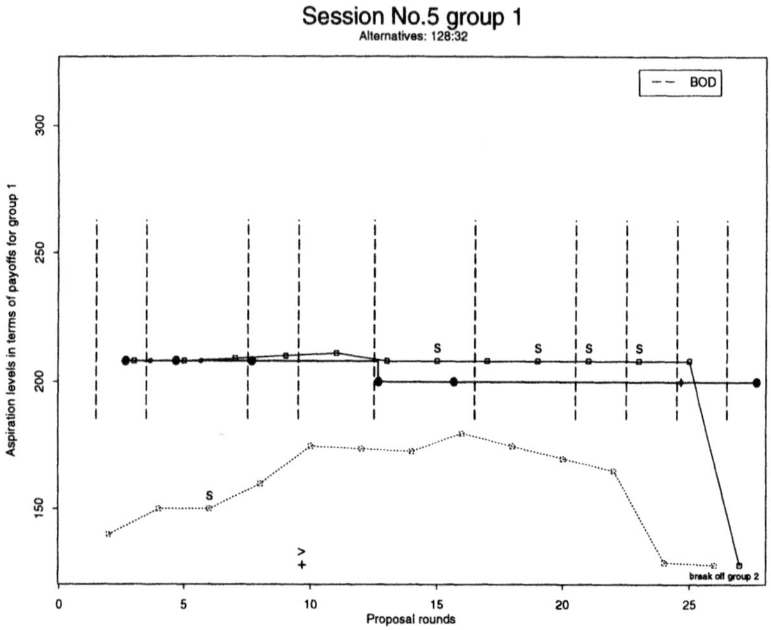
Session No.5 group 1
Alternatives: 128:32
BOD
Aspiration levels in terms of payoffs for group 1
Proposal rounds
break off group 2

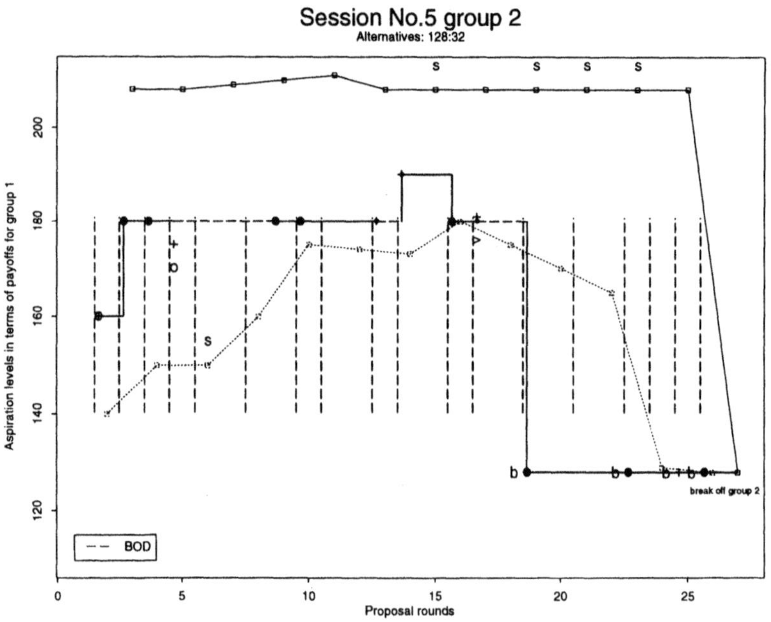
Session No.5 group 2
Alternatives: 128:32
BOD
Aspiration levels in terms of payoffs for group 1
Proposal rounds
break off group 2

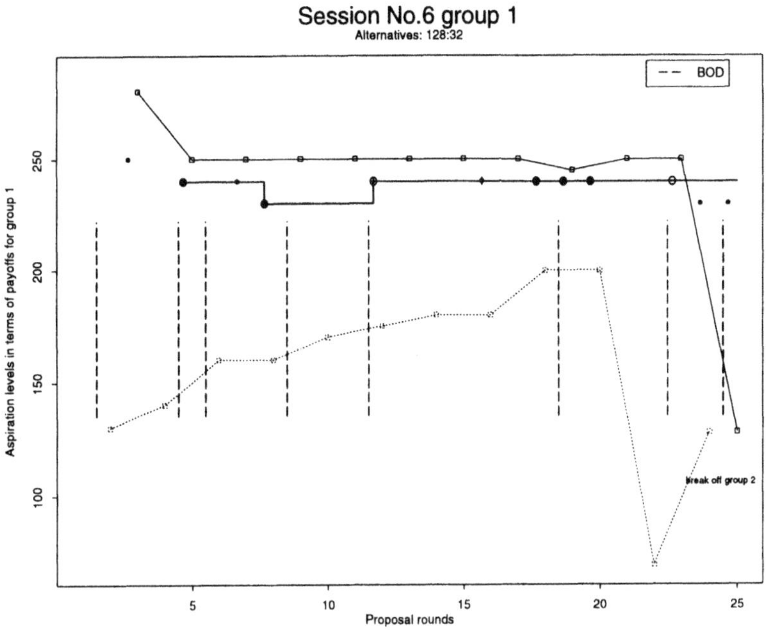
Session No.6 group 1
Alternatives: 128:32
BOD
Aspiration levels in terms of payoffs for group 1
Proposal rounds
break off group 2
100
150
200
250
5
10
15
20
25

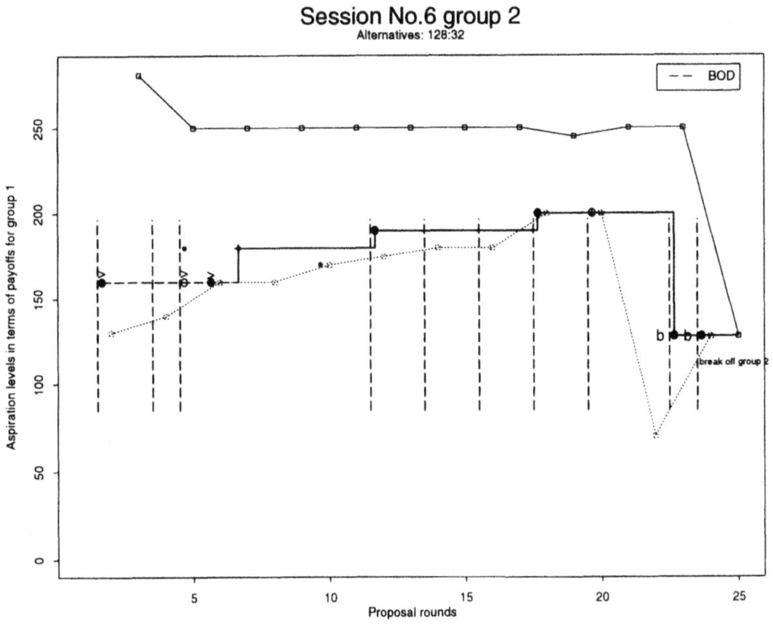
Session No.6 group 2
Alternatives: 128:32
BOD
Aspiration levels in terms of payoffs for group 1
Proposal rounds
break off group 2
0
50
100
150
200
250
5
10
15
20
25

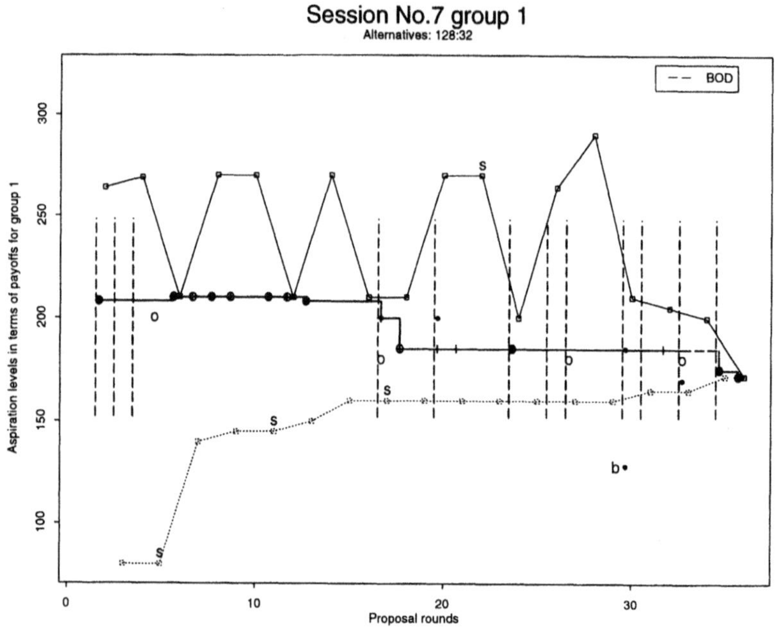
Session No.7 group 1
Alternatives: 128:32
BOD
Aspiration levels in terms of payoffs for group 1
Proposal rounds

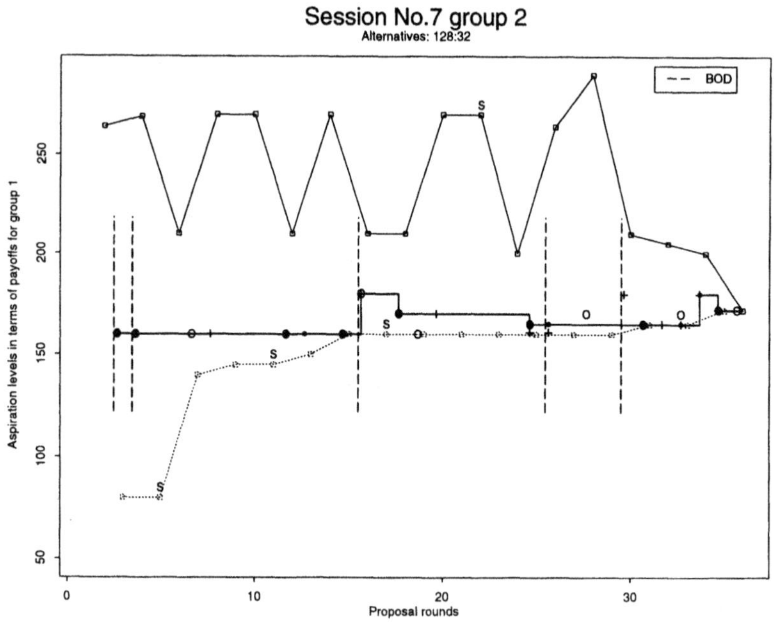
Session No.7 group 2
Alternatives: 128:32
BOD
Aspiration levels in terms of payoffs for group 1
Proposal rounds

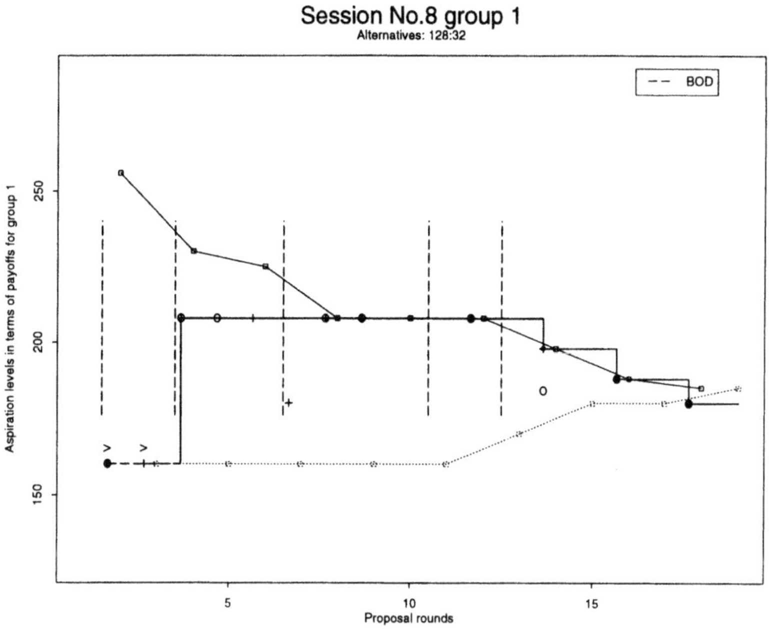
Session No.8 group 1
Alternatives: 128:32
-- BOD
Aspiration levels in terms of payoffs for group 1
150
200
250
5
10
15
Proposal rounds

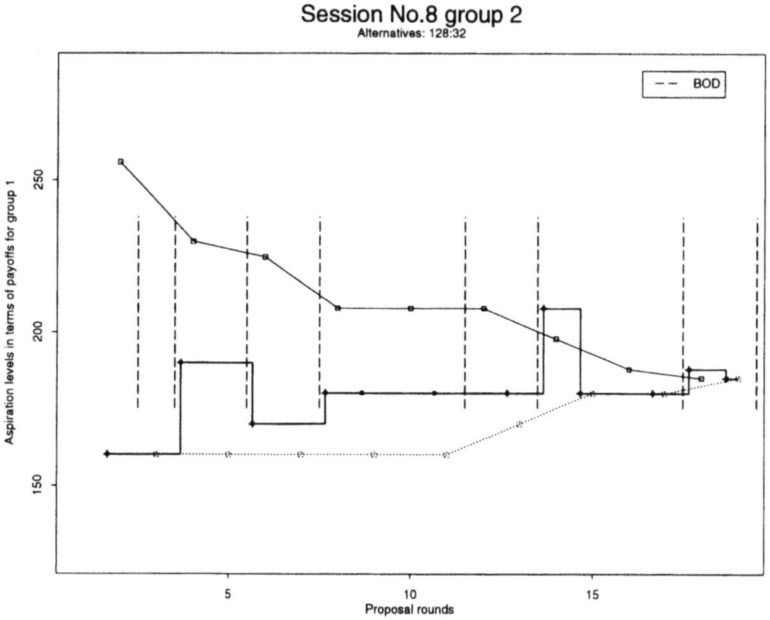
Session No.8 group 2
Alternatives: 128:32
-- BOD
Aspiration levels in terms of payoffs for group 1
150
200
250
5
10
15
Proposal rounds

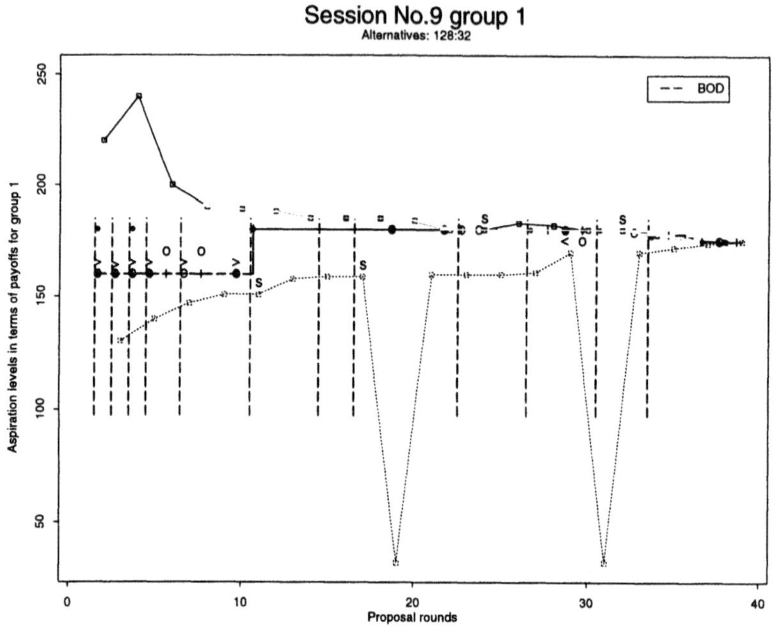
Session No.9 group 1
Alternatives: 128:32
BOD
Aspiration levels in terms of payoffs for group 1
Proposal rounds
0
10
20
30
40
50
100
150
200
250

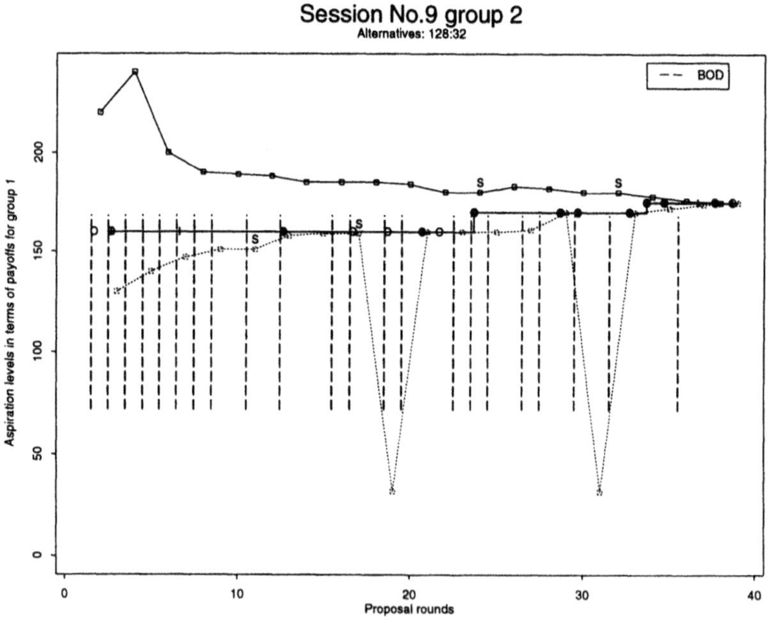
Session No.9 group 2
Alternatives: 128:32
BOD
Aspiration levels in terms of payoffs for group 1
Proposal rounds
0
10
20
30
40
0
50
100
150
200

Session No.10 group 1
Alternatives: 96:64

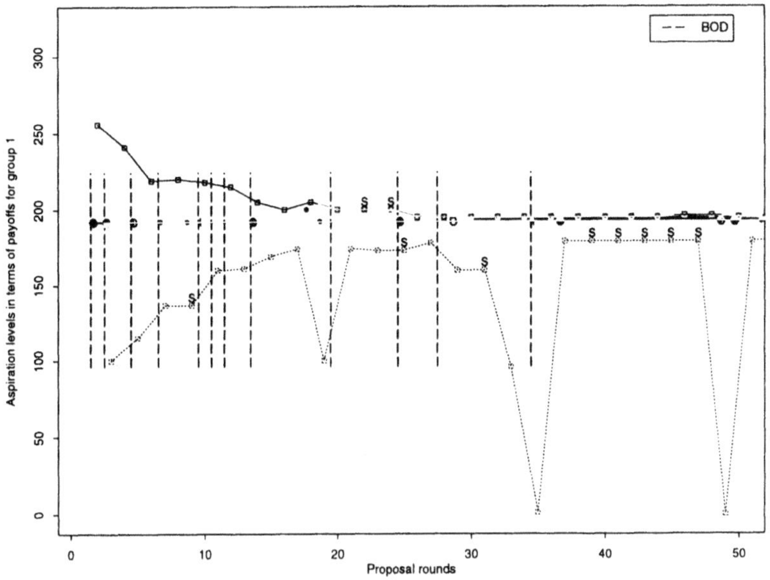

Session No.10 group 2
Alternatives: 96:64

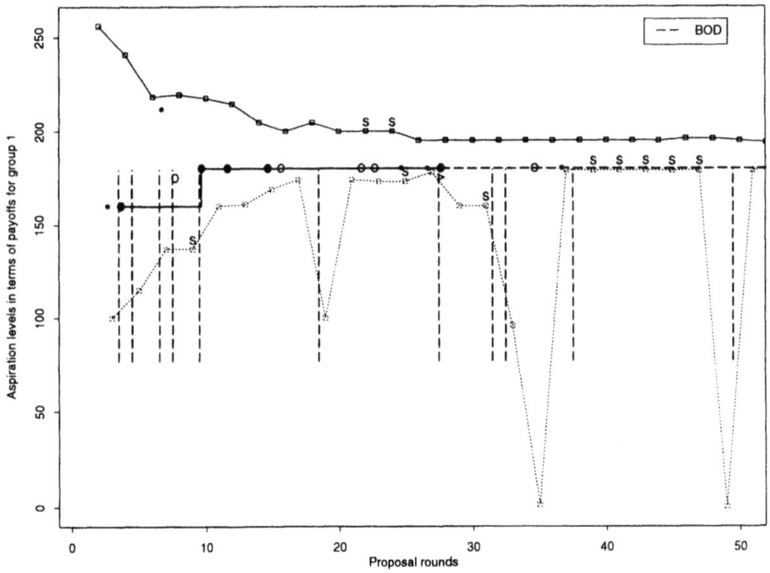

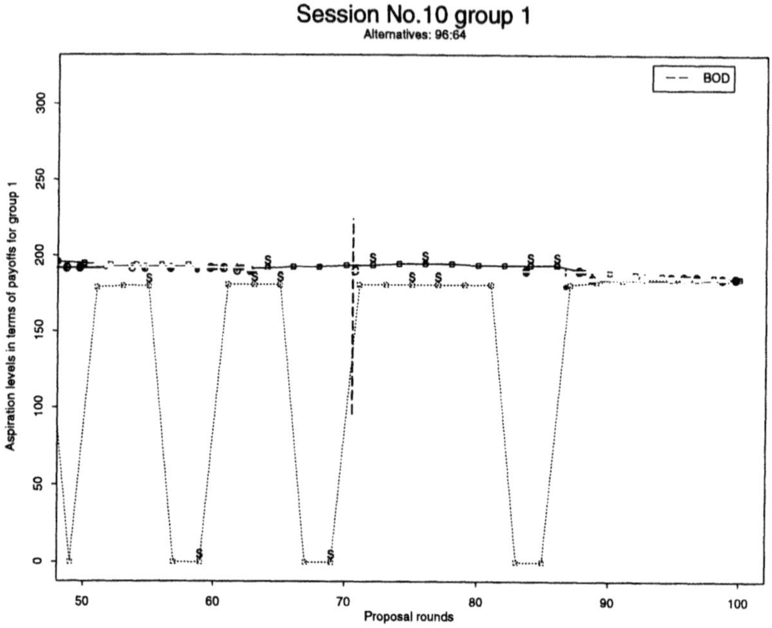

Session No.10 group 1
Alternatives: 96:64
BOD
Aspiration levels in terms of payoffs for group 1
Proposal rounds
0
50
100
150
200
250
300
50
60
70
80
90
100

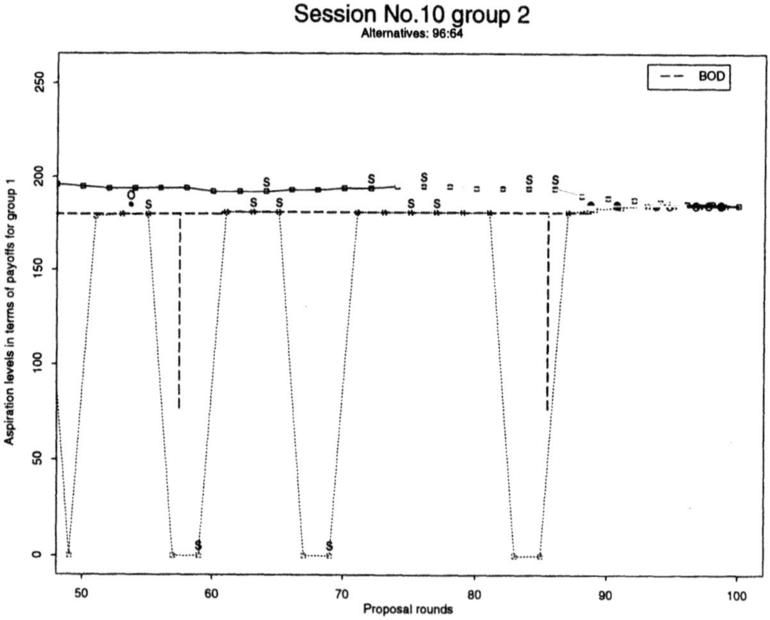

Session No.10 group 2
Alternatives: 96:64
BOD
Aspiration levels in terms of payoffs for group 1
Proposal rounds
0
50
100
150
200
250
50
60
70
80
90
100

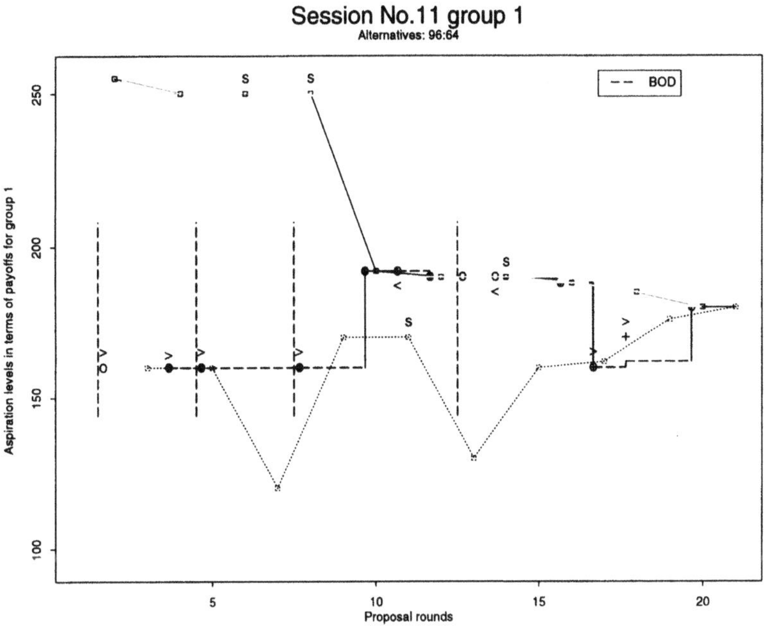
Session No.11 group 1
Alternatives: 96:64
BOD
Aspiration levels in terms of payoffs for group 1
Proposal rounds

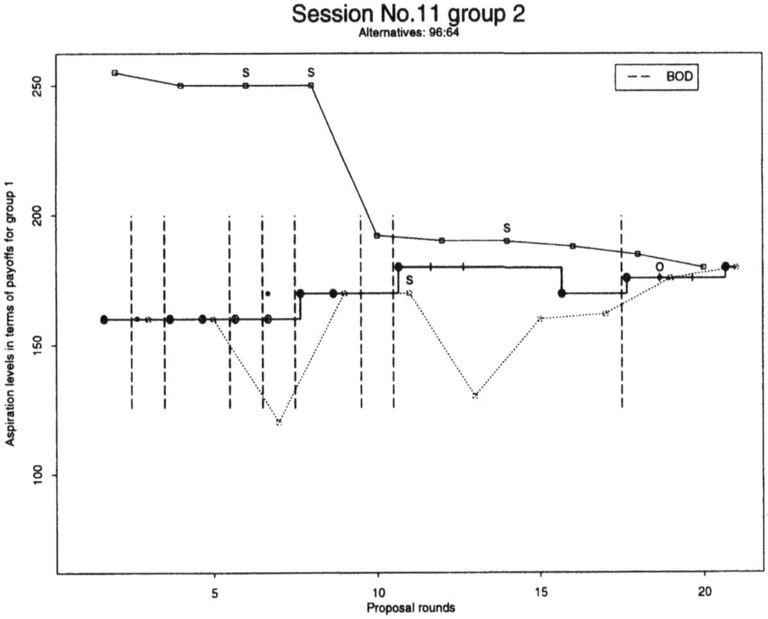
Session No.11 group 2
Alternatives: 96:64
BOD
Aspiration levels in terms of payoffs for group 1
Proposal rounds

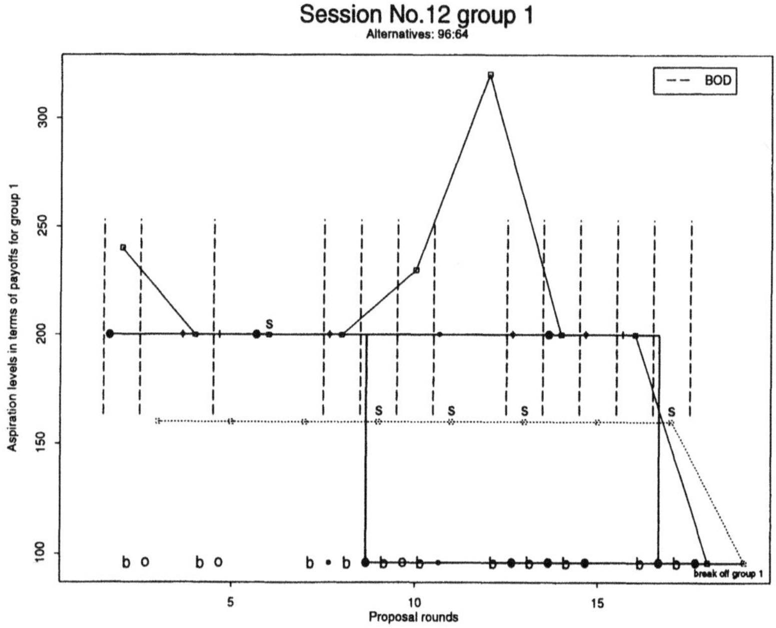
Session No.12 group 1
Alternatives: 96:64
BOD
Aspiration levels in terms of payoffs for group 1
Proposal rounds
break off group 1

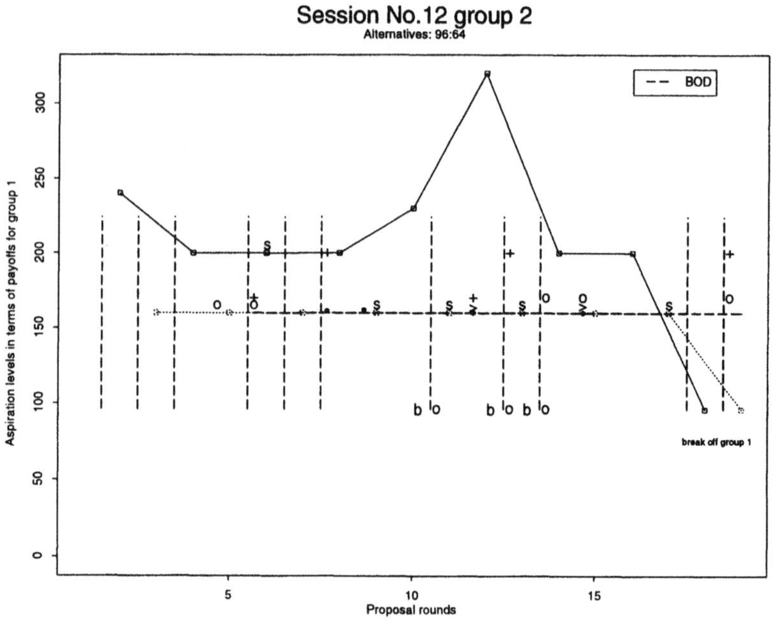
Session No.12 group 2
Alternatives: 96:64
BOD
Aspiration levels in terms of payoffs for group 1
Proposal rounds
break off group 1

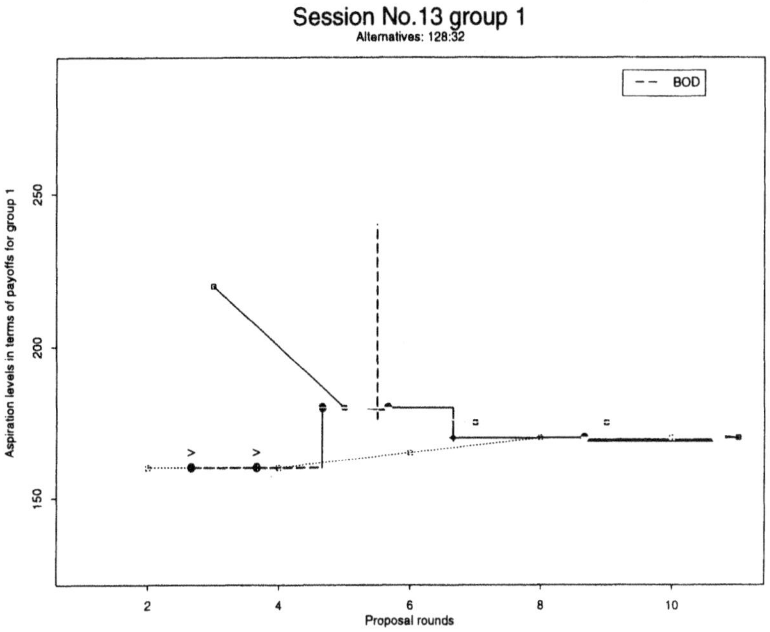
Session No.13 group 1
Alternatives: 128:32
BOD
Aspiration levels in terms of payoffs for group 1
150
200
250
2
4
6
8
10
Proposal rounds

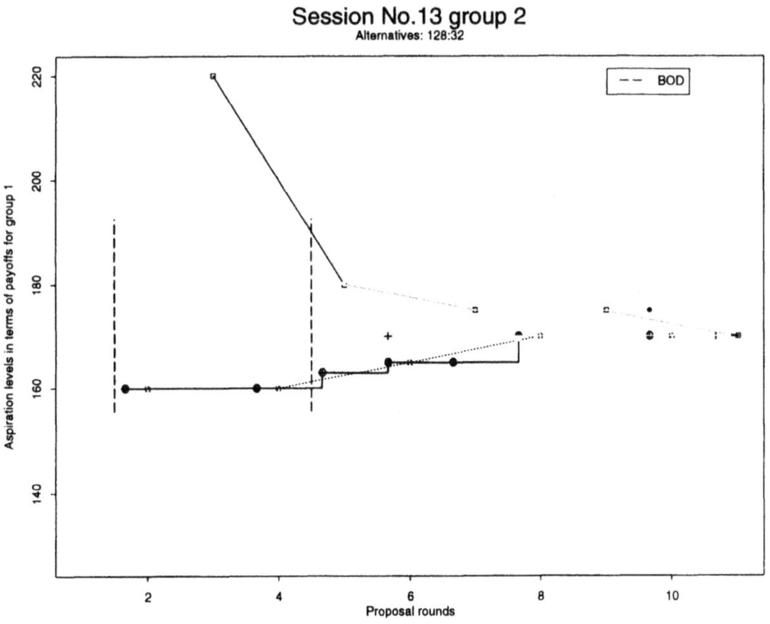
Session No.13 group 2
Alternatives: 128:32
BOD
Aspiration levels in terms of payoffs for group 1
140
160
180
200
220
2
4
6
8
10
Proposal rounds

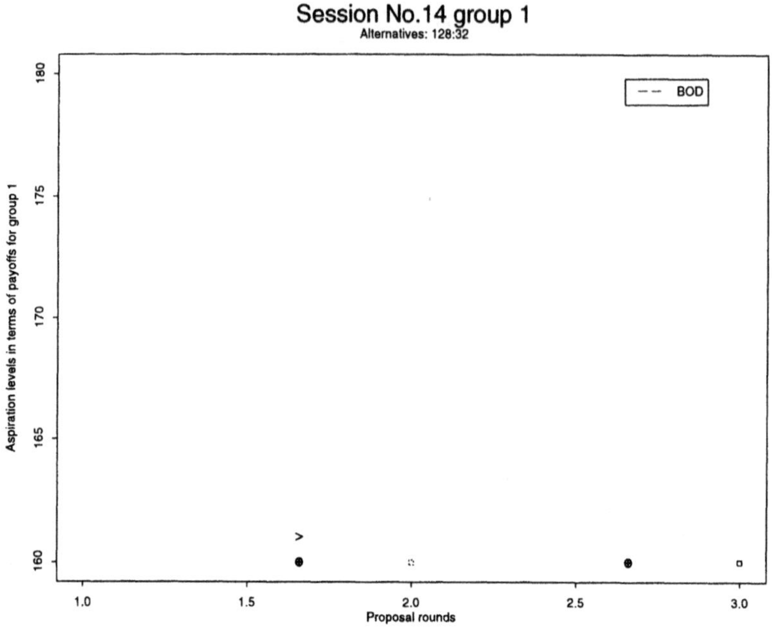

Session No.14 group 1
Alternatives: 128:32
BOD
Aspiration levels in terms of payoffs for group 1
Proposal rounds
160
165
170
175
180
1.0
1.5
2.0
2.5
3.0

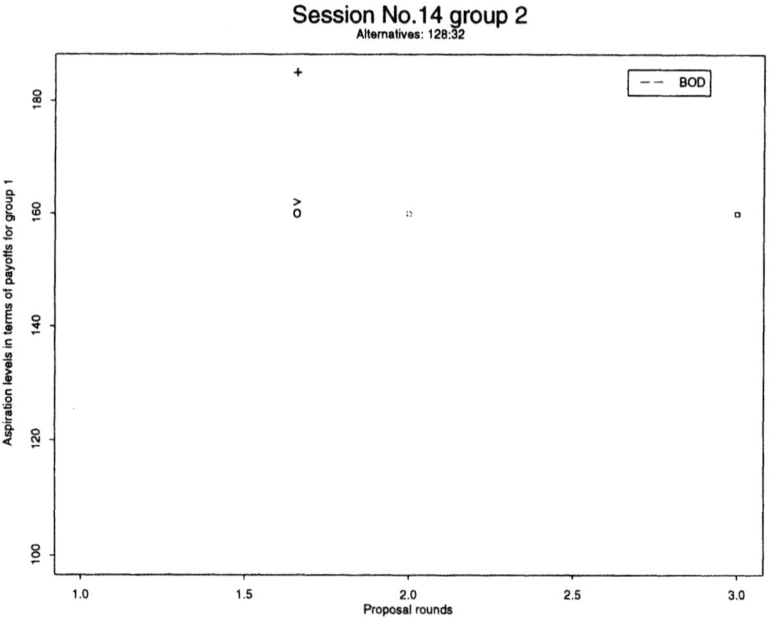

Session No.14 group 2
Alternatives: 128:32
BOD
Aspiration levels in terms of payoffs for group 1
Proposal rounds
100
120
140
160
180
1.0
1.5
2.0
2.5
3.0

Session No.15 group 1
Alternatives: 128:32

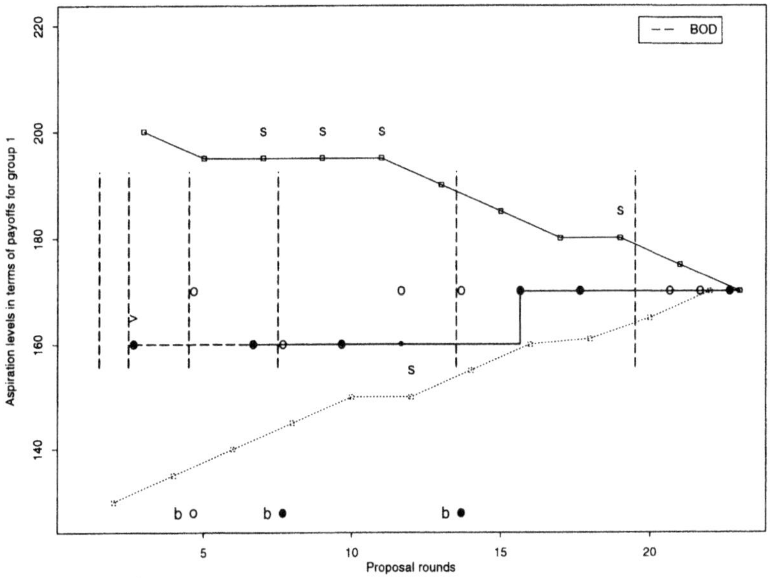

Session No.15 group 2
Alternatives: 128:32

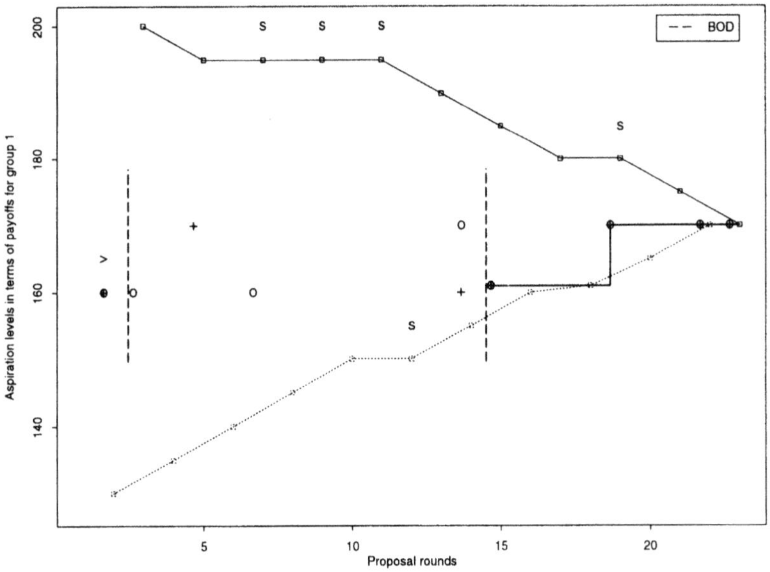

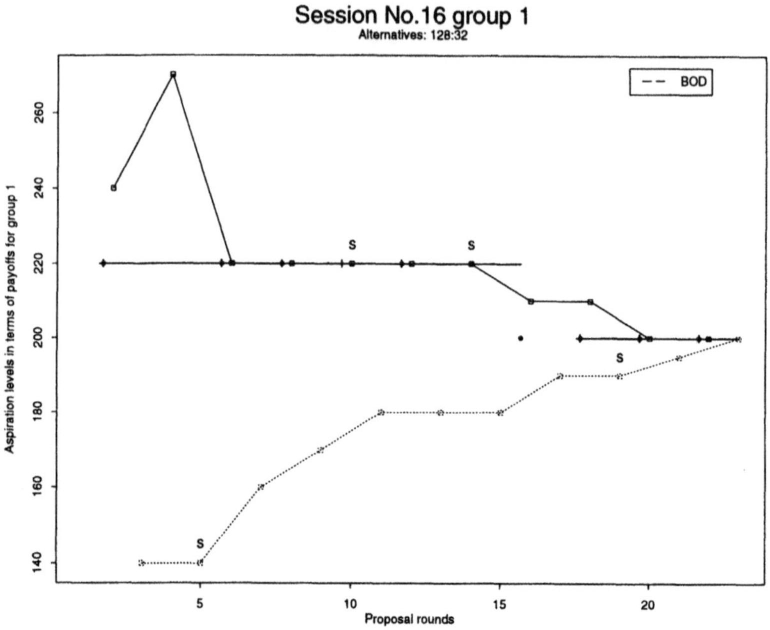
Session No.16 group 1
Alternatives: 128:32
BOD
Aspiration levels in terms of payoffs for group 1
Proposal rounds
S
S
S
S
140
160
180
200
220
240
260
5
10
15
20

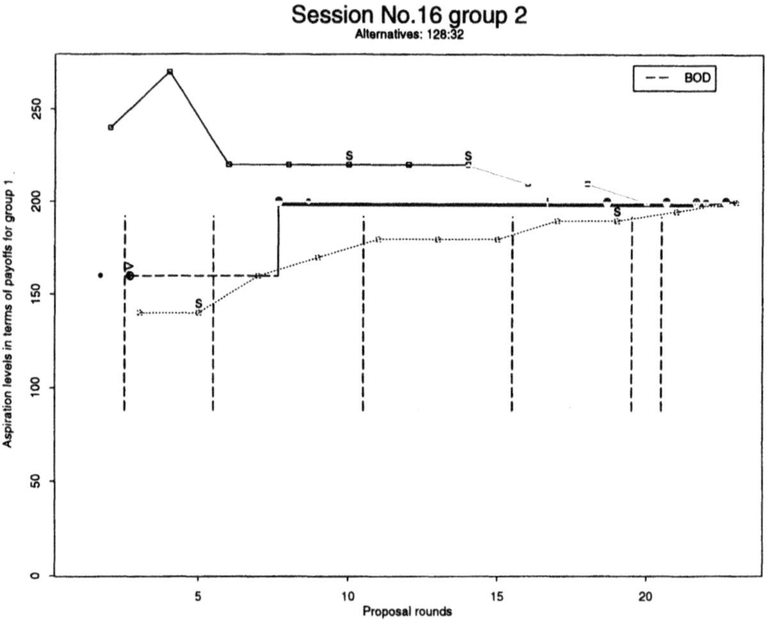
Session No.16 group 2
Alternatives: 128:32
BOD
Aspiration levels in terms of payoffs for group 1
Proposal rounds
S
S
S
S
0
50
100
150
200
250
5
10
15
20

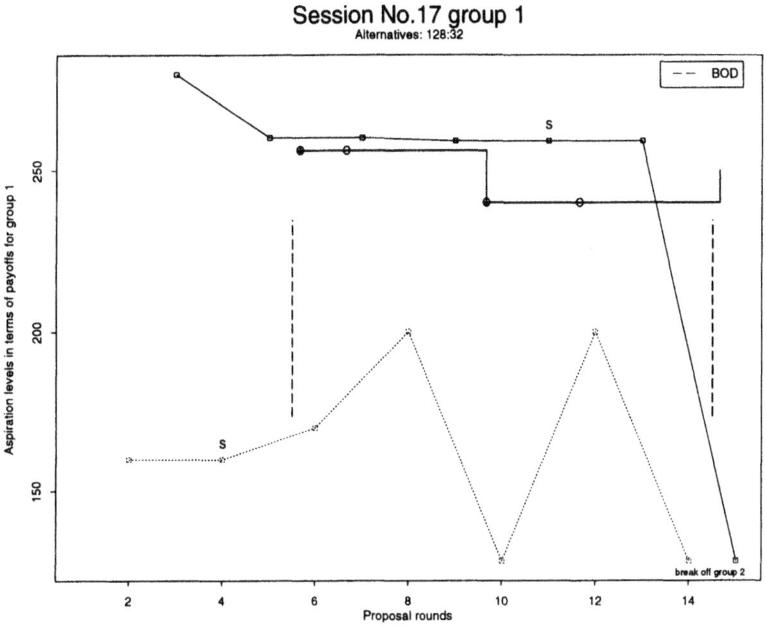
Session No.17 group 1
Alternatives: 128:32
BOD
s
s
Aspiration levels in terms of payoffs for group 1
250
200
150
break off group 2
2
4
6
8
10
12
14
Proposal rounds

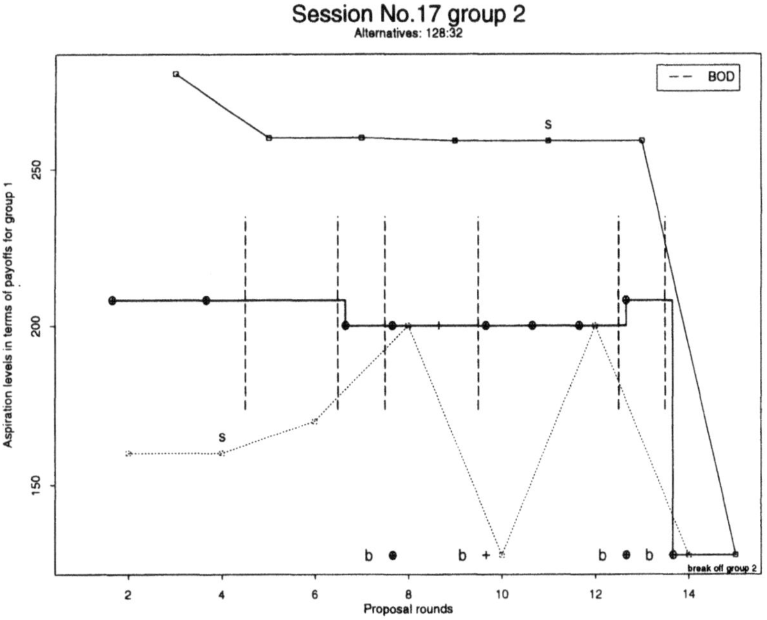
Session No.17 group 2
Alternatives: 128:32
BOD
s
s
b
b
+
b
b
Aspiration levels in terms of payoffs for group 1
250
200
150
break off group 2
2
4
6
8
10
12
14
Proposal rounds

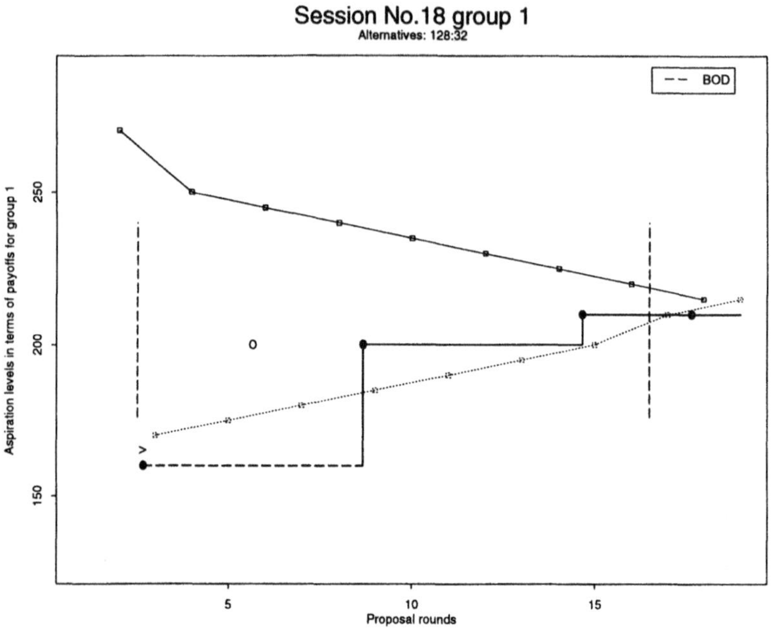
Session No.18 group 1
Alternatives: 128:32
BOD
Aspiration levels in terms of payoffs for group 1
150
200
250
5
10
15
Proposal rounds

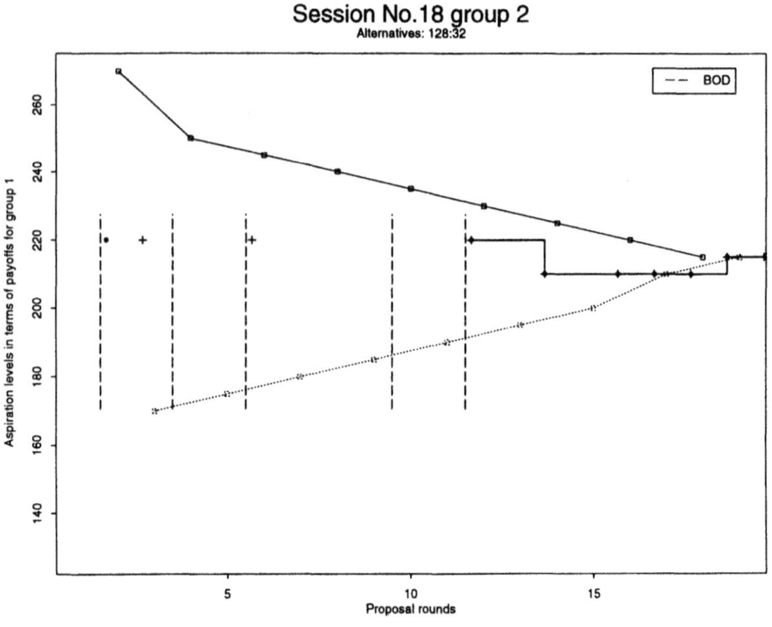
Session No.18 group 2
Alternatives: 128:32
BOD
Aspiration levels in terms of payoffs for group 1
140
160
180
200
220
240
260
5
10
15
Proposal rounds

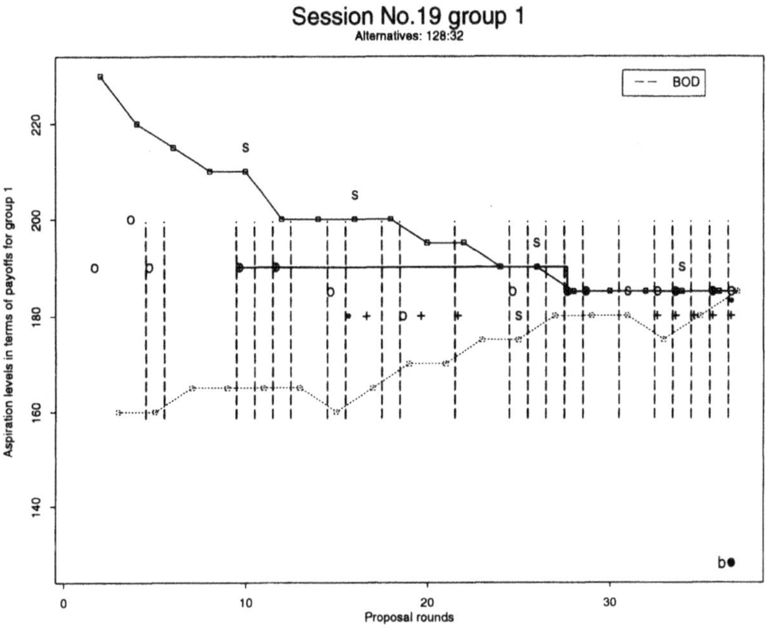
Session No.19 group 1
Alternatives: 128:32
BOD
Aspiration levels in terms of payoffs for group 1
Proposal rounds

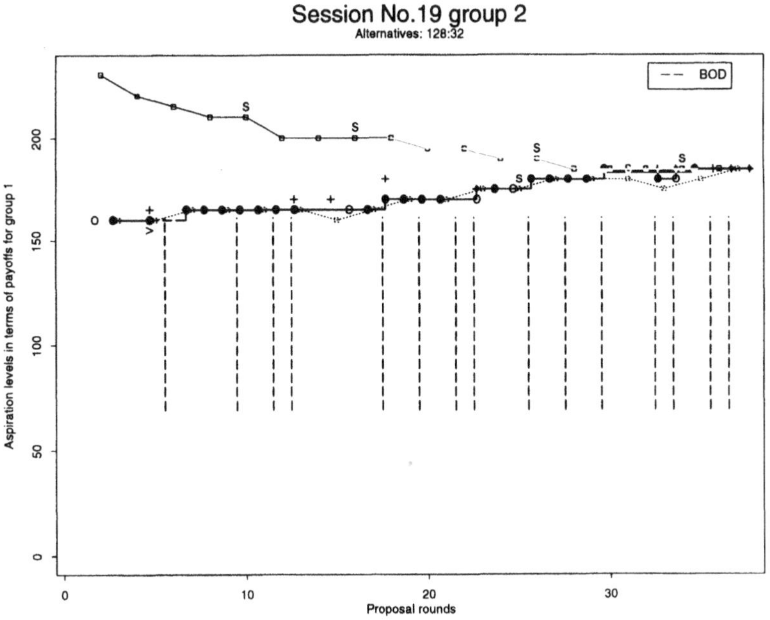
Session No.19 group 2
Alternatives: 128:32
BOD
Aspiration levels in terms of payoffs for group 1
Proposal rounds

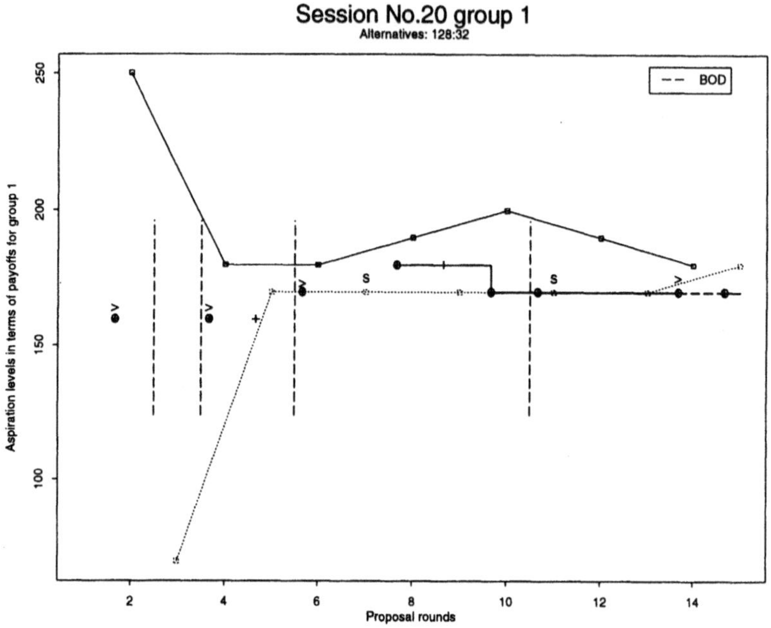
Session No.20 group 1
Alternatives: 128:32
BOD
Aspiration levels in terms of payoffs for group 1
Proposal rounds
S
S

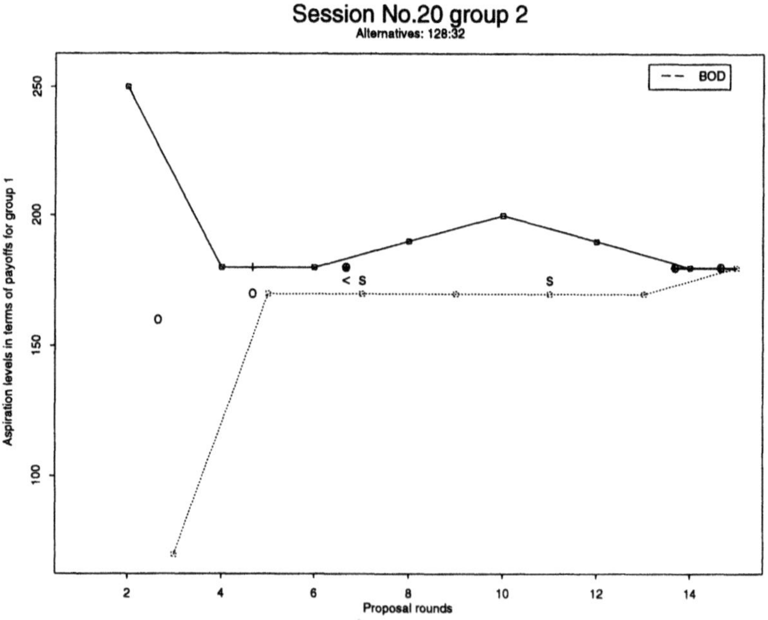
Session No.20 group 2
Alternatives: 128:32
BOD
Aspiration levels in terms of payoffs for group 1
Proposal rounds
S
S

Appendix G

Questionnaire for Business People

Suppose you are planning a joint venture with a stronger (weaker) partner. If both partners do not cooperate the profits each of them is able to realize correspond to a relation of 4:1, i.e. if you are the stronger partner your profit is 4 times higher than that of your potential companion, and vice versa. The joint venture is profitable since the gain from cooperation is twice as high as the sum of profits under noncooperation.

Example:

Profit of joint venture	1,000,000	100,000	500,000
Profit of A without cooperation	400,000	40,000	200,000
Profit of B without cooperation	100,000	10,000	50,000

Questions:

1. Which allocation you would be striving for if you are
   a) the partner being able to realize the **higher** profit without cooperation?
   b) the partner being able to realize the **lower** profit without cooperation?

   Please give the reasons why you are striving for this allocation.

2. Could you imagine breaking off the negotiation? Which offer of your potential partner would induce you to break off bargaining?

References

ADAMS, J. S. (1965) "Inequity in Social Exchange." In: L. Berkowitz (ed.), *Advances in Experimental Social Psychology*, vol. 2, 265–299, Academic Press, New York, London.

AKERLOF, G. A. AND W. T. DICKENS (1982) "The Economic Consequences of Cognitive Dissonance." *The American Economic Review*, 72, 307–319.

ALBERS, W. AND G. ALBERS (1983) "On the Prominence Structure of the Decimal System." In: R. Scholz (ed.), *Decision Making under Uncertainty*, 271–287, Elsevier Science Publishers B.V. (North Holland), Amsterdam et. al.

ARTALE, A. (1996) *Rings in Auctions: An Experimental Approach*, vol. 447 of *Lecture Notes in Economics and Mathematical Systems*. Springer Verlag, Berlin, Heidelberg, New York, London, Paris, Tokyo et. al.

AXELROD, R. (1984) *The Evolution of Cooperation*. Basic Books, Inc., New York.

BARTOS, O. J. (1970) "Determinants and Consequences of Toughness." In: P. Swingle (ed.), *The Structure of Conflict*, 45–68, Academic Press, New York and London.

BERG, J., J. DICKHAUT, AND K. MCCABE (1995) "Trust, Reciprocity and Social History." *Games and Economic Behavior*, 10, 122–142.

BERKOWITZ, L. AND L. R. DANIELS (1964) "Affecting the Salience of the Social Responsibility Norm: Effects of Past Help on the Response to Dependency Relationships." *Journal of Abnormal and Social Psychology*, 68, 275–281.

BEWLEY, T. F. (1997) *A Depressed Labor Market as Explained by Participants*. mimeo, Cowles Foundation, Yale University, New Haven.

BINMORE, K., A. SHAKED, AND J. SUTTON (1985) "Testing Noncooperative Bargaining Theory: A Preliminary Study." *American Economic Review*, 75, 1178–1180.

BINMORE, K., A. SHAKED, AND J. SUTTON (1989) "An Outside Option Experiment." *The Quarterly Journal of Economics*, 104, 753–770.

BOLLE, F. (1989) "Levels of Aspiration, Promises and the Possibility of Revaluation." In: K. Grunert and F. Oleander (eds.), *Understanding Economic Behaviour*, 199–211, Kluwer Academic Publishers, Dordrecht, The Netherlands.

BOLTON, G. E. (1991) "A Comparative Model of Bargaining: Theory and Evidence." *American Economic Review*, 81, 1096–1136.

BOLTON, G. E. AND R. ZWICK (1995) "Anonymity versus Punishment in Ultimatum Bargaining." *Games and Economic Behavior*, 10, 95–121.

BORNSTEIN, G., D. MINGELGRIN, AND C. RUTTE (1996) "The Effects of Within-Group Communication on Group Decision and Individual Choice in the Assurance and Chicken Team Games." *Journal of Conflict Resolution*, 40, 486–501.

BORNSTEIN, G., E. WINTER, AND H. GOREN (1997) "Cooperation in Intergroup and Single-Group - Prisoner's Dilemma Games." In: W. Albers, W. Güth, P. Hammerstein, B. Moldovanu, and E. van Damme (eds.), *Understanding Strategic Interaction. Essays in Honor of Reinhard Selten*, 418–429, Springer-Verlag, Berlin, Heidelberg, New York, Tokyo.

BURNSTEIN, E., A. VINOKUR, AND Y. TROPE (1973) "Interpersonal Comparison Versus Persuasive Argumentation: A More Direct Test of Alternative Explanations for Group-Induced Shifts in Individual Choice." *Journal of Experimental Social Psychology*, 9, 236–245.

CAMERER, C. (1997a) "Progress in Behavioral Game Theory." *Journal of Economic Perspectives*, 11, 167–188.

CAMERER, C. (1997b) "Rules for Experimenting in Psychology and Economics, and Why They Differ." In: W. Albers, W. Güth, P. Hammerstein, B. Moldovanu, and E. van Damme (eds.), *Understanding Strategic Interaction. Essays in Honor of Reinhard Selten*, 313–327, Springer-Verlag, Berlin, Heidelberg, New York, Tokyo.

CAMERER, C. AND R. H. THALER (1995) "Anomalies – Ultimatums, Dictators and Manners." *Journal of Economic Perspectives*, 9, 209–219.

CAMERON, L. (1995) *Raising the Stakes in the Ultimatum Game: Experimental Evidence from Indonesia*. Working Paper 345, Princeton University.

CHARNESS, G. (1996) *Attribution and Reciprocity in a Simulated Labor Market: An Experimental Investigation*. Discussion paper, UC Berkley, USA.

CYERT, R. M. AND J. G. MARCH (1963) *A Behavioral Theory of the Firm.* Englewood Cliffs, New Jersey, Prentice Hall.

DAHL, R. A. (1957) "The Concept of Power." *Behavioral Science*, 2, 201–215.

DAVIS, D. AND C. A. HOLT (1992) *Experimental Economics.* Princeton University Press, Princeton, N.J.

DEMBO, T. (1931) "Der Ärger als dynamisches Problem. Untersuchungen zur Handlungs- und Affektpsychologie." *Psychologische Forschung*, 15, 1–144.

DUFWENBERG, M. AND U. GNEEZY (1996) *Efficiency, Reciprocity, and Expectations in an Experimental Game.* Discussion Paper 9679, Center for Economic Research, Tilburg University.

ERICSSON, K. A. AND H. A. SIMON (1984) *Protocol Analysis – Verbal Reports as Data.* The MIT Press, Cambridge, MA., London.

FEHR, E. AND S. GÄCHTER (1998) "How Effective Are Trust- and Reciprocity-Based Incentives?" In: A. Ben-Ner and L. Putterman (eds.), *Economics, Values, Organizations*, Cambridge University Press.

FEHR, E. AND E. TOUGAREVA (1996) *Do High Monetary Stakes Remove Reciprocal Fairness? Experimental Evidence from Russia.* Discussion paper, Institute for Empirical Economic Research, University of Zürich.

FEHR, E. AND J.-R. TYRAN (1997) "Institutions and Reciprocal Fairness." *Nordic Journal of Political Economy*, 23, 133–144.

FEHR, E., G. KIRCHSTEIGER, AND A. RIEDL (1993) "Does Fairness Prevent Market Clearing? An Experimental Investigation." *The Quarterly Journal of Economics*, 108, 437–459.

FEHR, E., S. GÄCHTER, AND G. KIRCHSTEIGER (1996) "Reciprocal Fairness and Noncompensating Wage Differentials." *Journal of Institutional and Theoretical Economics (JITE), Zeitschrift für die gesamte Staatswissenschaft*, 152, 608–640.

FEHR, E., S. GÄCHTER, AND G. KIRCHSTEIGER (1997) "Reciprocity as a Contract Enforcement Device – Experimental Evidence." *Econometrica*, 65, 833–860.

FEHR, E., E. KIRCHLER, A. WEICHBOLD, AND S. GÄCHTER (1998a) "When Social Norms Overpower Competition – Social Exchange in Experimental Labor Markets." *Journal of Labor Economics*, 16, 321–354.

FEHR, E., G. KIRCHSTEIGER, AND A. RIEDL (1998b) "Gift Exchange and Reciprocity in Competitive Experimental Markets." *European Economic Review*, 42, 1–34.

FOURAKER, L. E. AND S. SIEGEL (1963) *Bargaining Bahavior.* McGraw-Hill, New York.

FRANK, R. H. (1988) *Passions within Reason.* W.W. Norton and Company, New York, London.

GEANAKOPLOS, J., D. PEARCE, AND E. STACCHETTI (1989) "Psychological Games and Sequential Rationality." *Journal of Games and Economic Behavior*, 1, 60–79.

GERGEN, K. AND M. M. GERGEN (1986) *Social Psychology.* Springer-Verlag, New York, 2nd edn.

GIBBONS, J. D. (1985) *Nonparametric Statistical Inference.* Marcel Dekker, Inc, New York and Basel.

GORANSON, R. E. AND L. BERKOWITZ (1966) "Reciprocity and Responsibility Reactions to Prior Help." *Journal of Personality and Social Psychology*, 3, 227–232.

GOULDNER, A. W. (1960) "The Norm of Reciprocity: A Preliminary Statement." *Americal Sociological Review*, 25, 161–178.

GREENBERG, J. (1978) "Effect of Reward Value and Retaliative Power on Allocation Decisions: Justice, Generosity, or Greed?" *Journal of Personality and Social Psychology*, 36, 367–379.

GREENBERG, M. S. AND D. M. FRISCH (1972) "Effect of Intentionality on Willingness to Reciprocate a Favor." *Journal of Experimental Social Psychology*, 8, 99–111.

GRUDER, C. L. (1970) "Social Power in Interpersonal Negotiation." In: P. Swingle (ed.), *The Structure of Conflict*, 111–154, Academic Press, New York and London.

GÜTH, W. (1994) "Distributive Justice. A Behavioral Theory and Empirical Evidence." In: H. Branstätter and W. Güth (eds.), *Essays on Economic Psychology*, 153–176, Springer Verlag, Heidelberg.

GÜTH, W. (1995) "On Ultimatum Bargaining Experiments - A Personal Review." *Journal of Economic Behavior and Organization*, 27, 329–344.

GÜTH, W. (1997a) *Boundedly Rational Decision Emergence - A General Perspective and Some Selective Illustrations.* Discussion Paper 9748, CentER for Economic Research.

GÜTH, W. (1997b) *Ultimatum Proposals - How Do Decisions Emerge?* Discussion Paper 9740, CentER for Economic Research.

GÜTH, W. AND R. TIETZ (1990) "Ultimatum Bargaining Behavior. A Survey and Comparison of Experimental Results." *Journal of Economic Psychology,* 11, 417–449.

GÜTH, W., R. SCHMITTBERGER, AND B. SCHWARZE (1982) "An Experimental Analysis of Ultimatum Bargaining." *Journal of Economic Behavior and Organization,* 3, 367–388.

HARSANYI, J. C. (1976) *Essays on Ethics, Social Behavior and Scientific Explanation.* D. Reidel Publishing Company, Dordrecht, Boston.

HECKHAUSEN, H. (1989) *Motivation und Handeln.* Springer Verlag, Berlin, Heidelberg, New York.

HENNIG-SCHMIDT, H. (1996a) *Bargaining between Groups as Players – Textprotocols of a Video Experiment.* Experimental Data Documentation Series 1.96, Sonderforschungsbereich 303, University of Bonn.

HENNIG-SCHMIDT, H. (1996b) *Behavior of Groups as Players in a Bargaining Experiment - Some Results on Negotiation Processes from a Video Experiment.* Discussion Paper B-355, Sonderforschungsbereich 303, University of Bonn.

HENNIG-SCHMIDT, H. (1996c) *Equity, Fairness and Prominence – Determinants for the Behavior of Player Groups in a Bargaining Video Experiment.* Discussion Paper B-356e, Sonderforschungsbereich 303, University of Bonn.

HENNIG-SCHMIDT, H. (1997) *Break-offs in Bargaining – Evidence from a Video Experiment.* Discussion Paper B-402, Sonderforschungsbereich 303, University of Bonn.

HERKNER, W. (1988) *Einführung in die Sozialpsychologie.* Verlag Hans Huber, Bern, Stuttgart, Toronto, 4th edn.

HILDENBRAND, W. (1994a) *Market Demand.* Princeton University Press, Princeton, N.Y.

HILDENBRAND, W. (1994b) *Réflexions sur le Contenu Empirique des Théories Économiques.* Leçon inaugural, Collège de France.

HILDENBRAND, W. (1998) "How Relevant Are Specifications of Behavioral Relations on the Micro-Level for Modelling the Time Path of Population Aggregates?" *European Economic Review*, 42, 437–458, The Joseph-Schumpeter-Lecture, given at the 12th Congress of the European Economic Association, Toulouse, France, August 31-September 2, 1997.

HOFFMANN, E., K. MCCABE, AND V. SMITH (1995) "Behavioral Foundations of Reciprocity: Experimental Economics and Evolutionary Psychology." mimeo.

HOFFMANN, E., K. MCCABE, AND V. SMITH (1997) "Reciprocity: The Behavioral Foundations of Socio-Economic Games." In: W. Albers, W. Güth, P. Hammerstein, B. Moldovanu, and E. van Damme (eds.), *Understanding Strategic Interaction. Essays in Honor of Reinhard Selten*, 328–344, Springer-Verlag, Berlin, Heidelberg, New York, Tokyo.

HOMANS, G. C. (1961) *Social Behaviour.* Routledge and Kegan Paul, London.

HUANG, P. H. AND H.-M. WU (1992) "Emotional Responses in Litigation." *International Review of Law and Economics*, 12, 31–44.

JACOBSEN, E. AND A. SADRIEH (1996) *Experimental Proof for the Motivational Importance of Reciprocity.* Discussion Paper B-386, Sonderforschungsbereich 303, University of Bonn.

KAHN, L. M. AND J. K. MURNIGHAN (1993) "A General Experiment on Bargaining in Demand Games with Outside Options." *American Economic Review*, 83, 1260–1280.

KAHNEMAN, D., J. L. KNETSCH, AND R. THALER (1986a) "Fairness and the Assumptions of Economics." *Journal of Business*, 59, 285–300.

KAHNEMAN, D., J. L. KNETSCH, AND R. THALER (1986b) "Fairness as a Constraint on Profit Seeking: Entitlements in the Market." *The American Economic Review*, 76, 728–741.

KARANDIKAR, R., D. MOOKHERJEE, D. RAY, AND F. VEGA-REDONDO (1998) "Evolving Aspirations and Cooperation." *Journal of Economic Theory*, 80, 292–331.

KELLEY, H. H. AND J. W. THIBAUT (1978) *Interpersonal Relations - A Theory of Interdependence.* John Wiley, New York, Chichester, Brisbane, Toronto.

KESER, C. (1992) *Experimental Duopoly Markets with Demand Inertia*, vol. 391 of *Lecture Notes in Economics and Mathematical Systems.* Springer Verlag, Berlin, Heidelberg, New York, London, Paris, Tokyo et. al.

KIRCHLER, E., E. FEHR, AND R. EVANS (1995) "Social Exchange in the Labor Market: Reciprocity and Trust versus Egoistic Money Maximization." *Journal of Economic Psychology*, 17, 313–341.

KLEMISCH-AHLERT, M. (1996) *Bargaining in Economics and Ethical Environments. An Experimental Study and Normative Solution Concepts*, vol. 436 of *Lecture Notes in Economics and Mathematical Systems*. Springer Verlag, Berlin, Heidelberg, New York, London, Paris, Tokyo et. al.

KOMORITA, S. S. AND D. A. KRAVITZ (1979) "The Effects of Alternatives in Bargaining." *Journal of Experimental Social Psychologie*, 15, 147–159.

KÖNIGSTEIN, M. (1997) *Convergence to Equitable Play in the Repeated Ultimatum Game with Advance Production.* Discussion paper, Humboldt-University at Berlin.

KRELLE, W. (1976) *Preistheorie*, vol. II. J.C.B. Mohr (Paul Siebeck), Tübingen.

KUON, B. (1994) *Two-Person Bargaining Experiments with Incomplete Information*, vol. 412 of *Lecture Notes in Economics and Mathematical Systems.* Springer Verlag, Berlin, Heidelberg, New York, London, Paris, Tokyo et. al.

KUON, B. AND G. R. UHLICH (1993) "The Negotiation Agreement Area: An Experimental Analysis of Two-Person Characteristic Function Games." *Group Decision and Negotiation*, 2, 323–345.

LAMM, H. AND D. G. MYERS (1978) "Group-Induced Polarization of Attitudes and Behavior." In: L. Berkowitz (ed.), *Advances in Experimental Social Psychology*, vol. 11, 145–195, Academic Press, New York, London.

LEVENTHAL, G. S. AND D. ANDERSON (1970) "Self-Interest and the Maintenance of Equity." *Journal of Personality and Social Psychology*, 15, 57–62.

LEWIN, K., T. DEMBO, L. FESTINGER, AND P. SNEDDEN SEARS (1944) "Level of Aspiration." In: J. M. Hunt (ed.), *Personality and the Behavior Disorders*, 333–378, Ronald Press, New York.

MCCABE, K. A., S. J. RASSENTI, AND V. L. SMITH (1996) "Game Theory and Reciprocity in Some Extensive Form Experimental Games." *Proceedings of the National Academy of Sciences of the USA*, 93, 13421–13428.

MCCLELLAND, D. (1975) *Power: The Inner Experience.* Irvington, New York.

MCCLELLAND, D. (1985) *Human Motivation.* Scott and Foresman, Glenview, Dallas et. al.

McClintock, C. G., R. M. Kramer, and L. J. Keil (1984) "Equity and Social Change in Human Relationships." In: L. Berkowitz (ed.), *Advances in Experimental Social Psychology*, vol. 17, 184–228, Academic Press, New York, London.

Mitzkewitz, M. and R. Nagel (1991) *Envy, Greed, and Anticipation in Ultimatum Games with Incomplete Information: An Experimental Study.* Discussion Paper B-181, Sonderforschungsbereich 303, University of Bonn.

Mitzkewitz, M. and R. Nagel (1993) "Experimental Results on Ultimatum Games with Incomplete Information: An Experimental Study." *International Journal of Game Theory*, 22, 171–198.

Nagel, R. (1998) "A Survey on Beauty Contest Experiments: Bounded Rationality and Learning." In: D. Budescu, I. Erev, and R. Zwick (eds.), *Games and Human Behavior: Essays in Honor of Amnon Rapoport*, Lawrence Erlbaum Associates Inc., New Jersey, forthcoming.

Nash, J. (1950) "The Bargaining Problem." *Econometrica*, 18, 155–162.

Nash, J. (1953) "Two-Person Cooperative Games." *Econometrica*, 21, 128–140.

Ochs, J. and A. E. Roth (1989) "An Experimental Study of Sequential Bargaining." *American Economic Review*, 79, 355–384.

Osborne, M. J. and A. Rubinstein (1990) *Bargaining and Markets.* Academic Press, San Diego.

Ostmann, A. (1990) "On Rationality Issues in the Bargaining Context." *Journal of Institutional and Theoretical Economics (JITE), Zeitschrift für die gesamte Staatswissenschaft*, 146, 673–683.

Ostmann, A. (1992a) "The Interaction of Aspiration Levels and the Social Field in Experimental Bargaining." *Journal of Economic Psychology*, 13, 233–261.

Ostmann, A. (1992b) "On the Relationship between Formal Conflict Structure and the Social Field." *Small Group Research*, 23, 26–48.

Ostmann, A. and U. Leopold-Wildburger (1997) "On Styles of Relating to Bargaining Partners." In: W. Albers, W. Güth, P. Hammerstein, B. Moldovanu, and E. van Damme (eds.), *Understanding Strategic Interaction. Essays in Honor of Reinhard Selten*, 430–443, Springer-Verlag, Berlin, Heidelberg, New York, Tokyo.

PALOMINO, F. AND F. VEGA-REDONDO (1997) *Convergence of Aspirations and (Partial) Cooperation in the Prisoner's Dilemma.* Working Paper 345.96., Universitat Autónoma de Barcelona.

RABIN, M. (1993) "Incorporating Fairness into Game Theory and Economics." *American Economic Review*, 83, 1281–1302.

RAPOPORT, A., E. WEG, AND D. FELSENTHAL (1990) "Effects of Fixed Costs in Two-Person Sequential Bargaining." In: S. H. Tijs (ed.), *Experimental Studies of Interactive Decisions*, 119–137, Kluwer Academic Publishers, Dordrecht, The Netherlands.

RAVEN, B. H. AND A. W. KRUGLANSKI (1970) "Conflict and Power." In: P. Swingle (ed.), *The Structure of Conflict*, 69–109, Academic Press, New York and London.

RHEINBERG, F. (1995) *Motivation.* W. Kohlhammer, Stuttgart, Berlin, Köln.

ROTH, A. E. (1995a) "Bargaining Experiments." In: J. H. Kagel and A. E. Roth (eds.), *The Handbook of Experimental Economics*, 253–348, Princeton University Press, Princeton, N.J.

ROTH, A. E. (1995b) "Introduction to Experimental Economics." In: J. H. Kagel and A. E. Roth (eds.), *The Handbook of Experimental Economics*, 3–109, Princeton University Press, Princeton, N.J.

RUBINSTEIN, A. (1982) "Perfect Equilibrium in a Bargaining Model." *Econometrica*, 50, 97–109.

SAUERMANN, H. AND R. SELTEN (1962) "Anspruchsanpassungstheorie der Unternehmung." *Zeitschrift für die gesamte Staatswissenschaft*, 118, 577–597.

SCHELLING, T. C. (1957) "Bargaining, Communication, and Limited War." *The Journal of Conflict Resolution*, 1, 19–36.

SCHELLING, T. C. (1958) "The Strategy of Conflict: Prospectus for a Reorientation of Game Theory." *The Journal of Conflict Resolution*, 2, 203–264.

SCHELLING, T. C. (1960) *The Strategy of Conflict.* Harvard University, Cambridge, MA., London.

SELTEN, R. (1967) "Die Strategiemethode zur Erforschung des eingeschränkt rationalen Verhaltens im Rahmen eines Oligopolexperimentes." In: H. Sauermann (ed.), *Beiträge zur experimentellen Wirtschaftsforschung*, 136–168, J.C.B. Mohr (Paul Siebeck), Tübingen.

SELTEN, R. (1978a) "The Chain Store Paradox." *Theory and Decision*, 9, 127 –159, reprinted in: R. Selten (1988), Models of Strategic Rationality, Dordrecht, Boston, London, Kluwer Academic Publishers, 33-65.

SELTEN, R. (1978b) "The Equity Principle in Economic Behavior." In: H. Gottinger and W. Leinfellner (eds.), *Decision Theory, Social Ethics, Issues in Social Choice*, 289–301, D. Reidel Publishing Company, Dordrecht, reprinted in: R. Selten (1988), Models of Strategic Rationality, Dordrecht, Boston, London, Kluwer Academic Publishers, 269-281.

SELTEN, R. (1981) "A Noncooperative Model of Characteristic-Function Bargaining." In: R. J. Aumann (ed.), *Essays in Game Theory and Mathematical Economics*, 131–151, Bibliographisches Institut AG, Mannheim, Wien, Zürich.

SELTEN, R. (1987) "Equity and Coalition Bargaining in Experimental Three-Person Games." In: A. E. Roth (ed.), *Laboratory Experimentation in Economics*, 42–98, Cambridge University Press, New York et. al.

SELTEN, R. (1990) "Bounded Rationality." *Journal of Institutional and Theoretical Economics (JITE)/ Zeitschrift für die gesamte Staatswissenschaft*, 146, 649–658.

SELTEN, R. (1991) "Properties of a Measure of Predictive Success." *Mathematical Social Sciences*, 21, 153–167.

SELTEN, R. (1993) "In Search of A Better Understanding of Economic Behaviour." In: A. Heertje (ed.), *The Makers of Modern Economics*, vol. 1, 115–139, Simon and Schuster.

SELTEN, R. (1996a) *Aspiration Adaptation Theory.* Discussion Paper B-389, Sonderforschungsbereich 303, University of Bonn.

SELTEN, R. (1996b) "Eingeschränkte Rationalität." Vorlesung im Wintersemester 1995/96 an der Rheinischen Friedrich Wilhelms-Universität Bonn. Lectures on Bounded Rationality, given at the University of Bonn, winter term 1995/96.

SELTEN, R. (1997) "Descriptive Approaches to Cooperation." In: S. Hart and A. Mas-Colell (eds.), *Cooperation: Game-Theoretic Approaches*, vol. 155 of *NATO ASI Series, Series F: Computer and Systems Sciences*, Springer-Verlag, Berlin, Heidelberg, New York, Tokyo.

SELTEN, R. (1998) "Features of Experimentally Observed Bounded Rationality." Presidential Address, given at the 12th Congress of the European Economic Association, Toulouse, France, August 31-September 2, 1997.

SELTEN, R. AND W. KRISCHKER (1983) "Comparison of Two Theories for Characteristic Function Experiments." In: R. Tietz (ed.), *Aspiration Levels in Bargaining and Economic Decision Making*, no. 213 in Lecture Notes in Economics and Mathematical Systems, 259–264, Springer Verlag, Berlin, Heidelberg, New York, Tokyo.

SELTEN, R. AND K. G. SCHUSTER (1970) "Psychologische Faktoren bei Koalitionsverhandlungen." In: H. Sauermann (ed.), *Beiträge zur experimentellen Wirtschaftsforschung*, vol. 2, 99–135, J.C.B. Mohr (Paul Siebeck), Tübingen.

SELTEN, R., M. MITZKEWITZ, AND G. R. UHLICH (1988) *Duopoly Strategies Programmed by Experienced Players.* Discussion Paper B-106, Sonderforschungsbereich 303, University of Bonn.

SELTEN, R., M. MITZKEWITZ, AND G. R. UHLICH (1997) "Duopoly Strategies Programmed by Experienced Players." *Econometrica*, 65, 517–555.

SEN, A. K. (1990) "Rational Fools: A Critique of the Behavioral Foundations of Economic Theory." In: J. Mansbridge (ed.), *Beyond Self-Interest*, 25–43, The University of Chicago Press.

SHAKED, A. AND J. SUTTON (1984) "Involuntary Unemployment as a Perfect Equilibrium in a Bargaining Model." *Econometrica*, 52, 1351–1364.

SIEGEL, S. (1956) *Nonparametric Statistics for the Behavioral Sciences.* McGraw-Hill, New York, Toronto, London.

SIEGEL, S. (1957) "Level of Aspiration and Decision Making." *Psychological Review*, 64, 253–262.

SIEGEL, S. AND J. CASTELLAN, N. J. (1988) *Nonparametric Statistics for the Behavioral Sciences.* McGraw-Hill, New York, Toronto, London et. al., 2nd edn.

SIEGEL, S. AND L. E. FOURAKER (1960) *Bargaining and Group Decision Making – Experiments in Bilateral Monopoly.* McGraw-Hill, New York, Toronto, London.

SIMON, H. A. (1955) "A Behavioral Model of Rational Choice." *Quarterly Journal of Economics*, 69, 99–118, reprinted in: H. A. Simon (1957), Models of Man, New York, John Wiley.

SIMON, H. A. (1957) *Models of Man.* John Wiley, New York.

SIMON, H. A. (1961) *Administrative Behavior.* Macmillan, New York, 2nd edn.

SIMON, H. A. (1962) "New Developments in the Theory of the Firm." *American Economic Review*, 52, 1–15.

SIMON, H. A. (1963) "Economics and Psychology." In: S. Koch (ed.), *Psychology: A Study of a Science*, 685–723, McGraw-Hill, New York.

SIMON, H. A. (1972) "Theories of Bounded Rationality." In: C. B. Radner (ed.), *Decision and Organization*, 161–176, North-Holland Publishing Company, Amsterdam, reprinted in: H.A. Simon (1982), Models of Bounded Rationality, vol. 2, Behavioral Economics and Business Organization, Cambridge, MA., London, MIT-Press.

STÅHL, I. (1972) *Bargaining Theory.* The Economic Research Institute, Stockholm.

THALER, R. H. (1988) "Anomalies: The Ultimatum Game." *Journal of Economic Perspectives*, 2, 195–206.

THIBAUT, J. W. AND H. H. KELLEY (1959) *The Social Psychology of Groups.* John Whiley and Sons, New York, London, Sydney.

TIETZ, R. (1972) "The Macroeconomic Experimental Game KRESKO – Experimental Design and the Influence of Economic Knowledge on Decision Behavior." In: H. Sauermann (ed.), *Beiträge zur experimentellen Wirtschaftsforschung/Contributions to Experimental Economics*, vol. 3, 267–288, J.C.B. Mohr (Paul Siebeck), Tübingen.

TIETZ, R. (1975) "An Experimental Analysis of Wage Bargaining Behavior." *Zeitschrift für die gesamte Staatswissenschaft*, 131, 44–91.

TIETZ, R. (1976) "Der Anspruchsausgleich in experimentellen Zwei-Personen-Verhandlungen mit verbaler Kommunikation." *Zeitschrift für Sozial Psychologie*, 2, 123–141.

TIETZ, R. (ed.) (1983) *Aspiration Levels in Bargaining and Economic Decision Making*, vol. 213 of *Lecture Notes in Economics and Mathematical Systems.* Springer Verlag, Berlin, Heidelberg, New York, Tokyo.

TIETZ, R. (1997) "Adaptation of Aspiration Levels - Theory and Experiment." In: W. Albers, W. Güth, P. Hammerstein, B. Moldovanu, and E. van Damme (eds.), *Understanding Strategic Interaction. Essays in Honor of Reinhard Selten*, 345–364, Springer-Verlag, Berlin, Heidelberg, New York, Tokyo.

TIETZ, R., W. DAUS, J. LAUTSCH, AND P. LOTZ (1988) "Semi-Normative Properties of Bounded Rational Bargaining Theories." In: R. Tietz, W. Albers, and R. Selten (eds.), *Bounded Rational Behavior in Experimental Games and Markets*, 142–159, Springer Verlag, Berlin, Heidelberg.

TVERSKY, A. AND D. KAHNEMAN (1986) "Rational Choice and the Framing of Decisions." In: R. E. Hogarth and M. W. Reder (eds.), *Rational Choice - The Contrast between Economics and Psychology*, 67–94, The University of Chicago Press, Chicago and London.

UHLICH, G. R. (1988) *An Area Theory for Experimental Two-Person Characteristic Function Games.* Discussion Paper B-105, Sonderforschungsbereich 303, University of Bonn.

UHLICH, G. R. (1990) *Descriptive Theories of Bargaining: An Experimental Analysis of Two- and Three-Person Characteristic Function Bargaining*, vol. 341 of *Lecture Notes in Economics and Mathematical Systems.* Springer Verlag, Berlin, Heidelberg, New York, London, Paris, Tokyo et. al.

WEBER, H. J. (1976) "Theory of Adaptation of Aspiration Levels in a Bilateral Decision Setting." *Zeitschrift für die gesamte Staatswissenschaft*, 132, 582–591.

WEBSTER (1966) *Webster's Third New International Dictionary.* G. and C. Merriam Company, Springfield, MA.

WEINER, B. (1987) "The Role of Emotions in a Theory of Motivation." In: F. Halisch and J. Kuhl (eds.), *Motivation, Intention and Volition*, 21–30, Springer-Verlag, Berlin, Heidelberg, New York, London, Paris, Tokyo.

YAARI, M. E. AND M. BAR-HILLEL (1984) "On Dividing Justly." *Social Choice and Welfare*, 1, 1–24.

Lecture Notes in Economics and Mathematical Systems

For information about Vols. 1–274
please contact your bookseller or Springer-Verlag

Vol. 280: H.T. Lau, Combinatorial Heuristic Algorithms with FORTRAN. VII, 126 pages. 1986.

Vol. 281: Ch.-L. Hwang, M.-J. Lin, Group Decision Making under Multiple Criteria. XI, 400 pages. 1987.

Vol. 282: K. Schittkowski, More Test Examples for Nonlinear Programming Codes. V, 261 pages. 1987.

Vol. 283: G. Gabisch, H.-W. Lorenz, Business Cycle Theory. VII, 229 pages. 1987.

Vol. 284: H. Lütkepohl, Forecasting Aggregated Vector ARMA Processes. X, 323 pages. 1987.

Vol. 285: Toward Interactive and Intelligent Decision Support Systems. Volume 1. Proceedings, 1986. Edited by Y. Sawaragi, K. Inoue and H. Nakayama. XII, 445 pages. 1987.

Vol. 286: Toward Interactive and Intelligent Decision Support Systems. Volume 2. Proceedings, 1986. Edited by Y. Sawaragi, K. Inoue and H. Nakayama. XII, 450 pages. 1987.

Vol. 287: Dynamical Systems. Proceedings, 1985. Edited by A.B. Kurzhanski and K. Sigmund. VI, 215 pages. 1987.

Vol. 288: G.D. Rudebusch, The Estimation of Macroeconomic Disequilibrium Models with Regime Classification Information. VII,128 pages. 1987.

Vol. 289: B.R. Meijboom, Planning in Decentralized Firms. X, 168 pages. 1987.

Vol. 290: D.A. Carlson, A. Haurie, Infinite Horizon Optimal Control. XI, 254 pages. 1987.

Vol. 291: N. Takahashi, Design of Adaptive Organizations. VI, 140 pages. 1987.

Vol. 292: I. Tchijov, L. Tomaszewicz (Eds.), Input-Output Modeling. Proceedings, 1985. VI, 195 pages. 1987.

Vol. 293: D. Batten, J. Casti, B. Johansson (Eds.), Economic Evolution and Structural Adjustment. Proceedings, 1985. VI, 382 pages.

Vol. 294: J. Jahn, W. Knabs (Eds.), Recent Advances and Historical Development of Vector Optimization. VII, 405 pages. 1987.

Vol. 295. H. Meister, The Purification Problem for Constrained Games with Incomplete Information. X, 127 pages. 1987.

Vol. 296: A. Börsch-Supan, Econometric Analysis of Discrete Choice. VIII, 211 pages. 1987.

Vol. 297: V. Fedorov, H. Läuter (Eds.), Model-Oriented Data Analysis. Proceedings, 1987. VI, 239 pages. 1988.

Vol. 298: S.H. Chew, Q. Zheng, Integral Global Optimization. VII, 179 pages. 1988.

Vol. 299: K. Marti, Descent Directions and Efficient Solutions in Discretely Distributed Stochastic Programs. XIV, 178 pages. 1988.

Vol. 300: U. Derigs, Programming in Networks and Graphs. XI, 315 pages. 1988.

Vol. 301: J. Kacprzyk, M. Roubens (Eds.), Non-Conventional Preference Relations in Decision Making. VII, 155 pages. 1988.

Vol. 302: H.A. Eiselt, G. Pederzoli (Eds.), Advances in Optimization and Control. Proceedings, 1986. VIII, 372 pages. 1988.

Vol. 303: F.X. Diebold, Empirical Modeling of Exchange Rate Dynamics. VII, 143 pages. 1988.

Vol. 304: A. Kurzhanski, K. Neumann, D. Pallaschke (Eds.), Optimization, Parallel Processing and Applications. Proceedings, 1987. VI, 292 pages. 1988.

Vol. 305: G.-J.C.Th. van Schijndel, Dynamic Firm and Investor Behaviour under Progressive Personal Taxation. X, 215 pages.1988.

Vol. 306: Ch. Klein, A Static Microeconomic Model of Pure Competition. VIII, 139 pages. 1988.

Vol. 307: T.K. Dijkstra (Ed.), On Model Uncertainty and its Statistical Implications. VII, 138 pages. 1988.

Vol. 308: J.R. Daduna, A. Wren (Eds.), Computer-Aided Transit Scheduling. VIII, 339 pages. 1988.

Vol. 309: G. Ricci, K. Velupillai (Eds.), Growth Cycles and Multisectoral Economics: The Goodwin Tradition. III, 126 pages. 1988.

Vol. 310: J. Kacprzyk, M. Fedrizzi (Eds.), Combining Fuzzy Imprecision with Probabilistic Uncertainty in Decision Making. IX, 399 pages. 1988.

Vol. 311: R. Färe, Fundamentals of Production Theory. IX, 163 pages. 1988.

Vol. 312: J. Krishnakumar, Estimation of Simultaneous Equation Models with Error Components Structure. X, 357 pages. 1988.

Vol. 313: W. Jammernegg, Sequential Binary Investment Decisions. VI, 156 pages. 1988.

Vol. 314: R. Tietz, W. Albers, R. Selten (Eds.), Bounded Rational Behavior in Experimental Games and Markets. VI, 368 pages. 1988.

Vol. 315: I. Orishimo, G.J.D. Hewings, P. Nijkamp (Eds), Information Technology: Social and Spatial Perspectives. Proceedings 1986. VI, 268 pages. 1988.

Vol. 316: R.L. Basmann, D.J. Slottje, K. Hayes, J.D. Johnson, D.J. Molina, The Generalized Fechner-Thurstone Direct Utility Function and Some of its Uses. VIII, 159 pages. 1988.

Vol. 317: L. Bianco, A. La Bella (Eds.), Freight Transport Planning and Logistics. Proceedings, 1987. X, 568 pages. 1988.

Vol. 318: T. Doup, Simplicial Algorithms on the Simplotope. VIII, 262 pages. 1988.

Vol. 319: D.T. Luc, Theory of Vector Optimization. VIII, 173 pages. 1989.

Vol. 320: D. van der Wijst, Financial Structure in Small Business. VII, 181 pages. 1989.

Vol. 321: M. Di Matteo, R.M. Goodwin, A. Vercelli (Eds.), Technological and Social Factors in Long Term Fluctuations. Proceedings. IX, 442 pages. 1989.

Vol. 322: T. Kollintzas (Ed.), The Rational Expectations Equilibrium Inventory Model. XI, 269 pages. 1989.

Vol. 323: M.B.M. de Koster, Capacity Oriented Analysis and Design of Production Systems. XII, 245 pages. 1989.

Vol. 324: I.M. Bomze, B.M. Pötscher, Game Theoretical Foundations of Evolutionary Stability. VI, 145 pages. 1989.

Vol. 325: P. Ferri, E. Greenberg, The Labor Market and Business Cycle Theories. X, 183 pages. 1989.

Vol. 326: Ch. Sauer, Alternative Theories of Output, Unemployment, and Inflation in Germany: 1960–1985. XIII, 206 pages. 1989.

Vol. 327: M. Tawada, Production Structure and International Trade. V, 132 pages. 1989.

Vol. 328: W. Güth, B. Kalkofen, Unique Solutions for Strategic Games. VII, 200 pages. 1989.

Vol. 329: G. Tillmann, Equity, Incentives, and Taxation. VI, 132 pages. 1989.

Vol. 330: P.M. Kort, Optimal Dynamic Investment Policies of a Value Maximizing Firm. VII, 185 pages. 1989.

Vol. 331: A. Lewandowski, A.P. Wierzbicki (Eds.), Aspiration Based Decision Support Systems. X, 400 pages. 1989.

Vol. 332: T.R. Gulledge, Jr., L.A. Litteral (Eds.), Cost Analysis Applications of Economics and Operations Research. Proceedings. VII, 422 pages. 1989.

Vol. 333: N. Dellaert, Production to Order. VII, 158 pages. 1989.

Vol. 334: H.-W. Lorenz, Nonlinear Dynamical Economics and Chaotic Motion. XI, 248 pages. 1989.

Vol. 335: A.G. Lockett, G. Islei (Eds.), Improving Decision Making in Organisations. Proceedings. IX, 606 pages. 1989.

Vol. 336: T. Puu, Nonlinear Economic Dynamics. VII, 119 pages. 1989.

Vol. 337: A. Lewandowski, I. Stanchev (Eds.), Methodology and Software for Interactive Decision Support. VIII, 309 pages. 1989.

Vol. 338: J.K. Ho, R.P. Sundarraj, DECOMP: An Implementation of Dantzig-Wolfe Decomposition for Linear Programming. VI, 206 pages.

Vol. 339: J. Terceiro Lomba, Estimation of Dynamic Econometric Models with Errors in Variables. VIII, 116 pages. 1990.

Vol. 340: T. Vasko, R. Ayres, L. Fontvieille (Eds.), Life Cycles and Long Waves. XIV, 293 pages. 1990.

Vol. 341: G.R. Uhlich, Descriptive Theories of Bargaining. IX, 165 pages. 1990.

Vol. 342: K. Okuguchi, F. Szidarovszky, The Theory of Oligopoly with Multi-Product Firms. V, 167 pages. 1990.

Vol. 343: C. Chiarella, The Elements of a Nonlinear Theory of Economic Dynamics. IX, 149 pages. 1990.

Vol. 344: K. Neumann, Stochastic Project Networks. XI, 237 pages. 1990.

Vol. 345: A. Cambini, E. Castagnoli, L. Martein, P Mazzoleni, S. Schaible (Eds.), Generalized Convexity and Fractional Programming with Economic Applications. Proceedings, 1988. VII, 361 pages. 1990.

Vol. 346: R. von Randow (Ed.), Integer Programming and Related Areas. A Classified Bibliography 1984–1987. XIII, 514 pages. 1990.

Vol. 347: D. Ríos Insua, Sensitivity Analysis in Multi-objective Decision Making. XI, 193 pages. 1990.

Vol. 348: H. Störmer, Binary Functions and their Applications. VIII, 151 pages. 1990.

Vol. 349: G.A. Pfann, Dynamic Modelling of Stochastic Demand for Manufacturing Employment. VI, 158 pages. 1990.

Vol. 350: W.-B. Zhang, Economic Dynamics. X, 232 pages. 1990.

Vol. 351: A. Lewandowski, V. Volkovich (Eds.), Multiobjective Problems of Mathematical Programming. Proceedings, 1988. VII, 315 pages. 1991.

Vol. 352: O. van Hilten, Optimal Firm Behaviour in the Context of Technological Progress and a Business Cycle. XII, 229 pages. 1991.

Vol. 353: G. Ricci (Ed.), Decision Processes in Economics. Proceedings, 1989. III, 209 pages 1991.

Vol. 354: M. Ivaldi, A Structural Analysis of Expectation Formation. XII, 230 pages. 1991.

Vol. 355: M. Salomon. Deterministic Lotsizing Models for Production Planning. VII, 158 pages. 1991.

Vol. 356: P. Korhonen, A. Lewandowski, J . Wallenius (Eds.), Multiple Criteria Decision Support. Proceedings, 1989. XII, 393 pages. 1991.

Vol. 357: P. Zörnig, Degeneracy Graphs and Simplex Cycling. XV, 194 pages. 1991.

Vol. 358: P. Knottnerus, Linear Models with Correlated Disturbances. VIII, 196 pages. 1991.

Vol. 359: E. de Jong, Exchange Rate Determination and Optimal Economic Policy Under Various Exchange Rate Regimes. VII, 270 pages. 1991.

Vol. 360: P. Stalder, Regime Translations, Spillovers and Buffer Stocks. VI, 193 pages . 1991.

Vol. 361: C. F. Daganzo, Logistics Systems Analysis. X, 321 pages. 1991.

Vol. 362: F. Gehrels, Essays in Macroeconomics of an Open Economy. VII, 183 pages. 1991.

Vol. 363: C. Puppe, Distorted Probabilities and Choice under Risk. VIII, 100 pages . 1991

Vol. 364: B. Horvath, Are Policy Variables Exogenous? XII, 162 pages. 1991.

Vol. 365: G. A. Heuer, U. Leopold-Wildburger. Balanced Silverman Games on General Discrete Sets. V, 140 pages. 1991.

Vol. 366: J. Gruber (Ed.), Econometric Decision Models. Proceedings, 1989. VIII, 636 pages. 1991.

Vol. 367: M. Grauer, D. B. Pressmar (Eds.), Parallel Computing and Mathematical Optimization. Proceedings. V, 208 pages. 1991.

Vol. 368: M. Fedrizzi, J. Kacprzyk, M. Roubens (Eds.), Interactive Fuzzy Optimization. VII, 216 pages. 1991.

Vol. 369: R. Koblo, The Visible Hand. VIII, 131 pages. 1991.

Vol. 370: M. J. Beckmann, M. N. Gopalan, R. Subramanian (Eds.), Stochastic Processes and their Applications. Proceedings, 1990. XLI, 292 pages. 1991.

Vol. 371: A. Schmutzler, Flexibility and Adjustment to Information in Sequential Decision Problems. VIII, 198 pages. 1991.

Vol. 372: J. Esteban, The Social Viability of Money. X, 202 pages. 1991.

Vol. 373: A. Billot, Economic Theory of Fuzzy Equilibria. XIII, 164 pages. 1992.

Vol. 374: G. Pflug, U. Dieter (Eds.), Simulation and Optimization. Proceedings, 1990. X, 162 pages. 1992.

Vol. 375: S.-J. Chen, Ch.-L. Hwang, Fuzzy Multiple Attribute Decision Making. XII, 536 pages. 1992.

Vol. 376: K.-H. Jöckel, G. Rothe, W. Sendler (Eds.), Bootstrapping and Related Techniques. Proceedings, 1990. VIII, 247 pages. 1992.

Vol. 377: A. Villar, Operator Theorems with Applications to Distributive Problems and Equilibrium Models. XVI, 160 pages. 1992.

Vol. 378: W. Krabs, J. Zowe (Eds.), Modern Methods of Optimization. Proceedings, 1990. VIII, 348 pages. 1992.

Vol. 379: K. Marti (Ed.), Stochastic Optimization. Proceedings, 1990. VII, 182 pages. 1992.

Vol. 380: J. Odelstad, Invariance and Structural Dependence. XII, 245 pages. 1992.

Vol. 381: C. Giannini, Topics in Structural VAR Econometrics. XI, 131 pages. 1992.

Vol. 382: W. Oettli, D. Pallaschke (Eds.), Advances in Optimization. Proceedings, 1991. X, 527 pages. 1992.

Vol. 383: J. Vartiainen, Capital Accumulation in a Corporatist Economy. VII, 177 pages. 1992.

Vol. 384: A. Martina, Lectures on the Economic Theory of Taxation. XII, 313 pages. 1992.

Vol. 385: J. Gardeazabal, M. Regúlez, The Monetary Model of Exchange Rates and Cointegration. X, 194 pages. 1992.

Vol. 386: M. Desrochers, J.-M. Rousseau (Eds.), Computer-Aided Transit Scheduling. Proceedings, 1990. XIII, 432 pages. 1992.

Vol. 387: W. Gaertner, M. Klemisch-Ahlert, Social Choice and Bargaining Perspectives on Distributive Justice. VIII, 131 pages. 1992.

Vol. 388: D. Bartmann, M. J. Beckmann, Inventory Control. XV, 252 pages. 1992.

Vol. 389: B. Dutta, D. Mookherjee, T. Parthasarathy, T. Raghavan, D. Ray, S. Tijs (Eds.), Game Theory and Economic Applications. Proceedings, 1990. IX, 454 pages. 1992.

Vol. 390: G. Sorger, Minimum Impatience Theorem for Recursive Economic Models. X, 162 pages. 1992.

Vol. 391: C. Keser, Experimental Duopoly Markets with Demand Inertia. X, 150 pages. 1992.

Vol. 392: K. Frauendorfer, Stochastic Two-Stage Programming. VIII, 228 pages. 1992.

Vol. 393: B. Lucke, Price Stabilization on World Agricultural Markets. XI, 274 pages. 1992.

Vol. 394: Y.-J. Lai, C.-L. Hwang, Fuzzy Mathematical Programming. XIII, 301 pages. 1992.

Vol. 395: G. Haag, U. Mueller, K. G. Troitzsch (Eds.), Economic Evolution and Demographic Change. XVI, 409 pages. 1992.

Vol. 396: R. V. V. Vidal (Ed.), Applied Simulated Annealing. VIII, 358 pages. 1992.

Vol. 397: J. Wessels, A. P. Wierzbicki (Eds.), User-Oriented Methodology and Techniques of Decision Analysis and Support. Proceedings, 1991. XII, 295 pages. 1993.

Vol. 398: J.-P. Urbain, Exogeneity in Error Correction Models. XI, 189 pages. 1993.

Vol. 399: F. Gori, L. Geronazzo, M. Galeotti (Eds.), Nonlinear Dynamics in Economics and Social Sciences. Proceedings, 1991. VIII, 367 pages. 1993.

Vol. 400: H. Tanizaki, Nonlinear Filters. XII, 203 pages. 1993.

Vol. 401: K. Mosler, M. Scarsini, Stochastic Orders and Applications. V, 379 pages. 1993.

Vol. 402: A. van den Elzen, Adjustment Processes for Exchange Economies and Noncooperative Games. VII, 146 pages. 1993.

Vol. 403: G. Brennscheidt, Predictive Behavior. VI, 227 pages. 1993.

Vol. 404: Y.-J. Lai, Ch.-L. Hwang, Fuzzy Multiple Objective Decision Making. XIV, 475 pages. 1994.

Vol. 405: S. Komlósi, T. Rapcsák, S. Schaible (Eds.), Generalized Convexity. Proceedings, 1992. VIII, 404 pages. 1994.

Vol. 406: N. M. Hung, N. V. Quyen, Dynamic Timing Decisions Under Uncertainty. X, 194 pages. 1994.

Vol. 407: M. Ooms, Empirical Vector Autoregressive Modeling. XIII, 380 pages. 1994.

Vol. 408: K. Haase, Lotsizing and Scheduling for Production Planning. VIII, 118 pages. 1994.

Vol. 409: A. Sprecher, Resource-Constrained Project Scheduling. XII, 142 pages. 1994.

Vol. 410: R. Winkelmann, Count Data Models. XI, 213 pages. 1994.

Vol. 411: S. Dauzère-Péres, J.-B. Lasserre, An Integrated Approach in Production Planning and Scheduling. XVI, 137 pages. 1994.

Vol. 412: B. Kuon, Two-Person Bargaining Experiments with Incomplete Information. IX, 293 pages. 1994.

Vol. 413: R. Fiorito (Ed.), Inventory, Business Cycles and Monetary Transmission. VI, 287 pages. 1994.

Vol. 414: Y. Crama, A. Oerlemans, F. Spieksma, Production Planning in Automated Manufacturing. X, 210 pages. 1994.

Vol. 415: P. C. Nicola, Imperfect General Equilibrium. XI, 167 pages. 1994.

Vol. 416: H. S. J. Cesar, Control and Game Models of the Greenhouse Effect. XI, 225 pages. 1994.

Vol. 417: B. Ran, D. E. Boyce, Dynamic Urban Transportation Network Models. XV, 391 pages. 1994.

Vol. 418: P. Bogetoft, Non-Cooperative Planning Theory. XI, 309 pages. 1994.

Vol. 419: T. Maruyama, W. Takahashi (Eds.), Nonlinear and Convex Analysis in Economic Theory. VIII, 306 pages. 1995.

Vol. 420: M. Peeters, Time-To-Build. Interrelated Investment and Labour Demand Modelling. With Applications to Six OECD Countries. IX, 204 pages. 1995.

Vol. 421: C. Dang, Triangulations and Simplicial Methods. IX, 196 pages. 1995.

Vol. 422: D. S. Bridges, G. B. Mehta, Representations of Preference Orderings. X, 165 pages. 1995.

Vol. 423: K. Marti, P. Kall (Eds.), Stochastic Programming. Numerical Techniques and Engineering Applications. VIII, 351 pages. 1995.

Vol. 424: G. A. Heuer, U. Leopold-Wildburger, Silverman's Game. X, 283 pages. 1995.

Vol. 425: J. Kohlas, P.-A. Monney, A Mathematical Theory of Hints. XIII, 419 pages, 1995.

Vol. 426: B. Finkenstädt, Nonlinear Dynamics in Economics. IX, 156 pages. 1995.

Vol. 427: F. W. van Tongeren, Microsimulation Modelling of the Corporate Firm. XVII, 275 pages. 1995.

Vol. 428: A. A. Powell, Ch. W. Murphy, Inside a Modern Macroeconometric Model. XVIII, 424 pages. 1995.

Vol. 429: R. Durier, C. Michelot, Recent Developments in Optimization. VIII, 356 pages. 1995.

Vol. 430: J. R. Daduna, I. Branco, J. M. Pinto Paixão (Eds.), Computer-Aided Transit Scheduling. XIV, 374 pages. 1995.

Vol. 431: A. Aulin, Causal and Stochastic Elements in Business Cycles. XI, 116 pages. 1996.

Vol. 432: M. Tamiz (Ed.), Multi-Objective Programming and Goal Programming. VI, 359 pages. 1996.

Vol. 433: J. Menon, Exchange Rates and Prices. XIV, 313 pages. 1996.

Vol. 434: M. W. J. Blok, Dynamic Models of the Firm. VII, 193 pages. 1996.

Vol. 435: L. Chen, Interest Rate Dynamics, Derivatives Pricing, and Risk Management. XII, 149 pages. 1996.

Vol. 436: M. Klemisch-Ahlert, Bargaining in Economic and Ethical Environments. IX, 155 pages. 1996.

Vol. 437: C. Jordan, Batching and Scheduling. IX, 178 pages. 1996.

Vol. 438: A. Villar, General Equilibrium with Increasing Returns. XIII, 164 pages. 1996.

Vol. 439: M. Zenner, Learning to Become Rational. VII, 201 pages. 1996.

Vol. 440: W. Ryll, Litigation and Settlement in a Game with Incomplete Information. VIII, 174 pages. 1996.

Vol. 441: H. Dawid, Adaptive Learning by Genetic Algorithms. IX, 166 pages.1996.

Vol. 442: L. Corchón, Theories of Imperfectly Competitive Markets. XIII, 163 pages. 1996.

Vol. 443: G. Lang, On Overlapping Generations Models with Productive Capital. X, 98 pages. 1996.

Vol. 444: S. Jørgensen, G. Zaccour (Eds.), Dynamic Competitive Analysis in Marketing. X, 285 pages. 1996.

Vol. 445: A. H. Christer, S. Osaki, L. C. Thomas (Eds.), Stochastic Modelling in Innovative Manufactoring. X, 361 pages. 1997.

Vol. 446: G. Dhaene, Encompassing. X, 160 pages. 1997.

Vol. 447: A. Artale, Rings in Auctions. X, 172 pages. 1997.

Vol. 448: G. Fandel, T. Gal (Eds.), Multiple Criteria Decision Making. XII, 678 pages. 1997.

Vol. 449: F. Fang, M. Sanglier (Eds.), Complexity and Self-Organization in Social and Economic Systems. IX, 317 pages, 1997.

Vol. 450: P. M. Pardalos, D. W. Hearn, W. W. Hager, (Eds.), Network Optimization. VIII, 485 pages, 1997.

Vol. 451: M. Salge, Rational Bubbles. Theoretical Basis, Economic Relevance, and Empirical Evidence with a Special Emphasis on the German Stock Market.IX, 265 pages. 1997.

Vol. 452: P. Gritzmann, R. Horst, E. Sachs, R. Tichatschke (Eds.), Recent Advances in Optimization. VIII, 379 pages. 1997.

Vol. 453: A. S. Tangian, J. Gruber (Eds.), Constructing Scalar-Valued Objective Functions. VIII, 298 pages. 1997.

Vol. 454: H.-M. Krolzig, Markov-Switching Vector Autoregressions. XIV, 358 pages. 1997.

Vol. 455: R. Caballero, F. Ruiz, R. E. Steuer (Eds.), Advances in Multiple Objective and Goal Programming. VIII, 391 pages. 1997.

Vol. 456: R. Conte, R. Hegselmann, P. Terna (Eds.), Simulating Social Phenomena. VIII, 536 pages. 1997.

Vol. 457: C. Hsu, Volume and the Nonlinear Dynamics of Stock Returns. VIII, 133 pages. 1998.

Vol. 458: K. Marti, P. Kall (Eds.), Stochastic Programming Methods and Technical Applications. X, 437 pages. 1998.

Vol. 459: H. K. Ryu, D. J. Slottje, Measuring Trends in U.S. Income Inequality. XI, 195 pages. 1998.

Vol. 460: B. Fleischmann, J. A. E. E. van Nunen, M. G. Speranza, P. Stähly, Advances in Distribution Logistic. XI, 535 pages. 1998.

Vol. 461: U. Schmidt, Axiomatic Utility Theory under Risk. XV, 201 pages. 1998.

Vol. 462: L. von Auer, Dynamic Preferences, Choise Mechanisms, and Welfare. XII, 226 pages. 1998.

Vol. 463: G. Abraham-Frois (Ed.), Non-Linear Dynamics and Endogenous Cycles. VI, 204 pages. 1998.

Vol. 464: A. Aulin, The Impact of Science on Economic Growth and its Cycles. IX, 204 pages. 1998.

Vol. 465: T. J. Stewart, R. C. van den Honert (Eds.), Trends in Multicriteria Decision Making. X, 448 pages. 1998.

Vol. 466: A. Sadrieh, The Alternating Double Auction Market. VII, 350 pages. 1998.

Vol. 467: H. Hennig-Schmidt, Gargaining in a Video Experiment. Determinants of Boundedly Rational Behavior. XII, 221 pages. 1999.

GPSR Compliance

The European Union's (EU) General Product Safety Regulation (GPSR) is a set of rules that requires consumer products to be safe and our obligations to ensure this.

If you have any concerns about our products, you can contact us on ProductSafety@springernature.com

In case Publisher is established outside the EU, the EU authorized representative is:

Springer Nature Customer Service Center GmbH
Europaplatz 3
69115 Heidelberg, Germany

Batch number: 10844675

Printed by Printforce, the Netherlands